Forgotten Saints

HARVARD MIDDLE EASTERN MONOGRAPHS

XLI

Forgotten Saints

History, Power, and Politics in the Making of Modern Morocco

Sahar Bazzaz

DISTRIBUTED FOR THE
CENTER FOR MIDDLE EASTERN STUDIES
OF HARVARD UNIVERSITY BY
HARVARD UNIVERSITY PRESS
CAMBRIDGE, MASSACHUSETTS
LONDON, ENGLAND

ISBN-13: 978-0-674-03539-3
ISBN-10: 0-674-03539-9
Printed in the United States of America

Library of Congress Cataloging-in-Publication Data

Bazzaz, Sahar.
Forgotten saints : history, power, and politics in the making of modern Morocco / Sahar Bazzaz.
p. cm. — (Harvard Middle Eastern monographs ; 41)
Includes bibliographical references.
ISBN 978-0-674-03539-3
1. Kattani, Muhammad ibn ʻAbd al-Kabir, 1873–1909. 2. Political activists—Morocco—Biography. 3. Islamic renewal—Morocco—History. 4. Morocco—Colonization—History. 5. France—Colonies—History. 6. Morocco—Historiography. 7. Historiography—Political aspects—Morocco. 8. Power (Social sciences)—Morocco—History. 9. Nationalism—Morocco—History. 10. Morocco—Politics and government. I. Title. II. Series.
DT324.92.K37B39 2010
964′.03092—dc22
[B]

2009044180

For
Fakhri (1933–2008) and Maarib

and for
Ammar and Dimitris

Contents

List of Figures

Acknowledgments

No work gets completed without the help, care, support, and love of others. There are many to whom I owe limitless gratitude. First, I would like to thank Susan Gilson Miller, without whose support, confidence, generosity, love, and kindness during this project—from its beginning as a dissertation to its completion as a book—this endeavor would never have borne fruit. Three scholars—Fawzi Abdelrazak, Khaled bin Shrir, and Jamaa Baida—were extremely generous with their time and knowledge regarding the marvelously rich archival materials on which *Forgotten Saints* is based. Through their patient help, the often oblique stories, aphorisms, and other information buried within the archives slowly began to make sense to me. For their willingness to share from their own private book and manuscript collections, I am ever grateful. Throughout the years, many brilliant friends and colleagues have given generously of their time and skill by commenting on book and grant proposals and wading through the numerous drafts of what has finally materialized as a book. My deepest and heartfelt gratitude goes to Diana Abouali, Shahab Ahmed, Anthony B. Cashman, Leila Farsakh, Israel Gershoni, Shirine Hamadeh, Cemal Kafadar, Jonathan G. Katz, Dimitris Keridis, Ilham Khuri-Makdisi, Julia Kruse, Susan Gilson Miller, Roger Owen, Eve Troutt Powell, Aaron Shakow, Karen Turner, Stephanie Yuhl, and Fatima

Zaidane. Numerous friends offered their support, put up with my whining and provided invaluable friendship and advice during the many phases of this long project. To them—Sinan Antoon, Mary Conley, Kouross Esmaeli, Bill Granara, Dimitris Kastritsis, Mary and Uli Kruse, Gwenn Miller, Dana Sajdi, Anna Stavrakopoulou, Ellen Trabka, Souhaib Yassin, Franz Ulm, Selma Farsakh Ulm, Tom Warne, and Michael West—I am especially indebted. I owe special thanks to Donna Fromberg, who has worked all these years to help me to realize this project (and other parts of myself). Teresa Iverson's masterful editing helped make this manuscript more readable and accessible, and my lovely cousin, Omar, showed up at just the right time: your presence made all the difference. My sincerest thanks to all those friends and colleagues in Morocco, who generously welcomed me, took me into their homes, facilitated my work, and made my stay there so fulfilling: Muhammad Bouam and his friends, Maʿṭī, ʿAbd al-Raḥmān and Bushrā; Daoud Casewit, Abdelhay Diouri, ʿAlī al-Kattānī and his family, Sadiyya Maski and the wonderful staff of the Moroccan American Commission for Educational and Cultural Exchange, Mina Mdaghri and her family, Geoffrey Porter, Khaled bin Shrir and his family, and Ahmed Tawfiq. This book could not have been completed without institutional and financial support from, the American Institute for Maghrib Studies, the Center for Middle Eastern Studies at Harvard University, the College of the Holy Cross, the Fulbright Commission, and Harvard University's Center for Hellenic Studies in Washington, D.C. Finally and most important, I am ever grateful for the love and support of my parents and brother, Fakhri, Maarib, and Ammar Bazzaz.

Note on Transliteration and Spelling

Forgotten Saints follows the transliteration scheme of the *International Journal of Middle Eastern Studies.* Words that are common in English usage (such as *shaykh, ulama, sharia, sultan, hadith, and jihad*) are printed in roman type and do not have diacritical markings. If the first term of an iḍāfa construction is feminine, then that word is spelled with *-at* to indicate elision in pronunciation (e.g., Salwat al-Anfās). Names of cities, towns, and other geographic and topographic features are spelled according to *The Times Comprehensive Atlas of the World,* twelfth edition (London: Times Books Group, 2007). The two exceptions are the cities of Fez and Marrakesh, which are written as *Fez* instead of *Fès* and *Marrakesh* instead of *Marrakech.* In the case where the name of a person is best known according to its Moroccan dialectical pronunciation, then transliteration follows pronunciation (e.g., *Bū Ḥmāra* instead of *Abū Ḥimāra* and *Sīdī* for *Sayyidī*). When quoting transliterated Arabic from another source, I have used the author's transliteration as it appears in the original text.

All dates are common era except when indicated by *AH*. If the Hijrī date is indicated, then the common era date will also be indicated with *CE*.

Glossary

ʿAlawīs Members of the ruling eponymous Moroccan dynasty and descendants of the Prophet.

bidʿa A term for heresy or an unlawful innovation in the Islamic legal tradition.

Fāsī A person from Fez. When preceding a noun, it indicates that the object or person comes from Fez.

Idrīsīs Descendants of the founder of Fez, Idrīs bin Idrīs, and descendants of the Prophet.

Kattāniyya The Kattāniyya mystical brotherhood.

makhzan The Moroccan government.

sharia Islamic law.

shaykh A leader of a sufi brotherhood or a person revered and followed due to their mystical knowledge.

shurafāʾ (sing. *sharīf*) Descendants of the Muslim Prophet, Muhammad.

Sufism A general term for Islamic mysticism.

Sufi Someone who practices Sufism.

sultan The ruler or political leader of the Moroccan state.

ṭarīqa A path referring to a specific mystical brotherhood and its rituals, practices, and religious exercises (e.g., *Ṭarīqa* Kattāniyya).

ulama (sing. *ʿālim*) Islamic legal scholars.

umma A community or people. When not preceded by an adjective such as Muslim or Christian, *umma* refers to the community of Muslims in its widest sense.

wazīr A political adviser or minister to the sultan.

wird A prayer specific to a particular mystical brotherhood, which is known to its disciples and distinguishes it from others.

zāwiya A lodge where Sufis practice their religious rituals.

Abbreviations of Archives

BG	Bibliothèque Générale, Rabat.
BH	Bibliothèque Ḥasaniyya, Rabat.
BS	Bibliothèque Ṣabīḥī, Salé.
DAR (TZ)	Direction des Archives Royales, Rabat (series *al-Tartīb al-Zamanī*).
DAR (TK)	Direction des Archives Royales, Rabat (series *al-Tartīb al-Khāṣṣ: al-Kattāniyyūn* collection and *Fez* collection).
EI2	*Encyclopedia of Islam.* Leiden: Brill, 1960–[i.e. 1954]–2009.

Map of Morocco

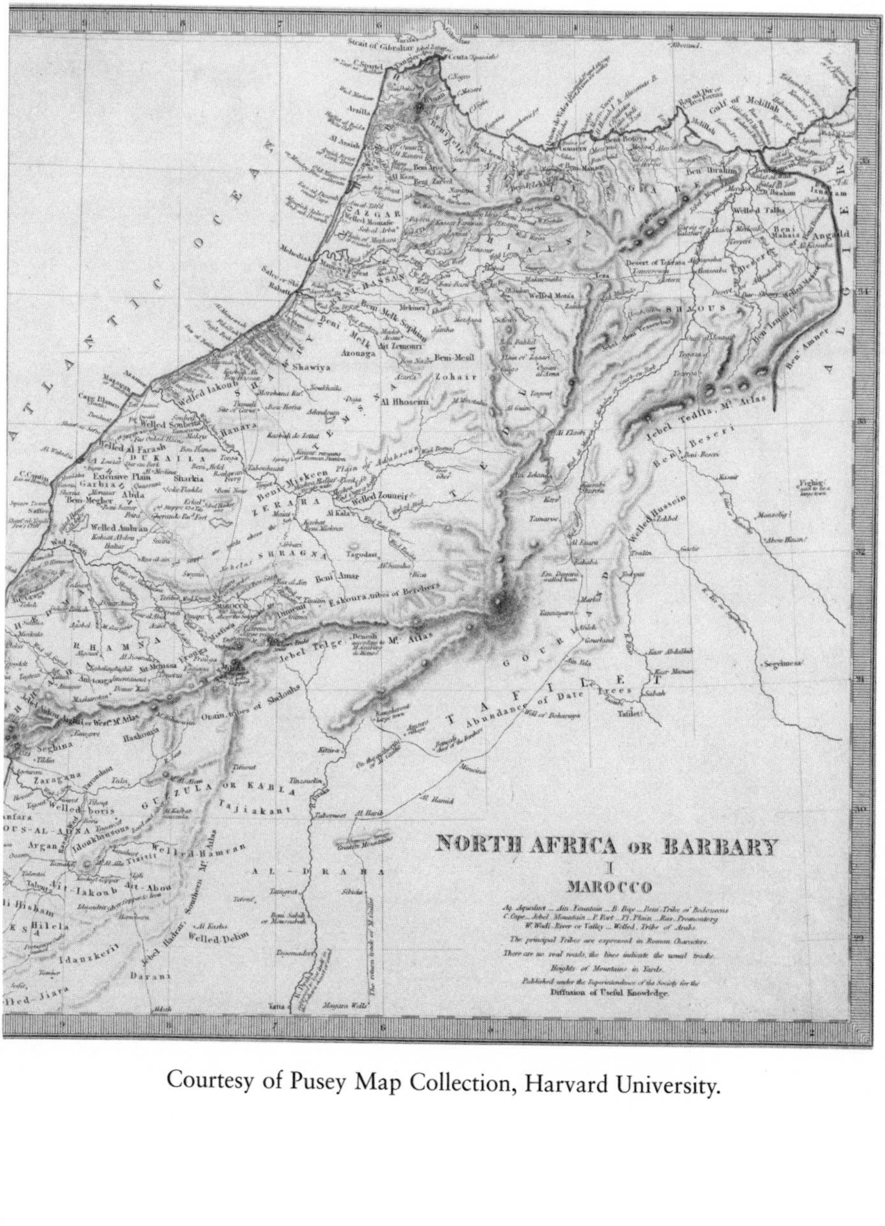

Courtesy of Pusey Map Collection, Harvard University.

Genealogical Table of the Principal Shurafā' of Morocco

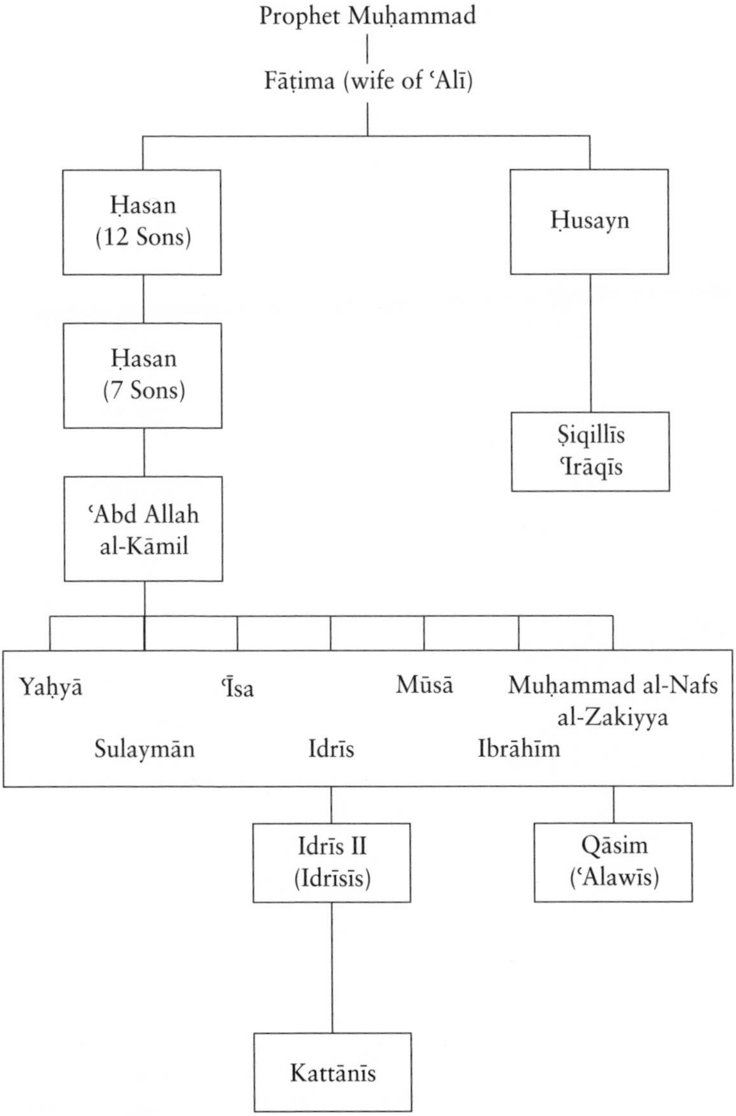

Based on Tableau 1 in Georges Drague, *Esquisse d'Histoire Religieuse du Maroc: Confréries et Zaouias*

"I do now have to say," said Don Quixote, "that the author of my history was no sage but some ignorant prattler, who started writing it in a haphazard and unplanned way and let it turn out however it would, like Orbaneja, the famous artist of Úbeda, who, when asked what he was painting, replied: 'Whatever emerges.'"

—Don Quixote, part 2, chapter 3, Miguel de Cervantes Saavedra

Introduction: Remembering Forgotten Saints

No memory of [ulama and ṣulaḥā'] remains unless written work is attributed to him or unless his grave is known [to people] by the building of a lofty structure.
—Muḥammad bin Ja'far al-Kattānī[1]

In April 1909, Moroccan newspapers reported the capture of a political dissident—Shaykh Muḥammad bin 'Abd al-Kabīr al-Kattānī—by soldiers of the Moroccan sultan, 'Abd al-Ḥafīẓ. A leader in the struggle against French colonialism in Morocco and a vocal critic of Sultan 'Abd al-Ḥafīẓ and his predecessor, Sultan 'Abd al-'Azīz, Muḥammad al-Kattānī had attempted to avoid imprisonment by fleeing Fez some weeks earlier. The sultan's guards paraded him, his family, and some of his disciples through the crowded streets of Fez on mules, the beasts of burden whose use in Morocco is associated with people of lower status. Legs shackled, beard shaven, turban humiliatingly removed, and his women exposed, al-Kattānī faced the throngs of people who had gathered to observe the procession of prisoners.[2] As they witnessed the unimaginable unfold before their eyes, those crowds expressed shock, dismay, sadness, and anger. Shaykh al-Kattānī—a descendant of the Prophet and a member of a notable family of Fez, who was widely recognized for his knowledge and piety—was being subjected to the humiliation of a common criminal. The English-language Tangier newspaper *al-Moghreb al-Aksa*—which crisply, although obliquely, approved of al-Kattānī's capture as a sign that the sultan was "a man quite capable of nipping insurrection in the bud"—still expressed dismay at the severity of the punishment being meted out to the prisoners: "Even the Shereef Kitani's [sic] family, women and children alike," were "imprisoned in irons," it reported.[3]

Some weeks later, word circulated throughout Fez that Muḥammad al-Kattānī had died, killed as a result of deep wounds from lashings inflicted by the sultan himself, and that his mangled and tortured body was "at once secretly buried at night."[4] Because of the widespread belief that the legacy, power, and authority of a holy person persisted after death through pilgrimages to their place of burial, the sultan had ordered that al-Kattānī's body be dumped in an unmarked grave so that his authority would die a quick death along with him. Furthermore, the sultan commanded the closing of Kattāniyya Sufi lodges throughout the country, while those disciples of al-Kattānī who had also fled received gruesome punishments.[5] With slight disdain yet tacit approval, one British diplomat residing in Fez at the time noted succinctly, "Such is the reward of traitors in this country."[6]

The significance of Muḥammad al-Kattānī's murder by the Moroccan sultan and the secret disposal of the corpse were not lost on the Kattānī family. As if anticipating Muḥammad al-Kattānī's gruesome end, one of his cousins—a prominent member of the ulama of Fez—had lamented some thirty years before that when pious folk *(ṣulahā')* died, their words and deeds would be lost for posterity "unless [their] grave[s] are known [to people]."[7] In response to his relative's death, the same cousin, along with other members of the esteemed yet greatly humiliated Kattānī family, decided to emigrate from Morocco permanently. That such an event could transpire in their society meant, for them, that Morocco was no longer part of the "abode of Islam" and that as pious Muslims they were obligated to practice *hijra*—to forsake Morocco and take up residence somewhere within the Dār al-Islām (that is, within the geographic realms in which the sharia—Islamic law—continued to be upheld and practiced).[8]

The extreme violence of Shaykh Muḥammad al-Kattānī's death, the humiliation of his entire family and his disciples, and the attempt to obliterate his memory represent one of the most dramatic and significant series of events in the history of the Moroccan pre-Protectorate period (c. 1860–1912). They mark both the culmination of a half century of Moroccan political and religious reform in which Muḥammad al-Kattānī and Sultan 'Abd al-Ḥafīẓ were leading figures as well as the demise of the Moroccan *ancien regime*—known as *Sharifism*—of which they were both beneficiaries. Enabled in part by the political vacuum created by the conflict, France established its Protectorate over Morocco soon after, in 1912, and remained in control of the country until 1956. In short, then, these calamitous events signal a turning point in the historical trajectory of Moroccan political modernity.

One hundred years have passed since Shaykh Muḥammad al-Kattānī's violent demise, yet the story of his life and legacy remain among the most obscure and understudied in the pages of modern Moroccan history. There is no scholarly study about al-Kattānī and his contributions to Moroccan history—not in Arabic, French, or English—and a biography written in 1962 is now out of print. *Tarjamat al-Shaykh Muḥammad al-Kattānī al-Shahīd (The Biography of the Martyr Muḥammad al-Kattānī)*, written by Muḥammad al-Bāqir al-Kattānī, al-Kattānī's grandson, is the single indigenous Moroccan source from which scholars writing about nineteenth-century Moroccan anticolonialism have drawn information about al-Kattānī. Yet the *Tarjama* avoids discussing or analyzing the conflict that led to Muḥammad al-Kattānī's death. Written by a member of the disgraced Kattānī family, it reads like a vindication of that family's honor through the celebration of its vanquished ancestor.[9] One goal of this book, then, is to shed light on these events by narrating the political biography of Shaykh Muḥammad bin ʿAbd al-Kabīr al-Kattānī (1873–1909) and of the movement he created in the closing years of the nineteenth century. During his life, Shaykh al-Kattānī mobilized Moroccans from across social divides, building in the process an Islamic revivalist movement—centered on the Kattāniyya sufi brotherhood associated with his family—that spanned the whole of Morocco. With important parallels to other anti–imperialist mobilizations in the Islamic lands (in particular, the Iranian constitutional revolution of 1906), Shaykh al-Kattānī's mass-based movement sought to challenge European encroachment in Morocco while simultaneously placing constraints on the consolidation of power in the hands of the Moroccan state. Indirectly, therefore, an aim of this book is to address striking lacunae in Moroccan intellectual and political history on the eve of the French conquest of Morocco and of the advent of French colonialism there.

However, my concern in narrating al-Kattānī's story goes beyond simply filling in this gap. I am also interested in considering why the gap exists and what it tells us about the historiography of the Moroccan pre-Protectorate period. Why is al-Kattānī virtually absent from the history of Moroccan nationalism? And how might the retelling of al-Kattānī's story alter our understanding of the Moroccan pre-Protectorate period and its historiography? More broadly, what does al-Kattānī's historiographical marginalization indicate about the relationships between history and politics in postcolonial contemporary Morocco?

It is tempting to explain al-Kattānī's sidelining in terms of the well-known adage that "history belongs to the victors." Since independence from France in 1956, the descendants of Sultan ʿAbd al-Ḥafīẓ (with whom al-Kattānī came into conflict) have ruled Morocco as kings—first through an alliance with the Moroccan nationalist movement, Istiqlāl, and later with consolidation of the power of the monarchy after 1962 under Ḥasan II (r. 1962–1999). The present king of Morocco, Muḥammad VI, is heir to this legacy. Today in Morocco, the monarchy is equated with the movement for national independence from France and is credited as the driving force behind the reform and development of Moroccan society in its march toward modernity. Moreover, skillful appropriation of the language of Islamic charismatic leadership associated with genealogical descent from the Prophet Muḥammad has solidified the dynasty's legitimacy to rule. Today, the kings of Morocco hold the title *Amīr al-Mu'minīn* (Commander of the Faithful).[10] Meanwhile, Muḥammad al-Kattānī's family declined as political actors, the importance and influence in Moroccan society of institutions with which they had been affiliated (Sufi brotherhoods and the Islamic colleges and schools) were greatly diminished and their mandates restricted, and the Moroccan religiopolitical elite to which al-Kattānī belonged lost the privileges and prestige that had defined its status before French colonialism. Why, then, focus on al-Kattānī when, in the end, he and those he represented and stood for lost? Such a tidy argument assumes that today there is consensus among Moroccans regarding Muhammad al-Kattānī's contribution to history and that there is a linear evolution of history. The research process itself—that is, the search for al-Kattānī in the archives—was powerful evidence that the answer to this question is vastly more complicated.

In archive after archive, librarians raised their eyebrows when I mentioned what I was hoping to find. Some seemed vaguely interested but confused about the identity of al-Kattānī: was it the famous nineteenth-century author (al-Kattānī's cousin), or was it perhaps the person who had founded the first Kattāniyya *zāwiya* (al-Kattānī's grandfather)? Others became stern and immediately rejected my requests for access to certain folios or simply denied having any knowledge of them. In yet another archival encounter, at first I was given access to a series of letters written in 1905 by government representatives (*makhzanī,* as they are known in Morocco), which offered veiled warnings about associations with al-Kattānī; but several days later (when the head archivist heard about my request), I was denied access to the same letters. In one library, a fellow researcher leaned over and asked what I was working on. When I replied "the Kattāniyya," he smiled, looked around suspiciously before whispering, "He's a hero," and quickly returned to his own work. To some extent, the obstructions I experienced were emblematic of research in the Moroccan archives, but clearly there was something specific about the project that elicited such responses. The fact that I was not Moroccan surely influenced these experiences although it is virtually impossible to know how.[11]

Eventually, I did locate the manuscripts, letters, and other documents that form the basis of this book. Nevertheless, these encounters were at once confusing and illuminating for several reasons. They were confusing because a strong positivist historical tradition has emerged in Morocco since independence. As a result, Moroccan archives and libraries are relatively accessible to scholars, and Moroccan scholars have used these sources effectively to write the history of their country.[12] They were illuminating because they suggested that beneath the historical silence surrounding al-Kattānī's life lay a Pandora's box of controversial and sensitive issues in contemporary Moroccan society. As several scholars have highlighted, among the most important of these concerns are the persistence of the authoritarian state, the existence of human rights abuses, and a vastly circumscribed space of open debate and limited possibilities for challenging the contemporary constellation of political, intellectual, and socioeconomic forces that dominate the political playing field in Morocco today.[13] More recently, as the place of Islam in political life has emerged as a point of debate in Morocco, the fate of Muslim activists and intellectuals has also become an issue of concern. Indeed, there are haunting similarities between the 1909 conflict (which resulted in the Muḥammad al-Kattānī's death and secret burial) and notorious episodes in the post independence period in which opponents of the Moroccan state were disappeared through the auspices of government security services.[14]

It would be reductive, however, to assume that the silence surrounding Muḥammad al-Kattānī is the result of state suppression of information or the threat of state violence. I am not suggesting that my archival encounters resulted from orchestration or conspiracy from above or from a specific government policy of censorship regarding the topic. Instead, they point to a process whereby concerns that have largely defined Moroccan nationalist politics in the postcolonial period—for example, consolidation of the newly independent nation-state, modernization and economic development and the search for an authentic national identity—have inscribed meaning on the grey areas of historical interpretation and thereby deemed certain protagonists and historical periods worthy of and amenable to study and scrutiny, while casting others aside.[15] The experience of the archives, in other words, was an important indication that in Morocco, as in many postcolonial societies, history is closely bound together with the politics of nationalism. Indeed, historian Prasanjit Duara has shown how popular allegiance to the nation-state—a new form of social and political organization—is intimately connected with the rise of positivist historical narratives. These narratives cast the nation as the "telos" of modernity and as historically transcendent—a "monistic subjecthood" traveling across historical time.[16] As I demonstrate in the pages that follow, al-Kattānī's historiographic obscurity therefore has much to do with the development of Moroccan nationalist historiography and the resulting interpretations of the pre-Protectorate era that it has produced.

Situated as it is on the cusp of the French colonial era (1912–1956) and marking the final years in which the Moroccan sultanate remained sovereign, scholars define the pre-Protectorate period (1860–1912) as an age of defensive action and reform on the part of the Moroccan state (known as the *makhzan*) as a means of preventing French encroachment. Unlike much of northern and sub-Saharan Africa, which had already come under the control of various European imperial powers by the end of the nineteenth century, the Moroccan sultanate remained independent until 1912. Nevertheless, since the conquest of neighboring Ottoman Algerian provinces by France in 1830, Moroccans began to experience the pressures of European encroachment. France, Britain, and to a lesser extent Germany and Spain competed for influence in internal affairs of the Moroccan sultanate, all the while hoping to secure the integration of Morocco on terms favorable to their respective national economies and geo-political interests.[17] Known also as the period of *iṣlāḥ* (correcting) that paralleled similar reform efforts in other regions of the Muslim Mediterranean[18] (namely, the Ottoman *tanzimat,* 1839–1876, and the efforts of Mehmet Ali Pasha in Egypt, r. 1811–1848), the Moroccan sultanate sought to transform society from above through implementation of changes that would result in modernization of its administration, military, and economy along contemporary European lines. Guided in these endeavors by various European advisers, the *makhzan* also employed members of an emerging Moroccan bureaucratic and mercantile elite who were familiar with social and political developments in Europe to implement these reforms.[19]

Broadly speaking, this historiography shows a tendency to focus on the initiatives of the reforming and centralizing state as both the major force for modernization and also the only legitimate bulwark against colonial incursions. It exhibits the influential but increasingly questioned language of modernization theory, which envisions a single trajectory of modernity based on European and American models and also posits a series of mutually exclusive analytical categories by which historians have understood and analyzed Moroccan society. The forces of tradition and atavism stand in contrast to those of modernity and progress, and the ideas of secular intellectuals enable development while those of religious ones impede the process.[20] Moroccan nationalist historiography of the pre-Protectorate period also displays a specific tendency to downplay the importance of Islamic mysticism—its doctrines and institutions—for the development of political modernity and nationalism. That is, heterodoxy/Sufism functions as a foil for orthodox Islam (or Islamic modernism/*Salafiyya*).[21] Hindered by the traditional religiopolitical elite and the institutions they dominated, argues this perspective, these efforts mostly came to naught and failed in preventing French conquest.[22] From this view, the history of the Moroccan pre-Protectorate periods reads like the mostly outdated great men of history. The Moroccan sultan, Ḥasan I (r. 1873–1894) is lionized as the Moroccan strongman who achieved a high degree of success in state centralization during his reign. He is compared to his weak and incompetent successor, ʿAbd al-ʿAzīz (r. 1894–1908), who led the country into financial ruin and opened the way for French colonization.[23] Indirectly, then, the state-centered view of history empties Moroccan society of processes of social negotiation and dissent—in short, of politics.[24] Current perspectives, therefore, reveal little about the ways in which 'society', articulated and negotiated the social, political, and intellectual/epistemological transitions that characterized the Moroccan nineteenth century.[25]

Yet as Muḥammad al-Kattānī's biography illustrates, Moroccan religious and political elites were active in facing the challenges of impending French conquest and in the reform of their society. As the backbone of precolonial Moroccan intellectual, cultural, and religious life, Sufism's doctrines and institutions enabled Muḥammad al-Kattānī to mobilize Moroccans from diverse social backgrounds—be they members of the elite ulama of Fez, merchants stationed in the expanding port cities of the sultanate, rural and tribal populations, urban artisans, or members of other mystical brotherhoods. As I argue below, al-Kattānī called for a "new key of politics" involving ulama activism and mass-based popular mobilization.[26] To do so, he synthesized Islamic mystical, rationalist and legal doctrines and tried to reconcile the universal Islamic concept of *tajdīd* (the renewal of religion) with local Moroccan concepts of political and religious power and authority. But unlike the *makhzan,* which sought to reign in and at times to marginalize the existing religiopolitical elite through its reform measures, al-Kattānī envisioned a place for them.

To avoid a framework of analysis that views the Moroccan

state and society as fundamentally oppositional forces, it is important to recognize that although al-Kattānī's political and intellectual vision challenged entrenched interests and attitudes throughout Moroccan society, the existence of various reform agendas did not lead the *makhzan* to seek al-Kattānī's immediate suppression and demise. Instead, competing visions of reform produced lively debates among Moroccans of al-Kattānī's generation. In fact, in 1895, when al-Kattānī became embroiled in a bitter conflict with the ulama of Fez, resulting in their efforts to have him tried as a heretic, the shaykh resolved the problem through delicate negotiations with the *makhzan* that lasted almost one year. From that time until his death, Muḥammad al-Kattānī and the *makhzan* had a strong relationship, and the sultan openly sanctioned and supported the shaykh's activities.

Morocco is one of only a few nation-states in the Muslim Mediterranean region to emerge in the twentieth century in which the current regime—a royal family—is simultaneously associated with precolonial reform *(tanzimat/iṣlāḥ)*, with the struggle for independence from colonial domination, and with efforts towards modernization and development in the post independence era. With few exceptions, populist and nationalist political movements overthrew the reforming administrators and political elites of the nineteenth and early twentieth-century Muslim Mediterranean. The Egyptian Free Officer movement, which overthrew the Egyptian monarchy (descendants of Mehmet Ali) in 1952, and the Kemalist regime, which sought to completely disassociate the Turkish Republic from its Ottoman-Islamic past in the post-World War I period, are the best examples of these movements.[27] Alternatively, the ruling Moroccan dynasty emphasizes its longevity and its embrace of tradition as a means of dominating the political fields. Its ability to initiate reforms in the nineteenth century, to survive the colonial period and to consolidate its power in the post independence era is a historical narrative that remains to be questioned in public discourse. But as Prasanjit Duara argues, to produce national history is necessarily to silence alternative historical voices and narratives regarding the experience of the transition to modernity.[28] As I hope to demonstrate in the pages that follow, Muḥammad al-Kattānī and his supporters envisioned a future Morocco on different terms. They would have been hard pressed to imagine the constellation of religious and political authorities that emerged in the postcolonial period. To narrate the story of Muḥammad al-Kattānī and the Sufi revivalist political movement that he furthered is to challenge the teleology of nationalist history, in which the consolidation of power in the hands of the state was a linear and uncontested process.

Chapter 1 of this study situates the Kattāniyya Sufi brotherhood and its leaders within the context of the declining Moroccan religious and political system known as Sharifism. Sharifism privileged the *shurafāʾ*—descendants of the Prophet Muḥammad—as political agents, as interlocutors between various sectors of society and as would-be dynasts of Morocco. Those who claimed prophetic descent constituted a kind of nobility and were believed to possess *baraka*. *Baraka* served as a way of assessing, articulating and evaluating the power of an individual within the system of Sharifism. A *baraka*-laden individual was someone who had social or political agency in Moroccan society and was capable of accumulating great wealth (in some cases); of arbitrating in disputes between individuals, families, and the sultanate; or on rare occasions, of raising armies against the sultanate.[29]

This chapter uses hagiography, a literary genre associated with Sharifism, as a window into Moroccan Muslim concepts of religious and political power and authority in the late nineteenth century when the *shurafāʾ* were in decline as political actors. By doing so, it introduces the reader to the language, metaphor, iconography, and symbolism associated with Sharifism, which the Kattāniyya leadership deployed to articulate its sense of political legitimacy in its effort to reassert the leadership role of the *shurafāʾ* lineage from which it claimed descent. It outlines the shifting political and economic relationships among social groups in the city against the backdrop of larger socioeconomic trends that affected Morocco and that were associated with nineteenth-century globalization (imperialism and capitalist integration). It also sets the stage for the emergence of the Kattāniyya as a religious and political movement in 1894 in Fez.

In chapter 2, I turn to the 1895 heresy trial of Muḥammad al-Kattānī and its eventual resolution. The heresy affair offers the first glimpses of Muḥammad al-Kattānī from the perspective of the Moroccan state when his activities became suspicious in the eyes of the *makhzan* and its legal team so to speak. Much like the sixteenth century trials of historian Carlo Ginzburg's Friuli heretics, Shaykh al-Kattānī's heresy trial and its eventual resolution can be seen as an example of microhistory when the limits of institutional religious authority was being tested.[30] That is, I use the heresy trial of Muḥammad al-Kattānī as a lens through which to examine the politics of piety in late nineteenth-century Morocco. Al-Kattānī's doctrinal challenge to the state and to religious orthodoxy as defined by political and religious elites represents an important moment of negotiation. It also marks the moment when Muḥammad al-Kattānī enters official history.

In chapters 3 and 4, I turn away from al-Kattānī's involvement in elite politics by examining unpublished and published epistolary exchanges related to the Kattāniyya. The focus of discussion shifts away from *makhzan* and Kattāniyya relations to explain how the Kattāniyya movement emerged from the heresy crisis to become a popular political force that was able to mobilize Moroccans during the 1907 Ḥafīẓiyya uprising. Chapter 4 explains the meteoric rise of the Kattāniyya movement after 1897 by emphasizing the contribution of the Kattāniyya to Moroccan debates about the nature of European power and the weakness of Islam in relation to it. This chapter examines the exchange of ideas among Kattāniyya supporters and opponents, focusing on interactions between the Kattāniyya brotherhood and other Moroccan mystical brotherhoods. Through a wide variety of primary sources, including political pamphlets written by members of the Kattāniyya movement, I demonstrate how Muḥammad al-Kattānī's *baraka* (that is, his power and authority) were grounded in his ability to provide an outlook that fulfilled the spiritual and intellectual needs of a diverse audience in a period characterized by crisis of leadership. Chapter 4 highlights how the universal concept of revival of Islam *(tajdīd)* was central to his vision. The chapter also looks at how the movement successfully harnessed printing and other modern technologies new to Morocco in its efforts to expand the movement beyond its traditional base and constituencies in Fez and environs to the south of the kingdom of Morocco and to the northern port city of Tangier.

Chapter 5 begins by narrating the events of the Ḥafīẓiyya uprising, which eventually led to the conflict between the Kattāniyya leader, Muḥammad al-Kattānī, and the sultan he helped to bring to power, ʿAbd al-Ḥafīẓ. This conflict marked the end of the system of Sharifism, which had existed for over two centuries. The highly diffuse and fluid system of power sharing between the *shurafāʾ*, the *makhzan* and the ulama came under fire during the nineteenth century as larger internal and external social and economic crises occurred. Although the concept of *sharaf* (political agency as a result of prophetic descent) still carried symbolic weight at the end of the nineteenth century, the new challenges posed by a centralizing state (guided by the demands of European political and economic agendas) meant that the Kattānīs as *shurafāʾ* had to recast themselves and redefine their roles as political actors to participate in the politics of reform. Paradoxically, the Kattānīs' efforts to expand the Kattāniyya and assert the political and religious role of the *shurafāʾ* furthered the demise of *sharaf* as a legitimizing principle. This occurred because, through their project of reviving Islam *(tajdīd)*, they ultimately enabled emerging elite classes—whose social status was connected to new capitalist relations of production or to the modernizing reforms of the state but who lacked social, political, or religious legitimacy—to rally Moroccans.

The final chapter presents an interpretive overview essay of Muḥammad al-Kattānī's life that also highlights the moment when historiographical "silencing" of his story begins. However, this narrative is neither exhaustive nor closed to reinterpretation. Rather, it seeks to describe the Moroccan age of reform and the role of the Kattāniyya in that process in terms of what historian Cemal Kafadar—in his study of the historiography of the rise of the Ottoman empire—describes as "the historically contingent product of a culturally complex, socially differentiated, and politically competitive environment rather than as the necessary result of a unitary line of developmental logic."[31] In the case of Morocco and other postcolonial societies of the Muslim Mediterranean region, the "unitary line of developmental logic" is that of the nation-state, which has failed to manifest the political, economic, or cultural characteristics or achieve the standards of living associated with European and North American modalities of modernity.

A WORD ABOUT SOURCES

The greatest challenge in writing about Muḥammad al-Kattānī and the Kattāniyya relates to sources. The Moroccan archives reveal only small and often opaque evidence of al-Kattānī's presence. These limited references come in the form of barely legible excerpts of handwritten letters from al-Kattānī to disciples; statements of unknown authorship that sometimes praise but often criticize al-Kattānī; oblique references to prayers and rituals scribbled on the margins of Islamic textual exegesis; esoteric epistles about God written in language comprehensible to only a select few; and letters that shift voice, tense, and subject from one sentence to the next and have ink blots that obfuscate the short vowels and diacritical marks necessary for correctly reading Arabic texts.

This study uniquely relies on previously unstudied or underutilized archival source materials in al-Kattānī's native Arabic. Besides information contained in the *Tarjama* (the *Biography*), what little else is known about al-Kattānī and his activism comes from European diplomatic sources and ethnographic studies written when al-Kattānī was alive. Although they are informative and useful, an over reliance on them has tended to diminish the views of Moroccans regarding these events. How Muḥammad al-Kattānī articulated his own vision and understood his mission and what his Moroccan contemporaries thought of him are largely unknown, while the story of al-Kattānī's challenge to the sultanate also remains obscure.[32]

The primary sources on which this book is based are broad. They include manuscripts, epistolary exchanges, printed texts (lithographic and mechanical press), newspapers, ethnographic studies, eyewitness accounts, and travel logs. The novelty of the source base lies in the literary, epistemological and linguistic diversity of these materials and in the fact that they offer vastly different perspectives about the meaning of developments of the Moroccan nineteenth century. Printed newspapers such as the Tangier weekly *Lisān al-Mahgrib,* which reflected positivist perspectives on the nation-state as a model for social and political organization, existed in tandem with hagiographic and genealogical hand-written texts that celebrate the lives of great Muslim saints. The diversity of Moroccan literary production is emblematic of the lively intellectual tenor of the era in which Muḥammad al-Kattānī lived.

Official correspondence originating from the *makhzan* generally described as *al-wathā'iq* (documents) is a rich source for the period of study. These documents cover a range of topics—affairs of state, negotiations with the European powers, and individual requests for the state's assistance in all manner of affairs both public and private. The *wathā'iq* used in the book are housed in the Direction des Archives Royales in Rabat and exist in two series, *al-tartīb al-zamanī* and *al-tartīb al-khāṣṣ*. The first series contains correspondence that is organized according to the year in which letters were written. Two collections in the second series—al-Kattāniyyūn and Fez—contain invaluable epistolary exchanges between Muḥammad al-Kattānī and his father, ʿAbd al-Kabīr al-Kattānī. These letters provide a rare perspective on the affairs of the Kattāniyya brotherhood and its affiliates and activities. The ease with which the correspondents move between subjects in these letters stands in contrast to the formal epistolary style found in the correspondence of the state. They allow the historian to step back from a state-centered perspective on the Kattāniyya and its activities.

One of the most valuable sources on which this book relies is *al-Maẓāhir al-sāmiyya fī al-nisba al-sharīfa al-Kattāniyya,* a four hundred page, unpublished manuscript written in 1911 by ʿAbd al-Ḥayy al-Kattānī, Muḥammad al-Kattānī's brother. It is a history of the Kattānī family written shortly after Muḥammad al-Kattānī's death. Besides celebrating the Kattānī family, the composition of *al-Maẓāhir* was an effort to exonerate the family while simultaneously critiquing Sultan ʿAbd al-Ḥafīẓ. To my knowledge, no researcher to date has used this manuscript to write about the Moroccan nineteenth century.[33]

NOTES

1. Muḥammad bin Jaʿfar al-Kattānī, *Salwat al-anfās wa muḥādathat al-akyās bi man uqbira min al-ʿulamāʾ wa al-ṣulaḥāʾ bi fās,* vol. 1., ed. with an introduction by ʿAbd Allah al-Kattānī et al. (Casablanca: Dār al-Thaqāfa, 2004), 5.
2. "The Situation in Fez," *Al-Moghreb al-Aqsa,* April 1, 1909, no. 1379. The capture of al-Kattānī is also documented (with similar details) in Major-General Lord Edward Gleichen, *Journal of our Mission to Fez (1909)* (London: Harrison and Sons, 1909), 51. I would like to thank Prof. Susan G. Miller for referring me to Gleichen's reference.
3. "Captured Rebels' Torture," *Al-Moghreb al-Aksa,* April 15, 1909, no. 1383.
4. Gleichen, *Journal of our Mission to Fez (1909),* 61.
5. "Captured Rebels' Torture," *Al-Moghreb al-Aksa,* April 15, 1909, no. 1383.
6. Gleichen, *Journal of our Mission to Fez (1909),* 61.
7. al-Kattānī, *Salwat al-anfās,* 1: 5.
8. See the Introduction to Muhammad bin Ja'far al-Kattānī, *Naṣīḥat ahl al-Islam,* ed. with an introduction by Idris al-Kattānī (Rabat: Maktabat al-Badr, 1989). On the concept of *hijra* see, Muhmmad

Khalid Massud, "The Obligation to Migrate: The Doctrine of *Hijra* in Islamic Law," in *Muslim Travelers: Pilgrimage, Migration and the Religious Imagination,* ed. Dale F. Eickelman and James Piscatori (Berkeley: University of California Press, 1990), 29–49.

9. Muḥammad al-Bāqir al-Kattānī, *Tarjamat al-Shaykh Muḥammad al-Kattānī al-Shahīd* (n.p., Maṭbaʿat al-Fajr: 1962).

10. On the role of Islamic political discourse in the consolidation of the power of the monarchy, see three chapters from Rahma Bourqia and Susan Gilson Miller, eds., *In the Shadow of the Sultan: Culture, Power and Politics in Morocco* (Cambridge: Harvard University Press, 1999): Rahma Bourqia, "The Cultural Legacy of Power in Morocco," 243–258; Elaine M. Combs-Schilling, "Performing Monarchy, Staging Nation," 176–214; and Abdellah Hammoudi, "The Reinvention of Dar al-Mulk: the Moroccan Political System and its Legitimation," 129–175.

11. It is impossible to know how my foreignness might have been perceived by the archivists who helped me in the various Moroccan archives in which I researched this project. However, I was told on numerous occasions by Moroccan colleagues that my not being Moroccan meant I would have access to materials they did not or, alternatively, that I would not be able to see certain materials that they could. In other words, these colleagues attempted to interpret my experiences in the archives on the basis of their own understandings of the workings of the archives, the personalities of the employees who worked in these institutions, and their conception of the ways in which such institutions operated. One Moroccan colleague suggested "strategies" for getting access to records in which I emphasized my connections to an elite American university. Another Moroccan archivist suggested that I should give something in exchange for use of the archives—books, access to libraries, or other research tools—since I came from a rich country. These experiences illustrate the subtleties, gradations of maneuvering in the archives, and underlying perceptions that influenced individual responses to my requests. It belies the vision of the historical research process that takes for granted access to archives and the power of individuals working in the archives to limit or provide access.

12. On the Moroccan archives and the creation of the modern Moroccan historical tradition, see Ahmed-Chouqui Binebine, *Histoire*

des bibliothèques au Maroc (Rabat: Faculté des Lettres et des Sciences Humaines, 1992); Edmund Burke, "The Creation of the Moroccan Colonial Archive, 1880–1930," *History and Anthropology* 18, no. 1 (March 2007): 1–9.

13. Abdellah Hammoudi points to the problem of the persistence of the authoritarian state in Morocco and the Middle East and North Africa generally. Abdellah Hammoudi, *Master and Disciple: The Cultural Foundations of Moroccan Authoritarianism* (Chicago: University of Chicago Press, 1997). In recent years, revelations regarding the violent methods used by state security forces—such as incarceration, torture, and in some cases, the disappearance of political prisoners—has opened debate about the suppression of dissent. See Susan Slyomovics's excellent discussion of human rights, political prisoners, and efforts to break the silence regarding political repression in Morocco. Susan Slyomovics, *The Performance of Human Rights in Morocco* (Philadelphia: University of Pennsylvania Press, 2005).
14. The most famous of these cases are those of Mehdi Ben Barka, kidnapped in 1965 and whose whereabouts are still unknown, and General Mohamed Oufkir and his family. See Slyomovics, *The Performance of Human Rights in Morocco,* 54–56 (esp. chapt. 6 on Islamic political prisoners).
15. On the efforts of "modernizing nationalists" to further these processes, see Prasanjit Duara, "Introduction: The Decolonization of Asia and Africa in the Twentieth Century," in *Decolonization: Perspectives from Now and Then,* ed. Prasanjit Duara (London: Routledge, 2004), 1–20.
16. Prasanjit Duara, *Rescuing History from the Nation: Questioning Narratives of Modern China* (Chicago: University of Chicago Press, 1995): 27, 16. An extensive bibliography exists on the relationships among history, nationalism, and the writing of nationalist history in postcolonial societies. See, for example, Benedict Anderson, *Imagined Communities: Reflections on the Origins and Spread of Nationalism* (London: Verso, 1991); Dipesh Chakrabarty, *Habitations of Modernity: Essays in the Wake of Subaltern Studies* (Chicago: University of Chicago Press, 2002); Partha Chatterjee, *The Nation and Its Fragments: Colonial and Postcolonial Histories* (Princeton, NJ: Princeton University Press, 1993). On national traditions, see the well-known work, Eric

Hobsbawm and Terence Ranger, eds., *The Invention of Tradition* (Cambridge: Cambridge University Press, 1983).

17. The signing of the 1904 Entente-Cordiale between Britain and France represents the culmination of inter-European competition over control of Morocco. It established Morocco as part of France's sphere of influence on the southern shore of the Mediterranean in exchange for undisputed control of Egypt and the Suez Canal by Britain. During the 1905 Moroccan Crisis, Germany attempted to derail French ambitions to secure its plan for restructuring of the Moroccan bureaucracy and economy. For an excellent and detailed discussion of competing European ambitions in Morocco in this period, see Jonathan G. Katz, *Murder in Marrakesh: Émile Mauchamp and the French Colonial Adventure* (Bloomington: Indiana University Press, 2006).
18. By the term Muslim Mediterranean I refer to the linguistically and religiously diverse societies of the Mediterranean and its hinterlands in which institutions and methods of governance prior to the twentieth century (the era of the emergence of nation states in the region) were articulated in terms of adherence to Islamic principles of law and social order. As I demonstrate in the chapters that follow, Islamic principles and social order are dynamic and historically and geographically determined despite the fact that those who advocate them (whether rulers, political activists, legal scholars, or the people) often claim them as universal and timeless. On a historicized understanding of Islam, see: Talal Asad, *Genealogies of Religion: Discipline and Reasons of Power in Christianity and Islam* (Baltimore: Johns Hopkins University Press, 1993), and Muhammad Qasim Zaman, *The Ulama in Contemporary Islam: Custodians of Change* (Princeton: Princeton University Press, 2002). More generally, Harjot Oberoi emphasizes the historicity of religious symbolism and rituals. He views "religion as a social and cultural process; not something given, but an activity embedded in everyday life, a part of human agency." Harjot Oberoi, *The Construction of Religious Boundaries: Culture, Identity and Diversity in the Sikh Tradition* (Oxford: Oxford University Press, 1994), 23.
19. The 1845 Moroccan delegation to France led by ʿAbd al-Qādir Ashʿāsh is the most studied example of this phenomenon whereby, through travel to Europe, Moroccans gained knowledge about political, social, and intellectual developments there. One member of

the delegation, Muḥammad al-Ṣaffār, produced an extensive journal of his observations while abroad. Susan Gilson Miller, trans. and ed., *Disorienting Encounters: Travels of a Moroccan Scholar in France in 1845–1846—The Voyage of Muḥammad al-Ṣaffār* (Berkeley: University of California Press, 1992). As I explain in chapter 1, the bureaucratic elite that emerged in the nineteenth century was also drawn from among members of the ulama class.

20. Several scholars have demonstrated the limitations of modernization theory as an analytical framework for studying non-Western societies since its advent and gaining popularity in the post-World War II era. For an excellent overview of the history of social science perspectives on modernization and development in the Third World, see Jeffrey C. Alexander, *Fin de Siècle Social Theory: Relativism, Reduction and the Problem of Reason* (London: Verso, 1995). For critiques of modernization theory and its legacy in Islamic and Middle Eastern studies see Dale Eickelman, "Islam and the Languages of Modernity," in *Multiple Modernities,* ed. Shmuel N. Eisenstadt (New Brunswick, NJ: Transaction Publishers, 2002), 119–135; Bryan S. Turner, *Orientalism, Postmodernism and Globalism* (London: Routledge, 1994); Zaman, *The Ulama in Contemporary Islam.* For a more general discussion of modernization theory and nineteenth century European imperialism, see Frederick Cooper, *Colonialism in Question: Theory, Knowledge, History* (Berkeley: University of California Press, 2005).

21. On the polemics against Sufism in the nineteenth and twentieth centuries, see Elizabeth Sirriyeh, *Sufis and Anti-Sufis: The Defence, Rethinking and Rejection of Sufism in the Modern World* (Richmond, Surrey: Curzon Press, 1999); R. S. O'Fahey and Bernd Radtke, "Neo-Sufism Reconsidered," *Der Islam* 70 (1993): 52–87. A notable exception to the erasure of Sufis from the history of modernity is Julia Clancy-Smith, *Rebel and Saint: Muslim Notables, Populist Protest, Colonial Encounters (Algeria and Tunisia, 1800–1904)* (Berkeley: University of California Press, 1994).

22. The Moroccan scholar Abdallah Laroui's groundbreaking *Les origines sociales et culturelles du nationalisme Marocain, 1830–1912,* is the best example of state-centered history. His work represents the most comprehensive history of the Moroccan pre-Protectorate period. Laroui was the first to attempt a synthetic history of the era in which he relied on indigenous Moroccan sources

instead of simply drawing on materials in European languages. Laroui's framework largely defines the historiography of this period. He argued that the reasons for the *makhzan*'s failure to reform Moroccan society in the wake of nineteenth-century European expansion had its basis in traditional Moroccan culture and society and its resistance to modern concepts. In particular, Laroui located the failure to modernize with the Moroccan religiopolitical elite—namely, the ulama (legal scholars versed in Islamic law), the *shurafā'*, the heads of mystical brotherhoods, and the indigenous institutions of Muslim learning (the *madrasas,* mosque colleges, and Sufi lodges). Abdallah Laroui, *Les origines sociales et culturelles du nationalisme Marocain* (Casablanca: Centre Culturel Arabe, 1993).

23. Edmund Burke has addressed the influence of nationalist ideology in Moroccan historiography of the French colonial period. However, to my knowledge, this issue has not been discussed for the pre-Protectorate period. Edmund Burke, "Theorizing the Histories of Colonialism and Nationalism in the Arab Maghrib," in *Beyond Colonialism and Nationalism in the Maghrib,* ed. Ali Abdullatif Ahmida (New York: Palgrave, 2000), 17–34.
24. Through her meticulous study of nineteenth-century Moroccan primary sources such as *bay'a* documents and hagiography, Bettina Dennerlein provides strong evidence of the complex and textured nature of politics, political negotiations, and power in pre-Protectorate society. Bettina Dennerlien, "Asserting Religious Authority in Late Nineteenth/Early Twentieth Century Morocco: Muhammad b. Ja'far al-Kattânî and His Kitâb Salwat al-Anfâs," in *Speaking for Islam: Religious Authorities in Middle Eastern Islam,* ed. G. Kramer and S. Schmidtke (Leiden: Brill, 2006), 128–152; Bettina Dennerlein, "Legitimate Bounds and Bound Legitimacy: the Act of Allegiance to the Ruler *(bai'a)* in Nineteenth Century Morocco," *Die Welt des Islams* 41, no. 3 (2001): 287–310; and Bettina Dennerlein, "Savoir religieux et débat politique au Maroc: une consultation des 'gens de Fès' en 1886," *Hespéris-Tamuda* 39 fasc. 2 (2001): 119–132.
25. Jonathan G. Katz's recent study, *Murder in Marrakesh,* offers a new perspective on the pre-Protectorate period by examining responses to French intervention by an urban mob in Marrakesh that attacked a French doctor believed to be spying for France. His

study provides an alternative to the state-centered view. Katz, *Murder in Marrakesh*. Edmund Burke's work on Morocco also shifts focus away from the *makhzan* by highlighting the socioeconomic history of the pre-Protectorate period. He examines the ways in which capitalist integration of the Moroccan economy influenced the forms of resistance that occurred in Morocco during the era, especially rural rebellions. Edmund Burke, *Prelude to Protectorate in Morocco: Precolonial Protest and Resistance, 1860–1912* (Chicago: University of Chicago Press, 1976). See also Edmund Burke, "The Moroccan Ulama, 1860–1912: An Introduction," in *Scholars, Saints, and Sufis: Muslim Religious Institutions in the Middle East since 1500,* ed. Nikki R. Keddie (Berkeley: University of California Press, 1972), 93–125. Some new perspectives have emerged regarding the role played by society in the transformations associated with the transition to modernity in the Middle East and North Africa. Some examples of this include Ilham Khuri-Makdisi, *The Eastern Mediterranean and the Making of Global Radicalism, 1860–1914* (Berkeley: University of California Press, 2010). Cemil Aydin, *The Politics of anti–Westernism in Asia: Visions of World Order in pan-Islamic and pan-Asian Thought* (New York: Columbia University Press, 2007); James McDougall, *History and the Culture of Nationalism in Algeria* (Cambridge: Cambridge University Press, 2006); Eve M. Troutt Powell, *A Different Shade of Colonialism: Egypt, Great Britain and the Mastery of the Sudan* (Berkeley: University of California Press, 2003); Ussama Makdisi, *The Culture of Sectarianism: Community, History and Violence in Nineteenth-Century Ottoman Lebanon* (Berkeley: University of California Press, 2002).

26. I borrow the phrase "new key of politics" from historian Carl Schoerske.
27. Lebanon, Israel, Jordan, and Saudi Arabia are exceptions.
28. Duara, *Rescuing History from the Nation.*
29. In the late nineteenth and early twentieth centuries during al-Kattānī's life, examples of such prestige certainly existed. For example, the Wazzānī *shurafā'* held vast landed estates north of Fez. In the southern part of the realm, Sharqāwī shaykhs mobilized rebellions against the *makhzan*. In some cases, claims to prophetic lineage—such as those of the rebel leader and pretender to

the throne, Bū Ḥmāra—helped in mobilizing forces against the *makhzan* between 1903 and 1909.

30. Here, I refer to Carlo Ginzburg's masterful study of the inquisition trials in sixteenth-century Friuli. Carlo Ginzburg, *The Cheese and the Worms: The Cosmos of a Sixteenth-Century Miller,* trans. John and Anne Tedeschi (Harmondsworth, NY: Penguin Books, 1982).
31. The quote refers to the mostly debunked decline paradigm in Ottoman studies, which situates the Ottoman golden age during the reign of Sultan Sulayman the Magnificent (1520–1566). Cemal Kafadar, *Between Two Worlds: The Construction of the Ottoman State* (Berkeley: University of California Press, 1995), 14.
32. Dipesh Chakrabarty explains the limitations of writing about non-Western societies using analytical categories associated with the European and American sociological tradition. He writes: "Unlike in the case of the mathematical sciences or other disciplines that allow formal presentation of problems, it is difficult for social-science categories to attain a universality that is completely free of historical and contingent differences between societies. While such categories are eminently translatable across societies and should, indeed, be translated in the interest of social justice, they are also dogged by problems that arise from such acts of translation. This happens because societies are not tabulae rasae. They come with their own plural histories that have already been imbibed by their members through certain shared dispositions, skills, competencies, and sentiments." Confusion and, in the case of al-Kattānī, obfuscation have more to do with "the problems of translation that we, academic intellectuals, encounter" in our efforts to describe non-Western societies "through the filter of European-derived social sciences and political philosophies." Chakrabarty, *Habitations of Modernity,* xxii–xxiii. On the use of the colonial archive and its shaping of scholarly discourse about North African societies see: Sahar Bazzaz, "Reading Reform beyond the State: Salwat al-Anfas, Islamic Revival and Moroccan National History," *Journal of North African Studies* 13, no. 1 (2008): 1–13; Burke, "The Creation of the Moroccan Colonial Archive, 1880–1930"; Edmund Burke, "The Image of the Moroccan State in French Ethnological Literature: A New Look at Lyautay's Berber Policy," in *Arabs and Berbers: From Tribe to Nation in North Africa,* ed. Ernest Gellner and Charles Micaud (London: Gerald Duckworth and Co., 1973),

175–199; Edmund Burke, "The First Crisis of Orientalism," in *Connaissances du Maghreb: sciences sociales et colonisation,* ed. Jean-Claude Vatin et al. (Paris: Editions du Centre National de la Recherche Scientifique 1984), 213–226; Julia Clancy-Smith, "In the Eye of the Beholder: Sufi and Saint in North Africa and the Colonial Production of Knowledge, 1830–1900," *Africana Journal* 15 (1990): 220–257; Abdelmajid Hannoum, "Colonialism and Knowledge in Algeria: The Archives of the Arab Bureau," *History and Anthropology* 12 (2001), 343–379.

33. On French Orientalism and its assessment of the Moroccan Muslim literary tradition, see Bazzaz, "Reading Reform beyond the State."

· ONE ·

Muḥammad al-Kattānī: Shaykh for a New Era

In the late nineteenth century, the Moroccan territory—known in the Islamic geographical tradition as al-Maghrib al-Aqṣā—was bounded by the Atlantic Ocean to the west, the Mediterranean Sea to the north, and Taza and the Atlas Mountains to the east and south, respectively.[1] Since the early Muslim conquests in the seventh century, Morocco had been ruled and controlled by numerous dynasties and would-be claimants seeking to establish themselves as rulers in the name of Islam. The extent and reach of any particular dynasty changed over time, sometimes reaching as far as Spain and parts of modern Algeria. At other times, Moroccan dynastic control was restricted to the region's hinterlands, with coastal cities occupied by foreign powers. The Ottoman conquest of Algeria in the mid-sixteenth century helped solidify the broad outlines of the Moroccan territory. Situated in the northwestern corner of the African continent and divided from Europe by the narrow nine-mile Straits of Gibraltar, Morocco shared a political, geographical, and symbolic space with other societies of the Mediterranean world—including the Ottoman empire, Spain and France, the numerous corsairs and crusaders who pirated the Mediterranean Sea, and before the unification of Italy in the nineteenth century, Venice and the papal states.[2] By the nineteenth century, a self-conscious

Moroccan polity had existed for some four hundred years with its own sense of political identity, of the concepts of power and authority that defined that identity, and of its relationship to the larger Muslim *umma* and other states in the region (such as Spain and the Ottoman empire).[3]

Until the establishment of the French Protectorate in 1912, the Moroccan state and society were defined by a system known as *Sharifism*. Sharifism privileged the *shurafāʾ*—descendants of the Prophet Muḥammad—as political agents, as interlocutors between various sectors of society, and as would-be dynasts. The *shurafāʾ* emerged as a loosely defined social and political group during the period of Merinid dynastic rule of Morocco in the thirteenth century, and their political role was enhanced as a result of their participation in the jihadist movement against the Iberian Catholic incursions into North Africa in the fifteenth century.[4] Under Sharifism, Moroccans of all social classes venerated the *shurafāʾ* as saints. The Moroccan cult of the saints found expression in rituals (such as celebrations of the birth of the Prophet) claims of possession of prophetic relics, and the rise of hagiographic tradition (which documented the lives, spiritual achievements, and miracles of saints). Pilgrimages to saints' tombs, *zāwiya*s, and shrines and the offering of donations for the purpose of healing or intercession formed the basis of sharifan material advantage. Furthermore, *shurafāʾ* sanctuaries and *zāwiya*s functioned as safe zones beyond the jurisdiction of the *makhzan*, where fugitives could seek sanctuary *(ḥurm)*. As extensions of the divine realm, spaces designated as *ḥurm* were deemed sacred and inviolable.[5] Mystical doctrines associated with the teachings of Abū ʿAbdallah Muḥammad ibn ʿAbd al-Raḥmān al-Jazūlī (d. 1465) provided the ideological basis for sharifan power and authority within Sharifism.[6] Based on the eschatological concept of *tajdīd* (renewal), al-Jazūlī and his followers viewed saints as spiritual and social exemplars with active roles to play in the preservation and reinvigoration of their societies.[7] Jazūliyya ideas enabled the involvement of the *shurafāʾ* in politics and also paved the way for the rise of political dynasties that drew their power and authority to rule on the basis of their descent from the Prophet.

One branch of the *shurafāʾ*, the ʿAlawīs, consolidated Sharifism when they ascended to power in the mid-seventeenth century. Although their origins were in the southern Moroccan Tafilalt Oasis, they extended their power throughout the Moroccan territory by creating alliances with the great *shurafāʾ* families of Fez, most notably those families who traced their lineage to the Idrīsīs—that is, those *shurafāʾ* who descended from the founder of Fez, Idrīs bin Idrīs. Their patron-client networks proved instrumental in controlling the city and in navigating the waters of Fāsī urban politics. In Sharifism, political power was highly decentralized and consisted of power-sharing arrangements between the various Moroccan *shurafāʾ* families and the dynasty that controlled the Moroccan state *(makhzan)*. Central to Sharifism was the concept of *baraka,* a vaguely defined term often translated into English as "charisma," which served as a way of assessing, articulating and evaluating the power of an individual within this system. A *baraka*-laden individual was someone who had social or political agency in Moroccan society. *Baraka* enabled such a person to challenge the sultanate as well as to support its decisions and actions.

To explain Shaykh Muḥammad al-Kattānī's exceptional activism and his motivations for dedicating his life to the reform of his society, scholars have had recourse to this concept of *baraka.* As conceived in the extant historical literature, *baraka* is a quality fixed across time and space and related to prophetic lineage, learning and piety.[8] According to this model of social action, what distinguishes one *baraka*-laden individual from another is his or her degree of *baraka* in relation to others. There is little in this conception of *baraka* to tell us about the social, political, and cultural context in which Moroccans came to view Muḥammad al-Kattānī as a *baraka*-laden saint. Nor does it help us understand why al-Kattānī considered himself to possess the quality of *baraka* and hence believed that he had a role to play in the reform of his society. Other interpretations posit al-Kattānī's popularity in terms of his ability to speak on different levels to various social groups—that is, to articulate "the despair of a people on the verge of being colonized." He did this by effectively utilizing widely recognizable cultural metaphors.[9] But while this reading furthers our understanding about why Moroccans rallied around Muḥammad al-Kattānī (that is, why Moroccans viewed him as a *baraka*-laden or charismatic individual), it does not provide insight into his motivations in assuming this role. The argument simply assumes that anticolonialism was the driving force behind the conflicts that emerged among Moroccans during the pre-Protectorate period.

To give meaning to Muḥammad al-Kattānī's *baraka*—the quality that endowed him with religious, political, and social authority—we must consider what historian Vincent Cornell terms the "parameters of sainthood." To be a saint, argues Cornell, is to be recognized as such by one's peers and to be endowed with power and authority by them. If we are to move beyond a phenomenological understanding of sainthood and toward a historicized one, we must then situate Muḥammad al-Kattānī, his supporters (and detractors), and the movement he created within the intellectual, cultural, and sociopolitical context of the period in which he lived.[10]

MUḤAMMAD AL-KATTĀNĪ AND CRISIS ON THE HORIZON

Muḥammad al-Kattānī's generation of Moroccans was influenced by a sense that a crisis was in the making. Born in 1873 in Fez, Morocco, al-Kattānī witnessed dramatic events, all of which pointed to the possibility that Morocco would fall to French control. By the time he had come of age and begun building the Kattāniyya religious brotherhood, almost one hundred years of important political, economic, and intellectual changes had occurred in Morocco and throughout the wider Muslim Mediterranean as a result of the extension of European power into the region. In Fez, the last quarter of the nineteenth century was marked by social discontent and urban rioting. A new social class of merchant and bureaucratic elites was confidently making its mark on the city and in government as trade with Europe in foodstuffs, wool, animal skins, cloth, yarns, tea, sugar and silk increased. Their conspicuous palatial constructions began to dot the city's landscape.[11] The traditional Fāsī elite to which Muḥammad al-Kattānī belonged—the *shurafāʾ*—lost ground to new social forces and to a new coterie of European advisers, diplomats and businessmen who arrived at the ʿAlawī court hoping to influence the course of Moroccan reform. Meanwhile, the trajectory of the *makhzan*'s reforms—the centralization of administration, authority, and finance—also threatened to undermine the already tenuous system of power sharing that had existed for over two hundred years between the *makhzan* and notable sharifan families, such as the Kattānīs. Heightened contact through increased trade, improved communications technology, and the arrival of Europeans to Morocco in large numbers greatly strained the Moroccan religiopolitical system and tested its limits to adapt and respond. Within this atmosphere of change, the challenge for Muḥammad al-Kattānī's generation was to harness the potential of the moment to address and navigate the transition.

In the first half of the century, concern among Moroccans regarding the nature of European power and the weakness of Islam in relation to it had already become a source of controversy and debate. European imperialism had resulted in the complete conquest of Algeria by France, the loss of vast Ottoman territories in the Balkans after 1878, the French occupation of Tunis in 1881, and the British occupation of Egypt in 1882. Although Morocco remained independent until 1912, by the mid-nineteenth century, it was already apparent that military and administrative reform on the part of the Moroccan state was necessary to shore up its power. After two disastrous military defeats at the hands of greatly superior European armies in 1844 (France) and 1861 (Spain), the Moroccan sultan, ʿAbd al-Raḥmān (r. 1822–1859), undertook the first in a series of reforms intended to put more power in the hands of the state. The most energetic of the nineteenth-century reformist sultans, Mawlāy Ḥasan (r. 1873–1894), spent virtually his entire reign on campaign throughout Morocco in an effort to assert central authority over outlying regions of the territory and extract much needed income for reforms in the form of taxes from recalcitrant tribes.[12] Like its Ottoman and Egyptian counterparts, though hardly as extensive in its scope or reach, Morocco had entered its own era of *tanzimat* or reform, which continued until the French conquest of Morocco and the establishment of the colonial order.

The *makhzan*'s military and economic reforms had proven mostly ineffective in preventing greater involvement of the European powers in Moroccan affairs. In 1880, those powers convened the Madrid Conference, at which they addressed their competing ambitions regarding Morocco. The result was the internationalization of the Morocco question and the further opening of Morocco to foreign intervention.[13] Furthermore, the expanding protégé system by which Moroccans received citizenships from various European states in exchange for providing services in trade and diplomacy also exposed the *makhzan*'s vulnerability.[14] In a rare expression of overt concern about the impending possibility of European conquest of Morocco, Muḥammad al-Kattānī's older cousin, an established *ʿālim* who taught at the Qarawīyīn University, offered a prayer *(duʿāʾ)* for the sultan, asking that God "strengthen him in the jihad against the unrelenting infidel."[15]

In 1873, the year of Muḥammad al-Kattānī's birth, the social unrest that had brewed beneath the surface in Fez since midcentury finally culminated in full-scale urban rebellion. In that year, the powerful tanners' guilds of Fez protested the *makhzan*'s implementation of an unpopular form of market tax known as the *mukūs* (sing. *maks*). The tanning of hides and production of leather goods for domestic and foreign export had been a mainstay of Fez's economy for generations. Urban legend had it that Mawlāy Idrīs, the city's founder, established the first tannery in Fez, an indicator of the degree to which these industries, at least among the city's common folk and artisan classes, were held in high esteem.[16] Therefore, the tanners' call for rebellion was heard by the "common folk" of Fez as wider discontent spilled over onto the streets of the city. The revolt turned violent when the tanners and their supporters took up arms against the government, barricading neighborhoods and restricting access to the *makhzan*'s tax collectors. Compelled by their anger and in need of a target at which to direct it, rioters sacked the houses of market officials, looting and stealing whatever they could in the process. In an ironic twist, one official who was fearful for his life, sought refuge at the tanners' esteemed place of worship, the sanctuary of Mawlāy Idrīs.[17]

Fez had experienced numerous rebellions before the Tanners' Rebellion of 1873.[18] However, the 1873 uprising was the first of its kind in Fez in which the rebels articulated their demands in terms of corporate identity. The rebellion was therefore significant not only because of the resulting violence and destruction but also because it marked the culmination of a trend toward the reconfiguration of social forces in Fez, which had begun almost a century before.[19]

The city of Fez had served as the imperial capital of the Moroccan sultanate for almost two hundred years by the time Muḥammad al-Kattānī came of age. As the first city built by Muslim conquerors in al-Maghrib al-Aqṣā in the early ninth century, Fez was famed as an abode of Islamic learning and as a center of trade and of pilgrimage for Muslims in western sub-Saharan and North Africa. Located at the juncture of a series of valleys providing natural passage through the Middle Atlas Mountains to the south and east, Fez was perfectly situated as a center for trade and for communications and as a main garrison for the sultan's army. From Fez, the *makhzan* launched its intermittent military campaigns *(ḥarka)* and negotiating parties against dissident tribes and regions. Mountain rivulets and springs ensured a steady water supply for the city's many gardens and cool fountains, for which Fāsī elites were renowned.[20] Fāsīs were well connected to other cities and regions of the sultanate from where news, pilgrims, produce, and goods for sale arrived. Sixty kilometers to the west of Fez lies the imperial city of Meknès. The small but prosperous town of Sefrou,[21] which caravans leaving Fez had passed on their way south to Tafilalt and the Sudan since the opening of trade in the seventeenth century, lies about twenty kilometers to the southeast. Taza, an important stop on the old pilgrimage route from Morocco and the gateway to Tlemcen and Algiers, lies almost directly east of Fez near the Algerian border. Finally, heading northwest from Fez through Ouezzane, travelers and caravans would reach the Atlantic ports of Larache and Tangier. The port cities with which Fez was connected facilitated contacts between Moroccans and Europeans and with the Islamic lands of the eastern Mediterranean.

"THE LIGHT OF THE LAMP OF PROPHECY"

Muḥammad bin ʿAbd al-Kabīr al-Kattānī was born to a Fāsī family of status and prestige. His family, among Fez's religious and political elite, had resided in the city continuously since the sixteenth century.[22] As a *sharīf*—a descendant of the prophet Muḥammad—Muḥammad bin ʿAbd al-Kabīr al-Kattānī was born a member of the religiopolitical elite of Moroccan society and was therefore a son of privilege and status. The al-Kattānī family—whose strong ties to the imperial city of Fez extended back several centuries—traced their genealogy to Fez's illustrious founder and patron saint, Idrīs bin Idrīs. According to the Islamic discursive tradition, Mawlāy Idrīs—himself a descendant of the holy family—had built Fez in the early ninth century, establishing the city as the capital of the eponymous Idrīsī dynasty. Although the Idrīsīs did not rule for long, numerous saint cults centered on the Idrīsī *shurafāʾ* arose after the alleged discovery of Mawlāy Idrīs's tomb in Fez in 1438.[23] Mawlāy Idrīs was "the sultan of the saints," explained one esteemed nineteenth-century Sufi and *ʿālim*. "If there were to be a prophet after Muḥammmad," the Sufi added, "[that prophet] would be Idrīs."[24] Thus, Muḥammad al-Kattānī's connection to Islam's holy family meant that he shared the same lineage as that of many of the highly revered Moroccan saints. And it was the same lineage as that of the 'Alawī sultans who ruled Morocco.

The Kattāniyyūn were also widely recognized in Fez for their generations of learned, pious, and spiritually exemplary men and women. The seventeenth-century Moroccan author, Muḥammad bin al-Ṭayyib al-Qādirī, celebrated the Kattānīs in his renowned chronicle of Fez, *Nashr al-mathānī.*[25] The tombs of Kattānī ancestors were sites of pilgrimage, and the mystical brotherhood associated with the Kattānī family was a place for spiritual contemplation.[26]

Peidgree aside, al-Kattānī was an exceptional child in his own right. From an early age, he exhibited many of the characteristics of Muslim sainthood—a desire for knowledge, profound piety and spiritual depth, and love of God and the Prophet. He was quick to memorize the Quran, the first step in his immersion into the world of Islamic knowledge, and he displayed a level of intellectual and spiritual acumen that had not been seen in Fez for many years.[27] Noting that the boy arrived at his classes each day carrying numerous leather-bound notebooks, his instructor inquired jokingly whether Muḥammad had a donkey that could carry them all for him.[28] "When he left home in the morning," explained Muḥammad's younger brother, "he would not return until the *maghrib* prayer, the entire time spent in study."[29]

In the tradition of many of his esteemed ancestors, Muḥammad al-Kattānī continued his studies at Fez's illustrious Qarawīyīn University, where he received instruction from a number of distinguished Moroccan ulama in the standard subjects of Islamic education—hadith, exegesis, scholastic theology, grammar, and commentaries on the works of the *Mālikī* school of law.[30] Firmly grounded in the theories of classical *fiqh,* young al-Kattānī decided to further his understanding of the "divine secrets" through the teachings of Islamic mysticism. Al-Kattānī's father, himself a prominent Sufi and spiritual guide, served as mentor to Muḥammad, guiding him in the doctrines and practices of Sufism through the writings of important mystics, including al-Suhrawardī, Ibn al-ʿArabī, and al-Tirmidhī. In the tradition of numerous mystics before him, Muḥammad al-Kattānī took on the attributes of asceticism, immersing himself in silent contemplation, shunning worldly concerns, and surviving "for three days with the same piece of bread in his pocket."[31]

Yet despite his commitment to asceticism, Muḥammad al-Kattānī understood that sainthood encompassed dimensions other than contemplation, quietism, and disengagement from the world.[32] In Arabic, the words *walāya* and *wilāya* are used interchangeably to mean sainthood. Vincent Cornell has emphasized, however, that the focus on a strictly etymological analysis by scholars (which favors the term *walāya*), obscures the fact that in the Quran, the meaning of *walī Allah* is closer to that of "God's assistant or manager." The interchangeable use of the two terms reflects two components of sainthood in the Islamic tradition—the spiritual and the political. That is, saints also had important roles to play in their societies. They were not simply people who were "close to God," as one meaning of the word *walī* (the Arabic word for *saint*) suggests. Rather they were also "God's helpers"—meaning that saints acted as God's agents on earth, keeping watch over the Muslim community and protecting it from decline and anarchy.[33] In his capacity as an aspiring spiritual leader and *walī,* Muḥammad al-Kattānī began to make public appearances with his father at gatherings of ulama and Sufis in Fez and other cities in Morocco. By 1895, Muḥammad had assumed a position of leadership in the Kattāniyya *zāwiya* in Fez alongside his father. Disciples among the Fāsī ulama and the popular classes came to the *zāwiya* to pray, to practice the mystical rituals of the Kattāniyya brotherhood, and to study with Muḥammad al-Kattānī. He received praise from prominent Sufis, who were impressed by the young man's intellectual and spiritual capacities. When al-Kattānī reached maturity, predicted a prominent Moroccan Tijāniyya shaykh, he would be among the select few who were "close to God and [capable of] guid[ing] [the Muslim community]."[34] Ten years later, at only thirty-four years of age, al-Kattānī's fame had spread throughout Morocco. He was poised to navigate his countrymen and women through the most important political upheaval in pre-Protectorate Moroccan history.[35]

The *mujaddid* tradition of Islam stipulated that, in every century, God sent someone to the Muslim community to restore and revive Islam. The *mujaddid* (renewer of the age) was a person in whom the Muslim community placed its hopes for such a revival.[36] Moreover, Moroccan mystical tradition explained that the *mujaddid* drew his inspiration from "the light of the Lamp of Prophecy."[37] Believing his unborn grandson would someday fulfill this role, Muḥammad al-Kattānī's grandfather had given a lantern to the expectant mother of the child yet to be born—an omen of "his miracles [to come]."[38]

The reference to the "Lamp of Prophecy" would not be lost to Moroccans of a particular spiritual inclination and mystical training. Illumination was a concept central to Islamic doctrines of sainthood. Quran 33:46, for example, refers to the Prophet Muḥammad as "a torch that illumines." Quran 5:15 states, "a light has come to you from God."[39] Mystical doctrine held that all the prophets before Muḥammad—Moses, Jesus, and others—had received a portion of divine truth, which traveled in the form of a light from one messenger of God to the next during their lifetimes. Because of the Muslim Prophet's ontological perfection, this light attained its complete and final manifestation in him. Muslim mystics called this fully formed state of illumination the Muḥammadan light *(al-nūr al-Muḥammadī)*.[40] It evoked a similar incident in the life of the Prophet. In *al-Sīra al-Nabawiyya,* for example, Ibn Hishām referred to a saying of the prophet: "[W]hen my mother was pregnant with me, a light emanated from her that lit all the palaces of al-Shām."[41] Similarly, Moroccans associated light and illumination to the story of the birth of Mawlāy Idrīs, from whom Idrīsī *shurafā'* such as Muḥammad al-Kattānī traced their lineage. According to the legend, when Mawlāy Idrīs was born, "a star from the east and the west whose first light was white and last light was red continued appearing to the people of this farthest Maghrib for seven days."[42]

The hagiographer reveals that Muḥammad al-Kattānī portrayed himself in the images of Moses and of the Moroccan mystic, Bū Ya'zā, both great saintly figures of the Moroccan Sufi tradition. As did the prophet Moses, al-Kattānī veiled his face.[43] According to the typology of Muslim saints elaborated by Ibn al-'Arabī, "When Moses returned from his Lord, God clothed his face in light as a sign of the authenticity of that which he declared; and so fierce was this light that no one could look on him without being blinded, so that he had to cover his face with a veil in order that those who looked in his face would not be taken ill when they saw him."[44] Mawlāy Bū Ya'zā (d. 572 AH/ 1177 CE), another veiled saint from the Middle Atlas region of Morocco, was widely veneretated in the Moroccan mystical tradition and among the population at large. His Sufi contemporaries referred to Bū Ya'zā as the "shaykh of the shaykhs."[45] Bū Ya'zā was "[a] Moses-like [type of saint] [*mūsawī al-wirth*], and God had bestowed on him the same miraculous sign: No one could look him in the face without losing their sight."[46]

Finally, to further highlight al-Kattānī's messianic role, the hagiographer recounts and then interprets a dream told to him about al-Kattānī. "The finest wheat I have ever seen was being ground at the Kattāniyya *zāwiya,*" explained the sufi, 'Abd al-'Azīz bin Aḥmad al-Dabbāgh. Soon after experiencing the dream, al-Dabbāgh ran into young Muḥammad al-Kattānī, perhaps at the *zāwiya* or in the street of the Ibn Ṣawwāl neighborhood where the Kattānīs resided. The encounter helped al-Dabbāgh realize the meaning of his dream. For some time previously, he had believed that God had forsaken the Muslims. "But now," said al-Dabbāgh, God offered them guidance "by the hand of al-Kattānī."[47]

THE DECLINE OF THE *SHURAFĀ'*

During the calamitous events in Fez of 1873, the ulama made an effort to resolve the crisis by intervening on behalf of the rebels. Traditionally, the ulama frowned on the state's market tax from both juridical and ideological perspectives. The Quran did not stipulate the *mukūs;* therefore, it was somewhat suspect among the ulama as an innovation on God's word. More significant was their fear that the *mukūs* would fall most heavily on the shoulders of the common folk, ultimately burdening the most vulnerable sectors of the population. Therefore, in an effort to avoid what seemed inevitable, the ulama unsuccessfully asked that the sultan rescind the despised *mukūs*. Instead, the sultan deferred to the opinion of a little-known *'ālim,* who drafted a legal opinion sanctifying its collection, thereby exposing the diminished agency of the ulama as political interlocutors.[48] After almost one year of intermittent conflict between the *makhzan*'s forces and the rebels and their supporters, the tanners accepted a deal whereby they would give their allegiance to the sultan.

The complete breakdown of traditional channels for the resolution of such crises as the Tanners' Rebellion was surely important in shaping awareness among members of Muḥammad al-Kattānī's generation of the danger that loomed in the not-too-distant future if the sultan were to lose his authority. As during the mid-eighteenth century, "time of troubles" (when the *makhzan*'s control of Fez was significantly reduced for about thirty years), Fez's traditional elites—the ulama and the *shurafā'* families like Muḥammad al-Kattānī's—had failed to bring order to the city. Instead, armed contingents of commoners (whom the *makhzan* traditionally recruited for policing duties) often, quite literally, called the shots, while the *makhzan* and religiopolitical elites marched to their rhythm.[49] Were this to happen in this latest crisis, Fez could go up in flames, and its elite families would go along with it.

These concerns were most certainly augmented by the fact

Figure 1. Fez, Zāwiya of Mawlāy Idrīs, Interior View
Courtesy of Islamic Collection, Fine Arts Library, Harvard University.

that traditional religiopolitical elites such as the Kattānīs watched as a new merchant class came to occupy unprecedented positions of power and influence among the sultan and his advisers. Before the nineteenth century, Moroccan merchants had few claims to political legitimacy and virtually no ability to influence the decisions of the *makhzan.* In Moroccan society, prestige and power had not been based on wealth but rather on belonging to or association with a noble family with genealogical ties to the Prophet Muḥammad and his descendants. Such families were more likely to gain wealth as a result of their noble descent or through access to the patron-client networks of these sharifan families.[50] In the 1830s, for example, a coalition of Fāsī merchants successfully pressured Sultan ʿAbd al-Raḥmān not to break relations with France following the conquest of Algeria. Commercial interests in Algeria were too valuable to be threatened by political conflicts.[51] Yet Moroccan merchants—both Muslim and Jewish—thrived after Sultan ʿAbd al-Raḥmān signed free-trade agreements with Britain in 1856, and later with France and Spain. Commercial ties between Moroccan merchants and European trading companies, knowledge of foreign languages as a result of such contacts, and familiarity with European methods of diplomacy and banking collectively made the enterprising Moroccan commercial elite extremely valuable to the *makhzan.* From midcentury onward, merchants filled positions in the expanding bureaucracy the *makhzan* created to facilitate Moroccan ties with the European powers. These newly created bureaucratic positions, such as the *umanāʾ* or tariff inspectors, were emblematic of the emerging order in Morocco in which prestige, power, and authority were linked to knowledge of European models of governance, administration, and economy.[52]

The Moroccan learned establishment articulated the changing Moroccan political, socioeconomic, and intellectual landscape in their literary production. Although Moroccan scholars of the nineteenth century did not explain the reasons for their renewed interest in historical genres, they embarked on a renaissance in historical forms of literary production—such as dynastic chronicles *(tārīkh)*, hagiographies *(manāqib)* and biographies *(tarājim)*—with the hope that they might influence the direction of change.[53] Composed to document "the vast number of ulama and *ṣulaḥā'* who resided in the city of Fez" from its foundation in the ninth century, *Salwat al-anfās*—a nine-hundred page hagiography of the *shurafā'*, saints, Sufis, ulama, and pious folk of Fez—is one of the most significant among these literary experiments. Written in the 1880s by Muḥammad al-Kattānī's cousin, Muḥammad bin Ja'far al-Kattānī—a legal scholar and mystic in his own right—*Salwat al-anfās* reasserted the prominence of the Idrīsī *shurafā'* (to which his family belonged) while simultaneously offering a veiled critique of the 'Alawī sultans for abandoning consultation with the learned elite *(dhū al-'ilm/dhū al-ma'rifa)* in political matters.[54]

"A LOFTY AND UNAMBIGUOUS LINEAGE": SAINTS, SUFIS, AND THE *SHURAFĀ'* IN NINETEENTH-CENTURY FEZ

In Fez, powerful sharifan families depended on good relations with the *makhzan* to maintain their status among the Fāsī religiopolitical elite and support their patron-client networks. In exchange for their loyalty to the 'Alawī dynasty, the Idrīsīs received numerous privileges, such as tax exemptions and the right to collect donations at the tombs of their ancestors. The more prestigious *shurafā'* even possessed power akin to ulama-bureaucrats to arbitrate in legal disputes because their *zāwiya*s and shrines also served as inviolable sanctuaries *(ḥurm)* or safe zones, where the reach of the *makhzan* was restricted.[55] But from the reign of Mawlāy Ismā'īl (r. 1672–1727), the *makhzan* began to check and document family lineages officially, weeding out fraudulent claims and limiting the number of families who could receive benefits and tax cuts provided to the *shurafā'*, thereby creating a heightened atmosphere of competition among Fez's notable families. Official recognition of a *nasab ṣāliḥ*—a sound genealogy—helped families secure their positions within the world of inter-*shurafā'* politics.[56]

Since the Merinid period, Moroccan dynasties had acknowledged the prominence of the Kattānīs because of "the unambiguity of their lineage and the loftiness of their position."[57] In more recent times, successive 'Alawī sultans also recognized the Kattānīyūn as members of the religiopolitical elite by granting the family rights to collect pilgrims' donations made at the tomb of Abū Maymūna Darrās b. Ismā'īl, around whom one of the earliest saint cults in Fez had emerged.[58] According to the royal decree, "[pilgrims' dontaions at the tomb] remain in the hands of the Kattānī clan of the Kattānī *shurafā'*. Only they should benefit from the donations, and [they have the right] to use them without conflict or opposition [that may arise] due to their weakness or state of poverty." This was a privilege due them "because of their relations to the Prophet of God, blessing and peace upon him."[59] After his departure from or return to Fez the 'Alawī sultan, 'Abd al-Raḥmān (r. 1822–1859), and his entourage performed a pilgrimage to the tomb of one of al-Kattānī's ancestors, a saint named Mawlāy al-Ṭayyib al-Kattānī (d. 1837/1838).[60] The 'Alawīs made additional gestures toward the Kattānī family beyond the usual genealogical recognition. In 1864, for example, Sīdī Muḥammad (r. 1859–1873), donated a *ḥubus* property that was held in his name for enlargement of the Kattāniyya *zāwiya* in Fez.[61] In the competitive world of sharifan politics, displays of support such as those of Sīdī 'Abd al-Raḥmān and Sīdī Muḥammad could prove significant in shoring up the prominence of the Kattānīs.

By the time Muḥammad al-Kattānī was born, the Kattānīs had made their mark on Fāsī intellectual, spiritual and political life, and his family was well situated to take their position on the stage of Fāsī politics according to the rules of Sharifism. More important, the family seemed to gain prominence even as the *shurafā'* were losing out. Yet as is shown in the following chapter, al-Kattānī's *baraka* was influenced by his willingness to challenge the political establishment—namely, the ulama and the makhzan—regarding the meaning of Islamic orthodoxy and who had the authority to determine its limits.

NOTES

1. Aḥmad bin Khālid al-Nāṣirī, *al-Istiqsā li akhbār duwal al-Maghrib al-Aqṣā,* ed. Jaʿfar and Muḥammad al-Nāṣirī (Casablanca: Dār al-Kitāb, 1997), 1: 127.
2. By emphasizing Morocco's relationship with the wider Mediterranean world, I do not mean to suggest that important relationships with other regions (such as sub-Saharan Africa) did not exist. However, although scholars of North Africa have begun to recognize and examine in detail the region's links with sub-Saharan Africa, they remain mostly unexplored. The American Institute of Maghrib Studies, the West African Research Association, and the Tangier-based American Legation Institute for Moroccan Studies recently convened (June 2009) the first in a two-part series of conferences entitled Saharan Crossroads I and II to develop this underexplored avenue of research.
3. Abderrahman el Moueddin discusses the importance of travel in shaping a distinct Moroccan Muslim identity. He argues that between the fourteenth and nineteenth centuries, the Hajj (as well as embassies sent to Europe and the Ottoman Empire to represent the Moroccan sultanate) helped strengthen the bonds between Morocco and the broader Islamic *umma,* while simultaneously highlighting differences. For example, the seventeenth-century Moroccan scholar and traveler Abū Salīm ʿAbdallah al-ʿAyyāshī expressed wonder about the bustle of Cairo's streets and markets. Yet he also noted with displeasure the low level of religious knowledge among the Bedouin populations of Arabia as compared with his own countrymen and perceived the Ottoman sharia courts to be plagued by corruption (presumably in comparison with those back home). Abderrahman el Moueddin, "The Ambivalence of *Rihla:* Community Integration and Self-definition in Moroccan Travel Accounts, 1300–1800," in *Muslim Travellers: Pilgrimage, Migration and the Religious Imagination,* ed. Dale F. Eickelman and James Piscatori (Berkeley: University of California Press, 1990), 78. On Ottoman-Moroccan relations, see Abderrahman el Moueddin, "Sharifs and Padishahs: Moroccan-Ottoman Relations

from the Sixteenth through the Eighteenth Centuries," Ph.D. diss., Princeton, University, Princeton, NJ, 1992.

4. Vincent Cornell, *Realm of the Saint: Power and Authority in Moroccan Sufism* (Austin: University of Texas Press, 1998), 162–164.
5. Mohamed el Mansour, "The Sanctuary *(Hurm)* in Precolonial Morocco," in *In the Shadow of the Sultan: Culture, Power, and Politics in Morocco,* ed. Rahma Bourqia and Susan Gilson Miller (Cambridge: Harvard University Press, 1999), 49–73.
6. Abdelahad Sebti, "Au Maroc: Sharifisme, Citadin, Charisme et Historiographie," *Annales ESC* 2 (Mars–Avril 1986): 437.
7. Al-Jazūlī called for the renewal of Islam by invoking the *mujaddid* tradition, which was grounded in eschatological discourse and based on a hadith that states, "God will send to this community at the turn of every century someone who will restore religion." Cornell, *Realm of the Saints,* 184. On the concept of cyclical reform, see Ella Landau-Tasserson, "The 'Cyclical Reform': A Study of the Mujaddid Tradition," *Studia Islamica* 70 (1989): 79–117. On the teachings of the Jazūliyya order and its importance for the involvement of Sufi saints in the political conflicts of the day, see Vincent Cornell, "Mystical Doctrine and Political Action in Moroccan Sufism: The Role of the Exemplar in the Tariqa al-Jazuliyya," *al-Qantara* 13, fasc. 1(1992): 202.
8. Most notably, Edmund Burke and Abdallah Laroui. Their focus was social history, not cultural or intellectual history. Burke, "The Moroccan Ulama, 1860–1912; Laroui, *Les origines sociales et culturelles du nationalism Marocain, 1830–1912.*
9. Henry Munson Jr. attempted to move debate about Muḥammad al-Kattānī beyond the existing framework of inquiry by acknowledging the centrality of saintly figures in challenging state authority. Munson reads al-Kattānī's life in terms of "the righteous man of God"—a charismatic figure who was held to be both righteous and saintly and whose authority as a scholar and a saint formed the basis for his ability to challenge the state. Rather than fall back on a reified notion of charisma, Munson emphasized that conceptions of charisma are embedded in historical circumstances. See chapter 3 in Henry Munson Jr., *Religion and Power in Morocco* (New Haven: Yale University Press, 1993), 76.
10. Cornell, Introduction, *Realm of the Saint.* See also Stephen T. Katz, Editor's Introduction, in *Mysticism and Philosophical Anal-*

ysis, ed. Stephen T. Katz (New York: Oxford University Press, 1978), 1–9.

11. Norman Cigar, "Socio-economic Structures and the Development of an Urban Bourgeoisie in Pre-colonial Morocco," *Maghreb Review* 6 (1981): 60–61. For an excellent discussion of the social and political ramifications of increased Moroccan trade with Europe in the nineteenth-century see, Daniel Schroeter, "Royal Power and the Economy in Pre-colonial Morocco: Jews and the Legitimation of Foreign Trade," in *In the Shadow of the Sultan: Culture, Power, and Politics in Morocco,* ed. Rahma Bourquia and Susan Gilson Miller (Cambridge: Harvard University Press, 1999), 74–102.
12. Jocelyne Dakhila shows how the *ḥarka* (the movement of the court from one region of the sultanate to another) was important for shoring up symbolic as well as military power of the state by emphasizing the ubiquity of royal authority. For instance, comparing the reigns of Mawlāy Ḥasan and his son and successor, ʿAbd al-ʿAzīz, one author wrote, "L'aigle vit dans les airs habite les déserts, tandis que le coq erre autour des maisons. La force de l'aigle lui confère un pouvoir absolu; mais le coq, que peut-il faire sinon effrayer les poules quand il chante?" ["The eagle lives in the skies and in the deserts, while the rooster wanders around homesteads. The eagle's strength confers on him absolute power. As for the rooster, what can he do other than frighten the chickens when he sings?"]. Jocelyne Dakhila, "Dans la mouvance du prince: la symbolique du pouvoir itinérant au Maghreb," *Annales ESC* 3 (Mai–Juin 1988): 737.
13. Burke, *Prelude to Protectorate,* 25–27.
14. Mohammed Kenbib, "Structures traditionnelles et protections étrangères au Maroc au XIXème siècle," *Hespéris-Tamuda* 22 (1984): 79–101.
15. al-Kattānī, *Salwa,* 3: 288. This *duʿā'* is one of the few overt expressions of a political agenda in *Salwa.* It appears in the biographical entry of Sultan ʿAbd al-ʿAzīz, who was the reigning sultan at the time *Salwa* went to press in 1898.
16. R. Le Tourneau and L. Paye, "La corporation des tanneurs et l'industrie de la tannerie à Fès," *Hespéris* 20–21 (1935): 167.
17. al-Nāṣirī, *al-Istiqsa,* 9: 137–138. For a detailed discussion of the Tanners' Rebellion as seen through Moroccan chronicles, see Abdelahad Sebti, "Chroniques de la contestation citadine: Fès et la

revolte des tanneurs (1873–1874)," *Hespéris-Tamuda* 29, fasc. 2 (1991): 283–312.

18. A rich body of scholarly literature on the sociohistorical significance of the crowd and the use of violence in popular protest movements has emerged in the last thirty-five years, most notably through the work of George Rudé and E. P. Thompson. While such a literature is less developed in the context of North African history, several authors have demonstrated the importance of popular protest movements and rebellions in influencing high politics in Fez. For example, regarding the 1873 rebellion in Fez, Bettina Dennerlein explains that the rebels never questioned the legitimacy of the sultan to rule but rather "the concrete extent of his power and more specifically to his capacity to effectively impose the levying of taxes." Popular rebellion merely constituted "one of the multitude of processes of legitimation and of political involvement and participation." Mohamed al-Mansour shows how popular anger and violence was instrumental in determining the bid for power by two contenders to the ʿAlawī sultanate in the late eighteenth century. He thereby challenges the notion that politics was merely the provenance of elites such as the *shurafāʾ* and ulama of Fez. Abdelahad Sebti uses the term *frondeur* to characterize Fez, arguing that popular rebellion was a recurring feature of Fāsī urban life and politics. He challenges characterizations of the city solely in terms of Islamic orthodoxy, of high culture and of allegiance to the *makhzan* (as opposed to rural syncretism and rebellion against the state). Dennerlein, "Legitimate Bounds and Bound Legitimacy," 296 and 288–289; Mohamed al-Mansour, "Urban society in Fez: The Rumat during the Modern Period (Seventeenth–Nineteenth Centuries)," *Maghreb Review* 22 (1997): 75–95; George Rudé, *The Crowd in History* (New York: Wiley, 1964); Sebti, "Chroniques de la contestation citadine," 283–284; E. P. Thompson, *The Making of the English Working Class* (New York: Vintage Books, 1963). On popular protest in the Middle East and North Africa, see also Stephanie Cronin, ed., *Subalterns and Social Protest: History from below in the Middle East and North Africa* (New York: Routledge, 2008).
19. Cigar, "Socio-economic Structures and the Development of an Urban Bourgoisie," 68. On the segmented nature of Fāsī social groups in the pre-Protectorate period and their reconfiguration see

Norman Cigar, "Conflict and Community in an Urban Milieu: Fez under the ʿAlawīs (ca. 1666–1830)," *Maghreb Review* 3, no. 10 (1978): 3–13.

20. The sixteenth-century traveler Leo the African and ʿAlī Bey, who visited Fez in 1805, both commented on the opulence of Fez's markets and attested to the advantages of the city's geographical location in facilitating trade. Roger Le Tourneau, *Fès avant le protectorat,* 2nd ed. (Rabat: Editions la Porte, 1987), 368.
21. Although a small town, Sefrou had importance both for the military and for commerce and trade. It marked the end of the district of Fez and served as the residence of the sultan's governors, whose presence was primarily directed at controlling the semi-independent and powerful tribes of Aït Yūsī and branches of the Banī Mglīd. In the late 1890s, a French traveler noted, "Enormous quantities of fruit, olives, citrons, cherries, [and] grapes, are sent from Sefrou to Fez, and even fairly good wine is made there. It is the entrepôt for almost all the oil of the surrounding region, which is rich in olive-trees." M. La Martinière, *Morocco: Journeys in the Kingdom of Fez and to the Court of Mulai Hassan* (London: Whittaker and Co., 1889), 400–401.
22. ʿAbd al-Ḥayy al-Kattānī, *al-Maẓāhir al-sāmiyya fī al-nisba al-sharīfa al-kattāniyya,* 1911, photocopy of original ms., private Collection of Dr. Fawzi Abdulrazak, Cambridge, MA., 14.
23. Mercedes Garcìa-Arenal and E. Manzano Moreno, "Idrissisme et villes Idrissides," *Studia Islamica* 82 (October 1995): 6. On the Idrīsīs, see also "Idrisids," *EI2* vol. 3, fasc. 57–58, pp. 1035–1037.
24. al-Kattānī, *Salwa,* 1: 82.
25. *Nashr al-mathānī* is mentioned in al-Kattānī, *al-Maẓāhir,* 2.
26. Ibid., 285, 331.
27. al-Kattānī, *Tarjama,* 11.
28. Ibid., 13.
29. Ibid.
30. Ibid., 12–13.
31. al-Kattānī, *al-Maẓāhir,* 71. This is a literary trope intended to illustrate al-Kattānī's piety and commitment to Sufism. Such expressions of piety and sainthood are formulaic and are often found in the *manāqib* literature and in chronicles. On the use of literary tropes in these literary genres, see Abdelahad Sebti, "Akhbār al-manāqib wa manāqib al-akhbār," in *al-Tārīkh wa adab al-*

manāqib (Rabat: al-Jamʿiyya al-Maghribiyya li al-baḥth al-tārīkhī, 1988), 93–112.

32. Michel Chodkiewicz explains that a basic problem associated with the discussion of sainthood in the Islamic tradition relates to translation. The term sainthood has most often been used to denote the Arabic term *walāya* or *wilāya* while a *walī* (pl. *awliyāʾ*)—the person who possesses the attributes of sainthood—is described in English as a saint. In the Christian tradition, sainthood is associated with the idea of purity and inviolability as in the Greek *hagios,* the Latin *sanctus* and the Hebrew *qadosh.* Etymologically speaking, such concepts correspond to the semantic field associated with the Arabic root letters q, d and s. Alternatively, the root ḥ, r, m would be expected to convey the notion of *sanctity* as reflected in the Greek *hieros* and the Latin *sacer.* In the Islamic tradition, neither root is used in association with a person who is described as a saint. Michel Chodkiewicz, *Seal of the Saints: Prophethood and Sainthood in the Doctrine of Ibn Arabi,* trans. Liadan Sherrard (Cambridge: Islamic Texts Society, 1993), 21.
33. Cornell, Introduction, *Realm of the Saint,* xvii–xxi.
34. al-Kattānī, *al-Maẓāhir,* 158. The Arabic is *"min ahl al-qarāba wa al-dalāla."*
35. Ibid., 31.
36. Landau-Tasserson, "The 'Cyclical Reform'," 82–83.
37. Abū ʿImrān Mūsā al-Wazzānī (d. 1562), *al-Kurrasa li Mawlāna al-Manṣūr al-Sulṭān al-Muẓaffar Muḥammad ibn Muḥammad al-Sharīf al-Ḥasanī fī mas'alat al-quṭb al-mushār ilayhi ahl al-ṭariqa al-ṣūfiyya* [no page], quoted in Cornell, "Mystical Doctrine and Political Action in Moroccan Sufism," 230.
38. al-Kattānī, *al-Maẓāhir,* 69.
39. Chodkiewicz, *Seal of the Saints,* 61.
40. The concept of *al-nūr al-Muḥammadi* ("the Muḥammadan light") was elaborated by the thirteenth century mystic, Muḥyīʾ al-Dīn ibn al-ʿArabī in his famous work *al-Futūḥāt al-makkiyya.* For an excellent explanation of the concept and its relation to the thinking of Ibn al-ʿArabī, see Chodkiewicz, *Seal of the Saints.* See also J. Spencer Trimingham, *The Sufi Orders in Islam* (New York: Oxford University Press, 1998), 161. For the reception of Ibn al-ʿArabī's ideas in the early modern period, see Alexander Knysh, "Ibn Arabi in the Later Islamic Tradition," *Muhyiddin Ibn Arabi:*

A Commemorative Volume, ed. by Stephen Hirtenstein and Michael Tiernan (Rockport, Ma.: Element, Inc., 1993), 307–327; Derin Terzioğlu, *"Sufi and Dissident in the Ottoman Empire: Niyazi-i Misri (1618–1694),"* Ph.D. diss., Harvard University, Cambridge, Ma., 1999.

41. Ibn Hishām, *al-Sīra al-nabawiyya,* ed. M. al-Saqaa, I. al-Abyaari, A. Shalabi, pt. 1, p. 166, quoted in Sebti, "Akhbār al-manāqib wa manāqib al-akhbār," 96.
42. Muḥammad b. Jaʿfar al-Kattānī, *al-Azhār al-ʿāṭira al-anfās bi dhikr maḥāsin qutb al-Maghrib wa tāj madinat Fās* (Lithographic Press: Fez, 1889), 195, quoted in Sebti, "Akhbār al-manāqib wa manāqib al-akhbār," 95.
43. Moses is known in the Islamic tradition as *kalīm Allah* or "the one who speaks with God." Several passages from the Quran speak of direct communication between God and Moses. Moses was formed in the image of the Prophet Muḥammad. "Musa," *EI2* vol. 7, fasc. 123–130: pp. 638–640; al-Kattānī, *al-Maẓāhir,* 133.
44. Muḥyī' al-Dīn ibn al-ʿArabī, *al-Futūḥāt al-makkiyya,* IV, 50–51, quoted in, Chodkiewicz, *Seal of the Saints,* 74.
45. Cornell, *Realm of the Saint,* 68. See also V. Loubignac, "Un saint berbère, Moulay Bou Azza," *Hespéris* 31 (1944): 5–34.
46. Chodkiewicz, *Seal of the Saints,* 74–75.
47. al-Kattānī, *al-Maẓāhir,* 165. ʿAbd al-ʿAzīz bin Aḥmad al-Dabbāgh, who related the dream to al-Kattānī, is not to be confused with the eighteenth-century Sufi ʿAbd al-ʿAzīz al-Dabbāgh. However, *al-Maẓāhir* does not provide specific information about the identity of ʿAbd al-ʿAzīz bin Aḥmad al-Dabbāgh such as the date of his birth or his genealogy, so it is difficult to know whether he was related to the eighteenth-century al-Dabbāgh, although it is likely.
48. Laroui, *Les Origines,* 294; Ibrāhīm Ḥarakāt, *al-tayyārāt al-siyāsiyya wa al-fikriyya bi al-maghrib khilāla qarnayn wa niṣf qabla al-ḥimaya* (Morocco?: s.n., 1985), 110.
49. el-Mansour, "Urban Society in Fez," 91.
50. Cigar, "Socio-economic Structures and the Development of an Urban Bourgeoisie in Pre-colonial Morocco," 60.
51. Ibid.
52. Sīdī Muḥammad established the *umanā'* corps in 1861. Other functionaries in the reformed bureaucracy worked in the ministry of foreign affairs—*wizārat al-baḥr.* Many of them were drawn or

came from delegations of Moroccan students who had visited Europe on official missions (between 1874 and 1888, eight delegations with about 350 people). Abdellah Laroui, *Esquisses Historiques* (Casablanca: Centre Culturel Arabe, 1992), 58.

53. Évariste Levi-Provençal, *Les historiens des chorfas* (Paris: Larose, 1922), 350.
54. Bazzaz, "Reading Reform beyond the State." On conceptions of power and authority in nineteenth-century Morocco, see Dennerlein, "Asserting Religious Authority in Late Nineteenth- Early Twentieth-Century Morocco."
55. el-Mansour, "The Sanctuary *(Hurm)* in Precolonial Morocco."
56. Sebti, "Au Maroc: Sharifisme, Citadin, Charisme et Historigraphie," 435–438.
57. al-Kattānī, *al-Maẓāhir,* 14.
58. Cornell, *Realm of the Saint,* 100.
59. al-Kattānī, *al-Maẓāhir,* 327.
60. Ibid., 285 and 331.
61. Ibid., 378.

· TWO ·

Debating Religious Power and Authority

All those who believe in Sufism are the elite among the believers. All those who understand Sufism are the elite among the elite.

—'Abd al-Kabīr al-Kattānī[1]

The first glimpse of Muḥammad bin 'Abd al-Kabīr al-Kattānī in the *makhzan*'s archival record comes in the form of a series of letters exchanged between the Qāḍī of Fez and the Moroccan regent, Aḥmad bin Mūsā, between 1895 and 1896. Word of Muḥammad al-Kattānī's popularity had reached the ears of higher authorities. Only two years after he took over the leadership of the Kattāniyya order and despite his promising start as a Sufi and shaykh, the *makhzan* and the ulama of Fez charged Muḥammad al-Kattānī with heresy and declared him "doctrinally corrupt."[2] In October 1896, the *makhzan* commanded the closing of the Kattāniyya *zāwiya* in Fez after a group of ulama charged with examining al-Kattānī's activities deemed them blasphemous.[3] Al-Kattānī fled Fez and headed for the southern imperial city of Marrakesh, where Sultan 'Abd al-'Azīz, his advisers, and his courtiers had recently taken up residence. Al-Kattānī spent the next five months trying to establish his innocence and negotiate his freedom.

Muḥammad al-Kattānī's biographer dismissed the accusation of heresy as an expression of the jealousies of Fez's ulama over the increasing popularity of the Kattāniyya order under young Muḥammad's leadership.[4] But Muḥammad al-Kattānī could not have taken the matter lightly, given the implications of such a verdict for him personally and for the fate of the Kattāniyya order. Typically, the stigma of heresy carried severe punishment. According to Aḥmad al-Wansharīsī's *al-Miʿyār,* a standard text used by Malikī jurists throughout the nineteenth century to determine precedence in legal cases, the penalty for heresy was death.[5] The accusation of heresy not only carried with it the possibility of a death sentence but also potentially undermined al-Kattānī's legitimacy in the eyes of would-be disciples and supporters. Historically, a charge of heresy reflected greater ideological debates that often played themselves out in the realms of politics and culture. Al-Kattānī's case was no different. To be a heretic was to question the social construction of religious truth while simultaneously challenging those authorities responsible for this process—the ulama.

The accusation of heresy against Muḥammad al-Kattānī and its resolution signaled the first significant response on the part of Moroccan religiopolitical elites to the crises that characterized Moroccan politics in the late nineteenth century. The heresy affair points to broader conflicts among the Moroccan religiopolitical elite at the end of the nineteenth century. Behind charges of heterodoxy lay a much deeper contest over spheres of power and authority among the parties involved in the conflict—the *makhzan,* the ulama, and the Kattāniyya leadership. The *makhzan*'s involvement in and strong response to the al-Kattānī affair reflected anxieties over its centralization efforts, while for the ulama from which the makhzan ultimately drew its legitimacy, al-Kattānī's gaining popularity potentially undermined their monopoly over interpretation of the sacred texts and ultimately challenged their position as the keepers of knowledge. Besides reflecting the conflict between al-Kattānī and the *makhzan,* on the one hand, and al-Kattānī and the ulama, on the other, the heresy affair also provided the *makhzan* an opportunity to attack the ulama—who were in a position to thwart its efforts to facilitate military and financial reforms on legal grounds.

In a letter written in June 1896, the sultan's most influential minister, Aḥmad bin Mūsā, criticized the Qāḍī of Fez for his inaction against Muḥammad al-Kattānī. Recently, as the head of the Kattāniyya *zāwiya,* al-Kattānī had been gaining disciples and followers from among artisans and craftsmen associated with the tanning industry of Fez. Bin Mūsā denounced al-Kattānī for "enticing foolish minds" and "seducing the common people," echoing charges often raised by juridically minded ulama about Sufi practices such as dancing, the use of musical instruments in their rituals, and claiming to have seen the Prophet Muḥammad. In Aḥmad bin Mūsā's mind, these were not matters to be taken lightly: "Whoever appears in an ecstatic state, must, by law, submit his words and deeds to measure on the scale of sharia."[6] The crux of the matter, however, was the *makhzan*'s sense that Muḥammad al-Kattānī's activities could pose a threat to its authority in Fez. Aḥmad bin Mūsā formulated the charge of heresy against al-Kattānī in terms of its political concerns and calculations. "The people [who deal with worldly affairs]," Mūsā argued, "have agreed that, for the imam [the sultan], the most worrisome phenomenon is the emergence of someone from among the flock . . . who brings the common folk together and seduce[s] their minds."[7]

In this period, the *makhzan* had not taken similar action against other Sufi orders known for their ecstatic practices. The Ḥamdasha and ʿIsāwiyya orders were notorious for rituals involving ecstatic dancing, self-flagellation, and bodily mutilation.[8] But only twenty years earlier, during the Tanner's Rebellion, the city of Fez had erupted in revolt. At that time, rioters attacked the home of the *makhzan*'s official in charge of collecting unpopular market taxes, which had been reinstated just before the rebellion broke out.[9] The popularity of the Kattāniyya order among the tanners of Fez certainly must have been a point of concern for the *makhzan,* especially because it had been away from Fez for the previous two years on military campaign.

Just over one month after Aḥmad bin Mūsā wrote his letter of condemnation against al-Kattānī, the ulama of Fez met together to question the shaykh about practices that "repulsed them." The group of prestigious religious scholars, including a cousin of Muḥammad al-Kattānī, agreed that the young Sufi had made statements that "if interpreted from their external meaning [*ʿalā ẓāhirihā*]" were blasphemous. Specifically, they took offense at claims al-Kattānī made to his disciples that reciting devotional prayers associated with the Kattāniyya Ṭarīqa was "better than sixty complete recitations of the Quran." Finally, the ulama charged al-Kattānī with altering the call to prayer—the *adhān*—and instructed him to abandon such practices. "The notary witnessed [al-Kattānī's] repentance . . . his [pledge to] follow the way of his ancestors, and [his pledge to avoid] delving into what leads him toward blasphemy."[10]

The ulama in charge of evaluating Muḥammad al-Kattānī's statements were not concerned with determining whether al-Kattānī believed in a particular Islamic doctrine or precept. Unlike Christianity, in which the term *heresy* generally connotes beliefs that contradict doctrinal orthodoxy as determined by an authoritative religious body, in the Islamic tradition, the heresy and orthodoxy dichotomy resides in the distinction—albeit a fluid one—between sharia (divine law) and *bidʿa* (innovation).[11] The well-being of the Islamic community (*umma*) lay in maintenance of the sharia, which stood as the sole moral and practical guide for the *umma* after the death of the Prophet.[12] Therefore, when the ulama of Fez evaluated al-Kattānī's words and deeds, they considered them in terms of whether they conformed to the law as established by the precepts of classical Islamic jurisprudence—that is, reliance on the authoritative texts (the Quran and the Hadith), interpretation by accepted legal principles *(qiyās),* and acceptance on the basis of consensus *(ijmāʿ)* of the pious and learned community.

WAYS OF KNOWING: SUFIS AND ULAMA DEBATE EPISTEMOLOGY

Like mystics before him, Muḥammad al-Kattānī believed that revelation comprised both exoteric *(al-maʿrifa al-ẓāhiriyya)* and esoteric *(al-maʿrifa al-bāṭiniyya)* dimensions.[13] But regardless of the path chosen by a disciple, the attainment of gnosis was predicated on a firm grounding in sharia. Esoteric and more legal-minded idioms of religious expression and practice were seen as different sides of the same body of the revelation bequeathed to the community of Muslims by God by way of the Prophet.[14] In the tradition of Sufism, therefore, al-Kattānī believed that mystical epistemology and practices associated with mystical forms of religious devotion were legal.[15] Contrary to the notion that mystical forms of worship fell outside boundaries of sharia and therefore represented vulgarized, unorthodox, and popular forms of Islam, Sufis saw themselves squarely within the tradition of orthodoxy as defined by the principles of sharia. Indeed, numerous ulama participated in mystical forms of worship and meditation from the early period of Islam, through the classical period, and throughout the eighteenth and nineteenth centuries.[16]

According to classical Sufism, the path or *ṭarīqa* consisted of a series of stages known as *maqāmāt*, each of which brought the disciple *(sālik al-ṭarīq)* closer to God. The pinnacle of the initiate's ascent toward God was associated with his or her total self-annihilation *(al-fanāʾ)*. Ascetic practices such as the rejection of worldly goods, isolation, and silent contemplation were held to facilitate the Sufi initiate's travel along the path of illumination and bring him (or her) closer to God.[17] Self-annihilation, in turn, prepared him or her to receive the truth of revelation. This was achieved through strict adherence to practices such as remembering God through *dhikr*, meditation, isolation, asceticism, and the shunning of worldly goods and possessions. Intoxication *(sukr)* occurred when the disciple reached the apex of his ascent toward God—a state characterized by complete annihilation of the self in which all things become one and during which the disciple is blinded by God's light. After reaching the divine presence *(iqtirāb)*, the *sālik* (one who travels the mystical path) was overcome by the beauty of God's light and could remain in its proximity forever. Although intoxication marked the pinnacle of the disciple's journey, his path could not be complete until he descended *(nuzūl)* to a state of sobriety. The totality of revelation could not be attained without returning to this state.[18]

The existence of two epistemologies within the Islamic tradition—discursive knowledge and mysticism—provided for a vast range of religious experiences and devotional practices, but it also formed the basis for competing spheres of expertise and knowledge—one emphasizing the primacy of the exoteric (sharia) and another favoring hermeneutics derived through mysticism *(ḥaqīqa)*. More juridically minded ulama were concerned that people with a lesser capacity to receive and understand mystical revelations were unable to resist the spiritual dangers inherent in the Sufi path. For these critics of mysticism, danger stemmed from the view that the state of intoxication might lead the disciple to utterances and behaviors that constituted apostasy. Diversity of opinion among the ulama regarding the degree to which common believers *(ʿāmm)* could (or should) delve into the vast and potentially dangerous realm of esotericism also determined their propensity to favor textual interpretation that was largely exoteric.[19] Advocates of this position stressed that interpretive authority should remain the sphere of the ulama (although even the more sharia-oriented ulama held vastly divergent opinions about esotericism and law). The most extreme theosophists rejected this notion on the grounds that juridical principles derived from rationalistic hermeneutics (as employed by the schools of law) were incapable of providing full understanding of revelation and therefore could not serve as the basis for legal decisions.[20] Again, from this perspective, the crux of conflict between those who emphasized the exoteric over the esoteric was not one of belief versus disbelief. Rather, it reflected different epistemological approaches to full comprehension of divine revelation.[21]

The epistemological conflict between the Sufis and the ulama does not fully explain why Muḥammad al-Kattānī's belief in the primacy of esotericism warranted such a strong response from the ulama of Fez and the *makhzan*. Even more juridically oriented ulama who condemned more ecstatic aspects of mystical practice such as dancing, singing, and using musical instruments in prayer rituals conceded that proximity to God *(iqtirāb)* was attained not only through discursive knowledge *(ʿilm or ʿilm ẓāhirī)* and study but also through gnosis *(maʿrifa or ʿilm bāṭinī)* attained by an individual. Such distinctions had even less significance in Morocco, where the notion of a jurist-Sufi blurring the lines differentiating mystics and doctors of law had long become doctrinally normative and integrated into Moroccan Islam.[22]

The strong response of the ulama of Fez was related to Muḥammad al-Kattānī's call for *tajdīd*—the revival of Islam. Indirectly, his revivalist agenda was a call to challenge the status quo and involved engagement with broader discussions regarding who had the authority to interpret sharia and on what basis.[23] Muḥammad al-Kattānī's claims regarding the efficacy of Kattāniyya prayers and rituals—claims for which the ulama of Fez condemned him in 1896—could easily be interpreted as a profession of interpretive authority on the basis of esotericism rather than on the principles of classical jurisprudence. Indeed, when called to defend his position in later years, al-Kattānī drew on a constellation of mystical concepts known as the *Ṭarīqa Muḥammadiyya* to justify his claims to interpretive authority.[24] In short, therefore, Muḥammad al-Kattānī raised the ire of the ulama of Fez because he attempted to redefine the parameters of sharia and innovation, of orthodoxy and heresy. Beyond this, the fact that al-Kattānī actually gained a following in Fez gave life to his ideas.

One must also consider the sensitivities of the ulama regard-

Figure 2. Letter documenting allegations of heresy against Muḥammad al-Kattānī, Direction des Archives Royales, Rabat, Morocco.

ing al-Kattānī in light of the *makhzan*'s encroachment on their sphere of authority—interpretation of the law. Outrage regarding the questionable practices of the Kattāniyya was a thinly veiled attack against the ulama, who, in the sultan's estimation, had failed in their obligation to protect the sharia by not taking an active stand against al-Kattānī when rumors of his activities began to circulate. Aḥmad bin Mūsā argued that "had they paid heed to his activities, then this mischief would not have spread." In Aḥmad bin Mūsā's view, "their silence, in reality, was the origin of that sin."[25]

From the mid-nineteenth century, relations between the *makhzan* and the ulama were marked by growing tension springing from the state's greater involvement and interest in matters of law that directly related to the state's ability to govern, tax, and command—that is, to sustain itself. The main points of contention centered on taxation and trade reflecting broader processes of integration of Morocco into the global economy and the ensuing monetary crisis that emerged as a result. Because trade with Europe became the major source of revenue for the *makhzan* from the mid-nineteenth century onward, the balance of trade shifted for the first time in Europe's favor, altering the Moroccan economy in significant and unprecedented ways. Local artisan production was essentially destroyed by the flooding of the market with cheaply made European products. Monetary crisis caused by repayment of reparations imposed on Morocco following its crushing defeat by Spain during the Hispano-Moroccan War in 1860 led to large-scale depreciation of the Moroccan currency. The result was an alarmingly tangible four fold increase in the price of wheat over the next ten years. Two catastrophic famines also occurred between 1867 and 1869 and later between 1878 and 1884, making such increases in the price of food stuffs even more serious. Peasants streamed into the cities to seek alternative sources of income, adding to the populations of traditionally marginal port cities such as Tangier and Casablanca.[26]

At the beginning of the nineteenth century, the Moroccan

ulama did not exist as a corporate group with distinctly defined interests. With the exception of a small number of top-ranking ulama, who held positions as professors at the Qarawīyīn University or official posts such as the Qāḍīship of Fez, few among them relied on a salaried position and state benefits. Moreover, in the absence of a system of state-sponsored and hierarchically organized professional judgships (such as in the Ottoman empire), the development of ulama family dynasties that relied on inherited judgeships for their social, economic, and intellectual prestige was limited. Although there are limited studies examining the process by which individual Moroccan ulama gained prominence, peer recognition seems to have been central to this process. For example, one nineteenth-century French observer of the activities of the Qarawīyīn in Fez noted that ulama who attracted large numbers of students to their lectures gained distinction over time. Ulama who achieved this distinction were entitled to sit at an elevated position above the students during instruction; this position was called *kursī,* or chair.[27] As is shown in the previous chapter, lack of corporate identity among the ulama was further enhanced by the fact that knowledge *(ʿilm)* was not the sole provenance of the lawyers but also included others who derived authority and privilege from their status as people of knowledge *(ahl al-ʿilm);* these included *shurafāʾ* and *zāwiya* shaykhs (i.e., Sufi-saints).[28] Although the Moroccan ulama rarely took collective decisions regarding matters of law or acted en masse in overturning decisions of the ruler, the symbolic importance of the power bestowed on them as guarantors of the sacred law should not be overlooked. The ulama played a key role in what Bettina Dennerlein has termed the "(re)production of the Moroccan polity"—namely, in their capacity as conferrers of the *bayʿa* for a new sultan. During the Tanner's Rebellion in 1873, for example, the ulama intervened on behalf of the tanners by presenting the sultan with their demand to abrogate the gate tax.[29]

Conflicts between the ulama and the state over matters of taxation and trade had erupted intermittently since the early period of the ʿAlawī dynasty. Indeed, such conflict was endemic due to the state's reliance on revenue generated from trade with Christian countries and the collection of extra-Quranic taxes, both of which were unacceptable from the perspective of the Mālikī ulama. They argued that such activities could be sanctioned only if they could be shown to be necessary for carrying out jihad (i.e., that the revenues would help the sultan wage jihad).[30] The ulama also claimed that extra-Quranic taxes constituted a commercial monopoly by taxing certain products and transactions. To justify a new tax, the legal argument in support had to show that its implementation was indispensable for the good of the community and that the burden of taxes would be evenly distributed. The argument that costly reparations paid to Spain by Morocco after the Hispano-Moroccan War of 1860 justified a new tax, for instance, was rejected on the counterargument that any truce was illegal as long as the enemy was on the offensive, which Spain was considered to be.[31]

Other measures taken by the ʿAlawī sultans further undermined the authority of the ulama. Mawlāy Ḥasan promoted and encouraged gatherings of ulama for the purpose of hadith study in which he participated and surrounded himself with scholars known to be hadith-oriented in their legal interpretations.[32] Perhaps the most marked example of this, although rarely mentioned, was Mawlāy Ḥasan's decree to the people, which he composed on the occasion of the turn of the thirteenth *hijrī* century (1882). In it, he urged the people to maintain the principles of religion and to exercise the injunction to "command the good and censure the evil."[33] This was a particularly bold attempt to define the principle in terms of specific duties—the fulfillment of duties on the part of governors and tribal *qāʾid*s, the education of people in rural areas, and the protection of the rights of the *dhimmī*s (non-Muslim monotheists) more specifically, of Moroccan Jews.[34] These measures—the promotion of hadith studies through organized study circles and the attempt to define explicitly the duties of the community—further threatened the already tenuous authority of the ulama. Paradoxically, however, as the power of the ulama was increasingly undermined by the *makhzan*'s reforms, more ulama were filling positions within a slowly expanding administrative apparatus. These positions within the new administration provided them income and closer dealings with the state. As holders of this ambiguous position, the arbiters of law were unable to come down definitively on the side of either the *makhzan* or its opponents in matters of law and reform.[35]

The ulama conveyed this ambiguity in their dealings with the *makhzan* regarding Muḥammad al-Kattānī. Responding to bin Mūsā's harsh words against the Qāḍī of Fez, his representative explained, "I commanded ['Abd al-Kabīr al-Kattānī] to completely silence his son and to close the *zāwiya* during times designated for spiritual exercises." He added that he instructed al-Kattānī's father to prevent him from "teaching or gathering people together [for that purpose]."[36] In al-ʿIrāqī's estimation, the charge of neglect was clearly unsubstantiated. The heterodox nature of al-Kattānī's activities was apparent to him before the *makhzan* was even aware of the situation. In fact, he argued, failure to censure al-Kattānī fell on the shoulders of the sultan and his advisers, because they failed to respond to the ulama's concerns about the young Sufi. Referring to the meeting among the ulama of Fez about al-Kattānī, he explained, "You did not command us to do anything about his situation."[37]

Although the *qāḍī*'s true feelings about the matter come through clearly in his carefully worded and highly detailed response (that the *makhzan* was at fault for not suppressing the heresy sooner), he was nevertheless unable to dismiss the matter. Instead, he engaged the *wazīr* by attempting to downplay the situation through disparaging remarks about the accused, who, he added, was still young and misguided in his beliefs.[38] The *qāḍī*'s most pointed and telling argument emphasized al-Kattānī's failure to sway the ulama in supporting him. He explained that, "not one Muslim submitted to him, especially from among the people of knowledge [ulama]."[39] The *qāḍī* highlighted the anonymity (and hence unimportance) of al-Kattānī's disciples:

"None among his followers is known, and all those that we have seen speaking about the matter . . . denounce [his words] as shameful."[40]

Regardless of the strength of his arguments and his conviction regarding Muḥammad al-Kattānī, the *qāḍī* in the last instance understood his position toward the *makhzan* and its sphere of authority. Thus, in his concluding sentences, he acknowledged that it was only through the beneficence of the sultan that his position as an *ʿālim* carried weight: "But after all this," wrote al-ʿIrāqī, "I concede that I am wrong in any case, and I grovel between your hands and before his highness, our master—may God make him victorious—and may he pardon me in front of God almighty . . . may he not banish me from his generous gate and not expel me from under his beautiful protection. For I am a man in weak condition, who has little [property] and [yet] many dependants, [who is] poor of health and who cannot [tolerate], hardship, banishment, or repudiation."[41] In one sweeping sentence, Muḥammad bin Rashīd al-ʿIrāqī confirmed his acceptance of the innate order of things and conceded that the needs of the *makhzan* would factor into his assessment of the heretical nature of Muḥammad al-Kattānī's activities.

HERESY FROM FEZ TO MARRAKESH

During the heresy affair, theological and spiritual matters stood at the center of debate; however, its resolution was mediated through the prism of more worldly concerns. Political considerations were important for all parties involved including Muḥammad al-Kattānī. Through the guidance of his father and spiritual mentor, ʿAbd al-Kabīr, Muḥammad managed to steer his movement clear of interference on the part of his detractors by establishing an alliance with the *makhzan*. The heresy affair stood to jeopardize the Kattāniyya *zāwiya* and threaten the position of the Kattāniyya family, who had enjoyed strong relations with the *makhzan* until this time.

When the heresy affair erupted, Muḥammad al-Kattānī went

to Marrakesh, where the sultan and his court had recently taken up residence after two years of military campaigning outside Fez. Marrakesh lay five hundred kilometers to the southwest of Fez and had served intermittently as the capital for the itinerant court since the foundation of the city in the eleventh century. Seated both at the foot of the High Atlas mountains and at the beginning of an extensive plain that stretches northwestward to the Atlantic coast and Casablanca, Marrakesh functioned as a regional center for the movement of goods and people between the Atlantic coast, the High Atlas, the Tafilalt Oasis, and the southern and primarily Amazigh-inhabited Souss region. Under the Sa‘dī dynasty (which chose Marrakesh as its capital in the sixteenth century), Marrakesh experienced an economic and cultural renaissance as a result of their extensive building efforts and patronage. It remained of secondary importance as an imperial city for the succeeding ‘Alawī dynasty until the mid-nineteenth century, when the ‘Alawī sultans began a series of military campaigns to bring the southern Souss region into its sphere of influence.

While in Marrakesh, Muḥammad al-Kattānī corresponded regularly with his father regarding exoneration by the *makhzan.* As soon as the *makhzan* issued its statement of condemnation against al-Kattānī, negotiations began between the Kattānīs and the *makhzan*'s representative, Aḥmad bin Mūsā. Letters exchanged between Muḥammad and his father between September and December 1896 reveal their degree of conviction regarding the possibility of an official pardon. ‘Abd al-Kabīr urged his son to "hurry in obtaining the decree from the sultan for the people of Fez," adding "your innocence and your standing [in the eyes of others] is dearer than anything."[42] Two months later, the elder al-Kattānī conveyed his concern about the outcome of Muḥammad's endeavors: "Did you have a talk with the *wazīr* . . . regarding the matter of the two utterances, and did he accept [your explanation] or not? We would like you to take up all these matters, which they commanded us to abandon, to show the *wazīr* the truth from what is groundless . . . show him a grand sight that envelopes his heart."[43] Finally, although emphasizing the importance of successfully convincing Aḥmad bin Mūsā of his position, ʿAbd al-Kabīr added optimistically, "The fruit of acceptance is [that he will] write about your innocence to the students and the [ulama]." So that al-Kattānī the younger would heed his advice, ʿAbd al-Kabīr emphasized the importance of Aḥmad bin Mūsā's statement of innocence—"for people are misguided and cast shadows over others."[44] ʿAbd al-Kabīr also directed Muḥammad to pursue other concerns with the *makhzan* such as assistance in repelling attacks against the Kattāniyya *zāwiya* by disciples and adherents of other orders. In what al-Kattānī senior clearly viewed as a small victory for the Kattāniyya, ʿAbd al-Kabīr described his happiness in hearing that Aḥmad bin Mūsā "was displeased with the actions of those students and that he promised you he would write to Mawlāy ʿArfa [the Khalīfa of Fez][45] so that he stop them."[46]

Although the year 1896 was colored by uncertainty for the Kattānīs, both father and son seemed undeterred in spite of the bleak situation. They communicated regularly about the status of the disciples and the need to continue the practice of prayers and rituals associated with the Kattāniyya *ṭarīqa*. By relaying news and information through epistolary exchanges, Muḥammad al-Kattānī remained well informed about the activities of disciples and students throughout the country.[47] For ʿAbd al-Kabīr, his son's letters provided relief and comfort during the difficult days of the crisis. They were filled with discussion about his spiritual condition and with "comforting knowledge and happy illuminations."[48] The letters between father and son also reveal a depth of conviction about the task at hand. Far from conveying a sense of standstill, defeat, or intimidation on the part of the Kattāniyya leadership these letters—filled with spiritual advice, information about the finances of the *zāwiya*, political discussions, minutia, and updates about the situation in each city—show that both Muḥammad al-Kattānī and his father were actively pursuing the business of the Kattāniyya, despite the setbacks of the heresy affair. Nevertheless, they did not take matters lightly. Their correspondence also focused on ways of protecting the reputation of the Kattāniyya brotherhood. ʿAbd al-Kabīr explained that he had "commanded [the disciples] to stay with the pact that they made . . . [about reciting] the Anmūdhjiyya prayer or other [prayers]." However, he urged his son to send him a written explanation *(sharḥ)* of the controversial prayers: "Send it to us, it is absolutely necessary."[49] With a great sense of relief, he added, "the disciples accepted it all, and none of them interfered—praise God—for there is nothing [in] their hearts [that they hold against the Kattāniyya]."[50] ʿAbd al-Kabīr enthusiastically awaited the arrival of the prayer his son had composed regarding the conditions necessary for encountering the Prophet in an awakened state.[51]

Neither Muḥammad nor his father denounced the practices of the Kattāniyya. Their correspondence affirms their depth of conviction about the importance of Sufism and esoteric knowledge for understanding and interpreting revelation. The Kattānīs wished to enlighten the *wazīr,* to "envelop his heart" because of their belief in the power and truth of mysticism.[52] Alluding to a common theme found in mystical discourse, which emphasizes that recognition and understanding of true illumination was limited to a select few, ʿAbd al-Kabīr, by way of citation, reassured his son of the depth of his spiritual experience: "All those who believe in this science [Sufism] are among the elite; and all those who understand it are among the elite of the elite; all those who are strengthened by it and who speak about it, they are the stars that are not recognized and the sea that does not dry up, inexhaustible."[53] He believed that those who viewed al-Kattānī favorably were granted illumination through God's will alone. In turn, those to whom God granted this illumination were "those whom God desired to reach Him through you."[54] Casting aside for a brief moment the world of the sublime, ʿAbd al-Kabīr also expressed his intimate human desire to see his son home safely and in good health: "We need nothing except to be [re]united with you."[55]

Given Aḥmad bin Mūsā's sharp censure of Muḥammad al-

Kattānī in his discussions with the ulama of Fez, al-Kattānī's decision to flee to the city where the *makhzan* was stationed is surprising. Even more surprising, however, was his reception by the *wazīr* and the degree of freedom he seems to have exercised during his stay in Marrakesh. Would it not be expected that the *makhzan* would restrict the shaykh's activities through incarceration or some other form of punishment? From the state's perspective, an alliance with the shaykh of an active and expanding Sufi movement held many possibilities. By drawing on Muḥammad al-Kattānī's gaining spiritual and social authority among the people of Fez, the *makhzan* stood to bolster its waning legitimacy there, particularly against the backdrop of its increasingly unpopular reforms. Apart from this, with the young shaykh in Marrakesh and away from Fez, it was possible for the *wazīr* to maintain close scrutiny over him while simultaneously limiting his ability to incite his adherents in Fez. In fact, only the Kattāniyya *zāwiya* in Fez was closed while Kattāniyya *zāwiya*s in other regions remained open.[56]

It is possible to imagine other motivations for Aḥmad bin Mūsā's eagerness to enter into discussion with the Kattānīs. Since the mid-nineteenth century, the *makhzan* had been interested in extending its drive for political centralization in the regions around Marrakesh, such as the southern Souss, the Tafilalt and the Sais Plain between Marrakesh and the Atlantic coast. For more than sixty years, the *makhzan* had exercised only nominal authority in the Souss region. Through the goal of integrating the south more completely into its orbit, the *makhzan* hoped to secure badly needed income through taxation.[57] Shaykh al-Kattānī could likely assist the *makhzan* as a negotiator between itself and the tribes of the region.[58] Moreover, for Muḥammad al-Kattānī—whose authority was based, in part, on his ability to mediate between both spiritual and worldly authorities on behalf of his followers—exercising his influence with the sultan might further empower him and elevate his status in the eyes of his adherents and disciples.[59]

The first real sign of a move on the part of the *makhzan* in fa-

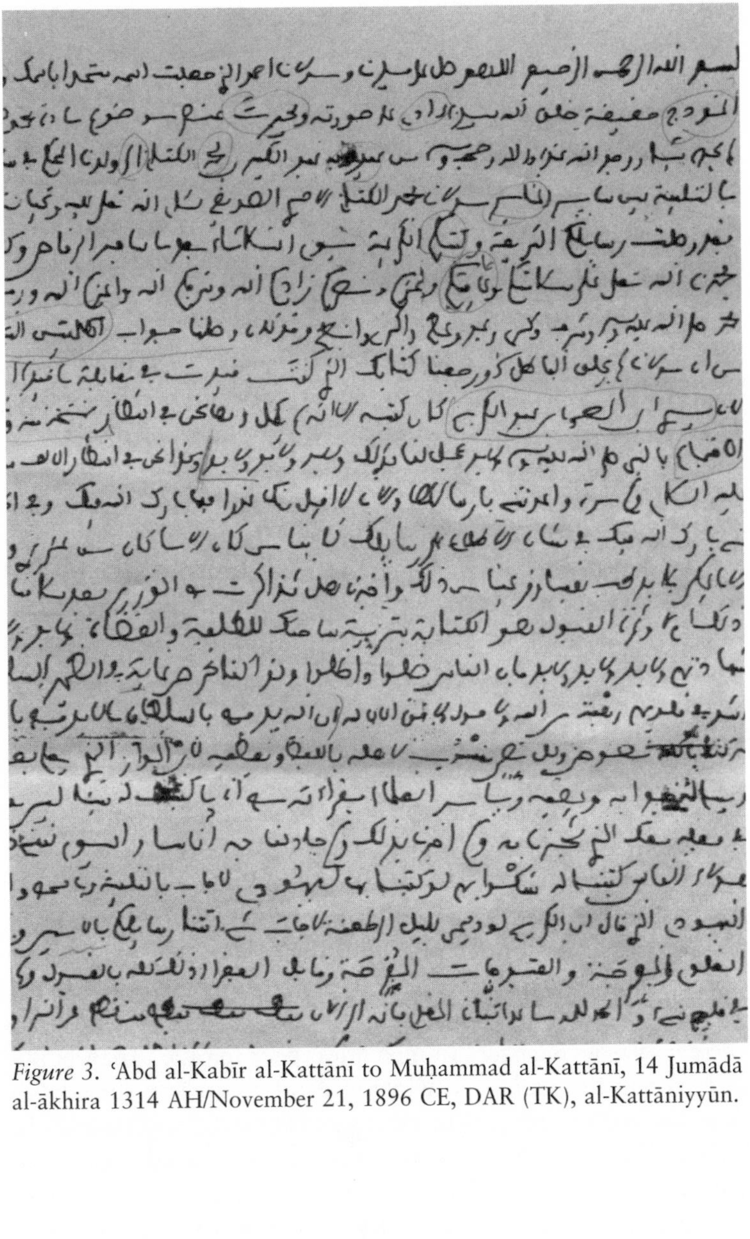

Figure 3. ʿAbd al-Kabīr al-Kattānī to Muḥammad al-Kattānī, 14 Jumādā al-ākhira 1314 AH/November 21, 1896 CE, DAR (TK), al-Kattāniyyūn.

vor of al-Kattānī occurred when, in December 1896, Shaykh Mā al-ʿAynayn al-Shanjīṭī—an *ʿālim,* Sufi, and head of the ʿAyniyya brotherhood—concluded that he found "nothing [in al-Kattānī's writings] to which I object and that would not sustain sound interpretation."[60] Mā al-ʿAynayn had spent many years involved in internecine conflicts in neighboring Mauritania, which led him to seek an alliance with the ʿAlawī sultans around 1859.[61] From that time, mutual political interests formed the basis for relations between the Moroccan *makhzan* and Mā al-ʿAynayn. Both Aḥmad bin Mūsā and Mawlāy Ḥasan had patronized ʿAyaniyya *zāwiyas* and participated in their prayer rituals.[62] Close political and devotional ties between the *makhzan* and Mā al-ʿAynayn surely influenced Aḥmad bin Mūsā's decision to submit the heresy controversy for his scrutiny. Shaykh Mā al-ʿAynayn was also known as a man of knowledge and learning. He produced numerous works on various topics relating to mystical devotion, religious sciences and jurisprudence.[63] Mā al-ʿAynayn shared some of al-Kattānī's ideas regarding *tajdīd,* which may have also influenced his verdict in favor of Muḥammad al-Kattānī.[64] Mā al-ʿAynayn's pronouncement opened the way for the Kattāniyya to operate freely in Marrakesh.

The rapid turn of events in Muḥammad al-Kattānī's favor had much to do with his father's ability to interpret the *makhzan*'s actions in terms of sharifan political logic. The cultivation of relations between the ʿAlawī *makhzan* and heads of Sufi bortherhoods formed a central pillar of Moroccan politics. In the absence of a strong central state, the Sufi orders provided important venues for arbitration and negotiation between different groups in society and the state.[65] In urban centers such as Fez, the *zāwiyas* were spaces of mediation between the urban populations and the *makhzan,* while in rural areas, Sufi shaykhs of popular orders acted as interlocutors between the state and the tribes. ʿAbd al-Kabīr al-Kattānī had been a savvy politician in his role as shaykh of the Kattāniyya before his son took over. For example, as a result of ʿAbd al-Kabīr's influence in the region of

Fez, in 1894 the *makhzan* summoned 'Abd al-Kabīr to mediate in a dispute between the people of Sefrou—a town southeast of Fez—and members of the Bahālīl tribe—a Middle Atlas tribal group that had numerous Kattāniyya disciples.[66]

In January 1897 and soon after Mā al-'Aynayn's definitive verdict pronouncing al-Kattānī's innocence, the young Sufi shaykh received an invitation from Aḥmad bin Mūsā to attend an annual party marking the arrival of Ramaḍān, the month of fasting.[67] As part of the ritual of royal power and authority, this gesture was understood by both parties as an acceptance of the new relationship between them. For those notable attendees, members of the royal household, and other prominent retainers participating in the festivities, al-Kattānī's presence was a sign that he now enjoyed the sultan's favor. Through the guidance of his father and spiritual mentor, Muḥammad al-Kattānī managed to steer his movement clear of interference on the part of his detractors by establishing an alliance with the *makhzan*. Muḥammad did not return to Fez until 1898 but remained in Marrakesh, where the sultan and his representative—al-Kattānī's new patrons—remained until 1902.

A SUFI PLAYS POLITICS

Muḥammad al-Kattānī's Marrakesh sojourn marked the beginning of a new relationship between the Kattāniyya and the *makhzan* that lasted for almost ten years. During this period, Muḥammad al-Kattānī provided services to the *makhzan* and, in return, utilized its support and protection. From the perspective of the state, an alliance with the shaykh of an active and expanding Sufi movement held many possibilities. By drawing on Muḥammad al-Kattānī's gaining spiritual and social authority, the *makhzan* stood to bolster its waning legitimacy. And for Muḥammad al-Kattānī, whose saintly authority was based, in part, on the ability to mediate between both spiritual and worldly authorities on behalf of his followers, exercising his influence with the sultan would further empower him and elevate his status in the eyes of his adherents and followers.[68]

Mutual agreement on the importance of this relationship was not determined by the interests of each party alone. Muḥammad al-Kattānī and the sultan were not thinking just in functionalist terms about how best to serve their interests. Rather, both parties also shared similar perspectives on the need for action to meet the cultural, social, and political challenges of the period. For the *makhzan,* political action was manifested in its efforts to implement financial and administrative reforms. For Muḥammad al-Kattānī, political action meant filling the vaccuum created by an increasingly compliant ulama class through the involvement of the religiopolitical elite—that is, of the Sufi-shayks and the *shurafāʾ* in guiding *tajdīd*—reforms that would lead to the revival of the Moroccan Muslim community. However, neither Muḥammad al-Kattānī nor the *makhzan* harbored false illusions about the possibility for conflict with their new ally. Both parties proceeded with caution in dealing with one another and understood the dangers associated with this alliance. The mercurial nature of relations with worldly authority and the vagaries of its behavior made it impossible to count on close ties with the *makhzan* for succor and support. Muḥammad reminded his father that "When we were in their favor, they did what had to be done in order to silence the people."[69] He righteously claimed that there were those among the people of Marrakesh "who feared the *makhzan* more than they feared God" but emphasized that God's sustenance was unwavering for those who followed the correct path.[70] The *makhzan* also took precautions in its dealings with Muḥammad al-Kattānī. ʿAbdallah bin Khaḍrāʾ, erstwhile Qāḍī of Fez and a prominent voice for the *makhzan* during the reigns of Mawlāy Ḥasan and ʿAbd al-ʿAzīz, warned against interaction with the Kattāniyya. In a missive written to a government official in Salé in 1906, bin Khaḍrāʾ warned that the makhzan did not want third parties involved with the Kattāniyya. Negotiations with the leadership of the order should remain the provenance of the state.[71]

Al-Kattānī's experience reveals that the politics of piety in late nineteenth-century Morocco were nuanced and complex. Intricately linked doctrinal and political concerns found their expression in debates that spanned geographic regions. Resolution of the crisis involved a six-month process of negotiation, which resulted in the emergence of new alliances between the Kattāniyya leadership and the *makhzan.* Although each party had its own reasons for conflict with the ulama, they were united in the position that interpretive authority must be wrested from their absolute control. However, if the *makhzan*'s release and subsequent promotion of Muḥammad al-Kattānī was a blow to the authority of the ulama regarding interpretation of the sharia, it also paved the way for its own demise. Indeed, support for Muḥammad al-Kattānī helped widen the parameters of debate regarding the limits of sharia and *bid'a,* thus paving the way for sharia-based arguments for the sultan's dethronement in 1907. Against the backdrop of the state's efforts to extend its power and rationalize its methods of administration throughout the nineteenth century, the struggle over authority to interpret the sharia was of great moment. Therefore, the outcome of the conflict between the ulama of Fez and Muḥammad al-Kattānī in al-Kattānī's favor further undermined the authority of the ulama of Fez while simultaneously enabling al-Kattānī and his followers and supporters. Thus, in the conflict over religiopolitical authority as represented by the heresy affair, al-Kattānī and his supporters emerged victorious.

Beyond the immediate controversy and antagonisms created by the heresy ordeal, the event marked an important transition in the history of the Kattāniyya brotherhood from a fairly localized and loosely connected series of *zāwiya*s to a more tightly and well-defined network. This event propelled the Kattāniyya to emerge as a force in the south, transcending its regional affiliations in Fez and its environs, and inevitably helped the Kattāniyya and its supporters rise to prominence during the turbulent months of 1907. If Muḥammad al-Kattānī was a heretic in Fez, in Marrakesh his adherence to sharia was unquestioned. The debate over the limits of sharia and *bid'a* also reflected differences between regional centers—Fez and Marrakesh.

NOTES

1. 'Abd al-Kabīr al-Kattānī to Muḥammad al-Kattānī, 3 Rabī' al-thānī 1314 AH/September 12, 1896 CE, DAR (TK), al-Kattānīyun.
2. Aḥmad bin Mūsā to 'Abd al-Raḥman al-Qarshī, 18 Muḥarram 1314 AH/June 30, 1896 CE, DAR (TK), al-Kattāniyyūn.
3. Muḥammad b. Rashīd al-'Irāqī to Aḥmad bin Mūsā, 29 Ṣafar 1314 AH/August 10, 1896 CE, DAR (TK), Fez 11, no. 6318.
4. al-Kattānī, *Tarjama,* 77.
5. The full name of the text is *al-Mi'yār al-Mu'rib wa al-Jami' al-Mughrib 'an Fatāwa ahl Ifriqiyya wa al-Andalus wa al-Maghrib.* The book was compiled by Aḥmad b. Yaḥyā al-Wansharīsī, born in 1430 in Algeria. For biographical information about al-Wansharīsī and about *al-Mi'yār,* see Émile Amar, Introduction, in *La pierre de touche des fétwas de Ahmad al-Wanscharīsī: choix de consultations juridiques des faqîhs du Maghreb,* trans. and ed. Émile Amar (Paris: E. Leroux, 1908), v–xiii.
6. Aḥmad bin Mūsā to 'Abd al-Raḥmān al-Qarshī, 18 Muḥarram 1314 AH/June 30, 1896 CE, DAR (TK), al-Kattāniyyūn. I have translated Aḥmad bin Mūsā's words *maqām* and *ḥāl* as "ecstatic state." A *ḥāl* is a "transitory spiritual 'state' of enlightenment or 'rapture' associated with passage along the Sufi path, while a *maqām* is a "stage or station along the Sufi Path." Trimingham, *The Sufi Orders in Islam,* 303 and 307.
7. Aḥmad bin Mūsā to 'Abd al-Raḥman bin al-Qarshī, 18 Muḥarram 1314 CE/June 30, 1896 CE, DAR (TK), al-Kattāniyyūn.
8. Joseph Thomson gives a disparaging yet colorful description of a procession of Ḥamdasha disciples in *Travels in the Atlas and Southern Morocco: A Narrative of Exploration* (London: George Philip and Son, 1889), 75–78. Other European travelers also commented on the practices of the two orders. During the period of this study, the sultans did not attempt to curtail the questionable activities of such orders, but their predecessor and a member of the same 'Alawī dynasty, Sultan Sulaymān (d. 1822), waged an intense campaign against the Sufi orders. His zealotry against what he per-

ceived as innovation included forbidding popular celebrations such as the celebration of the Prophet's birth *(al-mawlid al-nabawī)*. Although the visitation of saints' tombs was discouraged, the practice was not outlawed. Mohamed el-Mansour, *Morocco in the Reign of Mawlay Sulayman* (Cambridgeshire: Middle East and North African Studies Press, 1990); Ḥarakāt, *al-Tayyārāt.*

9. Sebti, "Chroniques de la contestation citadine."
10. Muḥammad bin Rashīd al-ʿIrāqī to Aḥmad bin Mūsā, 12 Jumādā al-ūlā 1314 AH/October 20, 1896 CE, DAR (TK), Fez 11, no. 6338.
11. For the purposes of this discussion, I draw on Jonathan Berkey's work on the debate over sharia and *bidʿa* during the medieval Islamic period. See Jonathan Berkey, "Tradition, Innovation and the Social Construction of Knowledge in the Medieval Islamic Near East," *Past and Present* 146 (February 1995): 38–65.
12. The concept of doctrinal deviation in Islam developed and changed over time. Heresy was closely linked to the emergence of the standardization of the juridical sciences and the standardization of the Sunna as an authoritative source for legal adjudication in the ninth century. The term *zandaqa* was used primarily in the early period of Islam to speak of Zoroastrian beliefs and thus is the closest to heresy in the Christian tradition. *Ridda,* another word that is sometimes translated as heresy refers to apostasy, or going back on Islam after declaring oneself a Muslim. And finally, *bidʿa,* which was the most widely employed accusation against the Sufis, literally means innovation. For the early history of heresy in Islam, see Roberto Giorgi, *Pour une histoire de la Zandaqa* (Firenze: La Nuova Italia, 1989).
13. This formulation was expressed by Muḥammad al-Kattānī in his *Lisān al-ḥujja al-burhāniyya fī al-dhabb ʿan al-sharāʾiʿ al-kattāniyya* (n.p., 1908?).
14. This principle was summarized most clearly by the eleventh century *ʿālim,* Abū al-Qāsim al-Qushayrī, who wrote, "The Sharia is concerned with the observance of the outward manifestations of religion [i.e., rites and acts of devotion *(ibādāt)* and duties *(muʿāmalāt)*]; whilst *Ḥaqīqa* [reality] concerns inward vision of the divine power [*mushāhadāt ar-rubūbiyya*]. Every rite not informed by the spirit of Reality is valueless, and every spirit of Reality not restrained by the Law is incomplete. The Law exists to regulate

mankind, whilst the Reality makes us to know the disposition of God. The Law exists for the service of God, whilst the Reality exists for contemplation of Him. The Law exists for obeying what He had ordained, whilst the Reality concerns witnessing and understanding the order He has decreed: the one is outer, the other inner." Abū al-Qāsim al-Qushayrī, *Al-Risāla al-qushayriyya,* cited in Trimingham, *The Sufi Orders in Islam,* 142. The writings of the late eighteenth century Moroccan Sufi, *ʿālim,* and founder of the eponymous Darqāwiyya order, al-ʿArabī al-Darqāwī, also reflect this concept. ʿAbd al-Majīd al-Ṣaghīr, *Al-Taṣawwuf ka waʿī wa mumārasa: dirāsa fī al-falsafa al-ṣufiyya ʿinda Aḥmad ibn ʿAjība* (Casablanca: Dar al-Thaqafa, 1999), 178–179. Aḥmad Ibn Idrīs, the founder of Idrīsī tradition (late eighteenth and early nineteenth centuries) also articulated the notion of the exterior and interior meaning of God's word in a similar manner. R. S. O'Fahey, *Enigmatic Saint: Aḥmad Ibn Idris and the Idrisi Tradition* (Evanston: Northwestern University Press, 1990), 196.

15. Trimingham, *The Sufi Orders in Islam,* 148. On the relationship between Sufism and sharia, see also Annemarie Schimmel, *Mystical Dimensions of Islam,* 5th ed. (Chapel Hill: University of North Carolina Press, 1983). Daniel Brown provides an excellent historical overview of the concept of the *sunna nabawiyya* as the basis for Islamic jurisprudence. See Daniel Brown, *Rethinking Tradition in Modern Islamic Thought* (Cambridge: Cambridge University Press, 1996).
16. See, for example, al-Kattānī, *Salwat al-anfās.*
17. Trimingham, *The Sufi Orders in Islam,* 153.
18. The stages of travel along the Sufi path according to the classical Sufi tradition are presented in Trimingham, *The Sufi Orders in Islam,* 153.
19. This refers to the principle that the depth of a disciple's mystical illumination *(fatḥ)* rested on his or her capacity to receive and understand such knowledge. This idea was expressed by the twelfth-century mystic Abū Madyān: "To flee from created being is one of the signs of a novice's sincerity. To reach God is a sign of the sincerity of his flight from created being. To return to created being is a sign of the sincerity of his having reached God." Chodkiewicz, *Seal of the Saints,* 171. The fifteenth-century Moroccan jurist and Sufi, Aḥmad Zarrūq (1442–1494), argued for an understanding of

a disciple's sincerity in terms of "external signs." Scott Kugle, *Rebel between Spirit and Law: Ahmad Zarruq, Sainthood, and Authority in Islam* (Bloomington: Indiana University Press, 2006), 144. The Indian Sufi Aḥmad Sirhindī (b. 1564) attributed his ecstatic declarations equating Islam and Christianity (and for which he was accused of heresy) to his state of intoxication. Yohanan Friedmann, *Shaykh Aḥmad Sirhindi: An Outline of His Thought and a Study of His Image in the Eyes of Posterity* (Montreal: McGill-Queen's University Press, 1971), 23. For the concept of ecstatic utterances in early Islam, see Carl W. Ernst, *Words of Ecstasy in Sufism* (Albany: State University of New York Press, 1985).

20. The tenth-century mystic al-Ḥakīm al-Tirmidhī believed that this was the case. Bernd Radtke et al., *The Exoteric Ahmad Ibn Idris: A Sufi's Critique of the Madhhab and the Wahhabis* (Leiden: Brill, 2000), 15. Doctrine relating to the concept of sainthood *(walāya)* in Islam was first elaborated by al-Tirmidhī. On al-Ḥakīm al-Tirmidhī, see also, Chodkiewicz, *Seal of the Saints.*
21. The most vitriolic attack against Sufis came from the Ḥanbalī jurist Ibn Taymiyya (d. 1328), whose writings were directed primarily against the teachings of the Sufi and *ʿālim,* Ibn al-ʿArabī (d. 1240). Ibn Taymiyya's ideas arose in the context of two parallel developments. The first was the sacking of Baghdad by the Mongols and the destruction of the Abbasid caliphate in 1258, signaling the final break-up of a unified Islamic ruling establishment. The second development was the institutionalization of the mystical orders and the systematization of mystical doctrine by Ibn al-ʿArabī.
22. Vincent Cornell labels this synthesis "juridical Sufism," a form of mysticism that "is epistemologically subservient to the authority of religious law." The juridical-Sufi paradigm, which developed out of a revived interest among medieval Spanish and North African Muslim *uṣūlī* scholars in the words and deeds of the prophet's companions *(al-salaf al-ṣāliḥ),* is "an ascetic, praxis-oriented, and jurisprudentially validated form of mysticism." Cornell, *Realm of the Saints,* 67 and 17. Scott Kugle discusses the efforts of the fifteenth-century Moroccan jurist-Sufi, Aḥmad Zarruq, to redefine this synthesis by developing the term *al-jāmiʿ* or "the one who brings together" (mysticism and law) in his writings about spiri-

tual growth. Kugle, *Rebel between Spirit and Law,* 132. On the polemics against the use of music and dancing in mystical rituals, see Arthur Gribetz, "The Sama' Controversy: Sufi vs. Legalist," *Studia Islamica* 74 (1991): 43–62.

23. Attempts to revive hadith study signaled a wider debate over the definition of normative Islam. The eighteenth-century traditionalists drew on ideas that, throughout the medieval period, had been maintained by Ḥanbalī jurists. Brown, *Rethinking Tradition in Modern Islamic Thought,* 22. For an excellent overview of the implications of hadith revival, see chapter 2 in Brown, ibid. See also Ahmad Dallal, "The Origins and Objectives of Islamic Revivalist Thought, 1750–1850," *Journal of the American Oriental Society* 113, no. 3 (July–September 1993): 341–359.
24. Kattānī, *Lisān al-Ḥujja,* 43. On ʿAbd al-Wahhāb al-Shaʿrānī (d. 1565) and the concept of the Ṭarīqa Muḥammadiyya, see Radtke et al., *The Exoteric Ahmad Ibin Idris.* The authors explain that a monograph on the *Ṭarīqa Muḥammadiyya* has yet to be completed. On al-Shaʿrānī's ideas, see Michel Chodkiewicz "Quelques remarques sur la diffusion de l'enseignement d'Ibn Arabi," in *Modes de transmission de la culture religieuse en Islam,* ed. Hassan Elboudrari (Institut Français d'Archeologie Orientale du Caire: Cairo, 1993), 201–224.
25. Aḥmad bin Mūsā to ʿAbd al-Raḥmān bin al-Qarshī, 18 Muḥarram 1314 AH/June 30, 1896 CE, DAR (TK), al-Kattāniyyūn.
26. Burke, *Prelude to Protectorate in Morocco,* 20–24. For the most important and detailed account of the effects of Moroccan integration into the expanding capitalist economy in the nineteenth century see Jean-Louis Miège, *Le Maroc et l'Europe, 1830–1894,* 4 vols. (Paris: Presses Universitaires de France, 1961–1963). On the famines of the nineteenth century and their effects on Morocco see Stacy Holden, "Modernizing a Moroccan Medina: Commercial and Technological Innovations at the Workplace of Millers and Butchers in Fez, 1878–1937," Ph.D. diss., Boston University, 2005.
27. M. A. Perité, "Les medrasas de Fès," *Archives Marocaines* 18 (1912): 317. Dale Eickelman's work on the Yusufiyya Mosque in Marrakesh also suggests the importance of peer recognition in the social construction of ulama power and authority. Dale Eickelman, *Knowledge and Power in Morocco: The Education of*

a Twentieth-Century Notable (Princeton, NJ: Princeton University Press, 1985), 87.

28. Edmund Burke also identifies this phenomenon as a factor in contributing to lack of corporate identity. Burke, "The Moroccan Ulama, 1860–1912: An Introduction," 96. For the bureaucratization of the Ottoman ulama, see Madeline Zilfi, *The Politics of Piety: The Ottoman Ulema in the Postclassical Age, 1600–1800* (Minneapolis: Bibliotheca Islamica, 1988).
29. Burke, "The Moroccan Ulama, 1860–1912: An Introduction," 101. Bettina Dennerlein argues that "even prior to the modern bureaucratic nation-state, political belonging was not simply the effect of unquestioned beliefs, but was brought about by a multitude of processes of legitimization and of political involvement and participation," including that of the ulama. Dennerlein, "Legitimate Bounds and Bound Legitimacy," 288–289.
30. During the ʿAlawī period, trade with Europe was grudgingly accepted by the ulama on the principle that it was the sultan's prerogative. This willingness was justified in two ways. First, the sultan used intermediaries (Jewish subjects) to trade on behalf of the *makhzan,* thus avoiding having to deal directly with non-Muslims. And second, piracy carried out with the sanction of the *makhzan* against European shipping satisfied the injunction that trade could be justified only if it could be shown to benefit the Muslims through the promotion of jihad. Schroeter, "Royal Power and the Economy in Precolonial Morocco," 77.
31. This particular line of reasoning was a central doctrine of the Malikī *madhhab.* Laroui, *Les origines sociales et culturelles du nationalisme marocain,* 291–294.
32. Muḥammad al-Fallāḥ al-ʿAlawī, *Jāmʿi al-qarawiyyīn wa al-fikr al-salafī, 1873–1914* (Casablanca: Maṭbaʿat al-Najāḥ al-Jadīd, 1994), 68.
33. The injunction to "command the good and censure the evil" *(al-amr bi al-maʿrūf wa al-nahī ʿan al-munkar)* appears in a number of places in the Quran, including 3:104, 110, 114, 9:112, 22:41, 31:17. Berkey, "Tradition, Innovation and the Social Construction of Knowledge in the Medieval Islamic Near East," 51. On the development of this concept, see Michael A. Cook, *Commanding Right and Forbidding Wrong in Islamic Thought* (Cambridge: Cambridge University Press, 2000).

34. Ḥarakāt, *al-Tayyārāt,* 107–108.
35. See Burke, "The Moroccan Ulama, 1860–1912." For a case study of the career path of a Moroccan *ʿālim* in the nineteenth century, see Kenneth Brown, "Profile of Nineteenth-Century Moroccan Scholar," in *Scholars, Saints, and Sufis: Muslim Religious Institutions in the Middle East since 1500,* ed. Nikki R. Keddie, 127–148. (Berkeley: University of California Press, 1972).
36. Muḥammad b. Rashīd al-ʿIrāqī to Aḥmad bin Mūsā, 29 Ṣafar 1314 AH/August 10, 1896 CE, DAR (TK), Fez 11, no. 6318.
37. Ibid.
38. Ibid.
39. Ibid.
40. Muḥammad b. Rashīd al-ʿIrāq to Aḥmad bin Mūsā, 29 Ṣafar 1314 AH/10 August 1896 CE, DAR (TK), Fez 11, no. 6318. What is significant here is that Muḥammad al-Kattānī was categorically rejected by the "people of knowledge" according to the *qāḍī,* al-ʿIrāqī. Although it appears that al-Kattānī's following among the intellectual elite of Fez was probably minimal at this time, we know that the Kattāniyya brotherhood had gained a following among the popular classes in Fez, particularly among members of the tanners' guilds *(al-dabbāghūn).* In the regions in the southwest of the district of Fez, disciples from among the Bahālīl and Aït Ḥamza (of the Tafilalt region) tribes were also growing in number. However, among his adherents and disciples in other cities and regions of the kingdom, some were considered learned scholars, for example, Aḥmad Bannānī (d. 1340 AH/1921–22 CE), who served as Qāḍī of Rabat.
41. Muḥammad b. Rashīd al-ʿIrāqī to Aḥmad bin Mūsā, 29 Ṣafar 1314 AH/August 10, 1896 CE, DAR (TK), Fez 11, no. 6318.
42. ʿAbd al-Kabīr al-Kattānī to Muḥammad al-Kattānī, 3 Rabīʿ al-thānī 1314 AH/September 12, 1896 CE, DAR (TK), al-Kattānīyun.
43. ʿAbd al-Kabīr al-Kattānī to Muḥammad al-Kattānī, 14 Jumādā al-ākhira 1314 AH/November 21, 1896 CE, DAR (TK), al-Kattāniyyūn.
44. Ibid.
45. Mawlāy ʿArfa was an uncle of Sultan ʿAbd al-ʿAzīz and his *khalīfa* in Fez.
46. ʿAbd al-Kabīr al-Kattānī to Muḥammad al-Kattānī, 14 Jumādā al-

ākhira 1314 AH/November 21, 1896 CE, DAR (TK), al-Kattāniy-yūn.

47. This correspondence is explored in more detail in chapter 3, which deals with networks and the circulation of information among the Kattāniyya *zāwiya*s throughout Morocco.
48. ʿAbd al-Kabīr al-Kattānī to Muḥammad al-Kattānī, 14 Jumādā al-ākhira 1314 AH/November 21, 1896 CE, DAR (TK), al-Kattāniy-yūn.
49. Ibid.
50. Ibid.
51. ʿAbd al-Kabīr al-Kattānī to Muḥammad al-Kattānī, 14 Jumādā al-ākhira 1314 AH/November 21, 1896 CE, DAR (TK), al-Kattāniy-yūn. The term *ijtimāʿ bi al-nabī* refers to a mystical station in which the disciple meets the Prophet Muḥammad in flesh and blood and has intimate, daily association with him. It does not mean unification with the Prophet, as in the mystical station referred to as "passing away" *(fanāʾ)* in the divine being. O'Fahey and Radtke, "Neo-Sufism Reconsidered," 70.
52. ʿAbd al-Kabīr al-Kattānī to Muḥammad al-Kattānī, 3 Rabīʿ al-thānī 1314 AH/September 12, 1896 CE, DAR (TK), al-Kattāniy-yūn.
53. The author tells us that this book was composed by "al-Ṣiqillī" and was titled, *Anwār al-Qulūb fī ʿilm al-Mawhūb bihi.* ʿAbd al-Kabīr al-Kattānī to Muḥammad al-Kattānī, 3 Rabīʿ al-thānī 1314 AH/September 12, 1896 CE, DAR (TK), al-Kattāniyyūn.
54. Ibid. ʿAbd al-Kabīr was referring to the role of the shaykh in leading his disciples toward God.
55. ʿAbd al-Kabīr al-Kattānī to Muḥammad al-Kattānī, 13 Rabīʿ al-thānī 1314 AH/September 12, 1896 CE, DAR (TK), al-Kattāniy-yūn.
56. "They were not obligated to [abandon it] in all the *zāwiya*s, but only in the Fez *zāwiya*. Therefore, it doesn't mean it has to be given up by others except if you permit them to do so." ʿAbd al-Kabīr al-Kattānī to Muḥammad al-Kattānī, 14 Jumādā al-ākhira 1314 AH/November 21, 1896 CE, DAR (TK), al-Kattāniyyūn.
57. Before becoming sultan of the kingdom in 1873, Mawlāy Ḥasan served as his father's *khalīfa* in the Souss region, and therefore, had close relations with the tribes of the region and understood their customs and needs. Mohamed Ennaji and Paul Pascon, *Le*

Makhzan et Le Sous Al-Aqsa: la correspondance politique de la maison d'Iligh, 1821–1894 (Paris: Editions du CNRS, 1988), 19.

58. Al-Kattānī's stay in Marrakesh coincided with a revolt by the Raḥāmna—a tribe located to the northwest of Marrakesh in the plains that, between 1892 and 1912, rebelled against the *makhzan* over succession of the sultan and taxation. On the Raḥāmna in the nineteenth century and relations with the *makhzan,* see Ellen Titus Hoover, "Among Competing Worlds: the Rehamna of Morocco on the Eve of French Conquest," Ph.D. diss., Yale University, 1978. There is no specific mention of al-Kattānī's participation in negotiations between the Raḥāmna and the *makhzan* in Hoover's thesis.
59. For a discussion on relations between the *makhzan* and the *zāwiya*s see Abdallah Hammoudi, "The Reinvention of Dar al-Mulk," 136.
60. al-Kattānī, *Tarjama,* 86–87.
61. B. G. Martin, *Muslim Brotherhoods in Nineteenth-Century Africa* (Cambridge: Cambridge University Press, 1976), 127.
62. On the advice of Aḥmad bin Mūsā, Sultan ʿAbd al-ʿAzīz granted the shaykh a place for the establishment of an ʿAyniyya *zāwiya* and established it as a pious endowment or *ḥubus,* which was to be controlled by Mā al-ʿAynayn and his descendants. Later, other *zāwiya*s were established in Fez and Salé with the financial support of the sultan. As a gesture to the shaykh, the sultan joined the ʿAyniyya brotherhood, apparently at the insistence of the *wazīr,* who was himself a member of the order. Ibid, 134–135.
63. Ibid., 147.
64. Muḥammad al-Kattānī and Mā al-ʿAynayn have been viewed by some authors as intellectual peers because they both supported jihad, both were Sufis and *ʿālim*s, and both men called for reform of the Sufi orders on the basis of unity. See, for example, Fawzī ʿAbd al-Razzāq, *Mamlakat al-Kitāb: Tārīkh al-Ṭibāʿa fī al-Maghrib, 1865–1912* (Rabat: Maṭbaʿat al-Maʿārif al-Jadīda, 1986). However, it is necessary to emphasize that Mā al-ʿAynayn's writings have not been systematically studied, and most of them remain in manuscript form as is also the case with Muḥammad al-Kattānī's writings. For an overview of Mā al-ʿAynayn's writings, see Martin, *Muslim Brotherhoods in Nineteenth–Century Africa,* 147.
65. For example, the Wazzāniyya *zāwiya.*

66. Muḥammad al-ʿAlamī bin Muḥammad al-Ḥasanī to Aḥmad bin Mūsā, 22 Rabīʿ al-awwal 1312 AH/September 22, 1894 CE, DAR (TK), Fez 10, no. 6617.
67. Aḥmad bin Mūsā to Muḥammad al-Kattānī, 24 Shaʿbān 1314 AH/ January 29, 1897 CE, DAR (TK), al-Kattāniyyūn. The name of this celebration is Nuzhat Shaʿbān. This large feast was held each year during the month of Shaʿbān to mark the arrival of Ramaḍān.
68. See Hammoudi, "The Reinvention of Dar al-Mulk," for a discussion on relations between the *makhzan* and brotherhoods, 136.
69. Muḥammad al-Kattānī to ʿAbd al-Kabīr al-Kattānī, 19 Ramaḍān 1314 AH/February 22, 1897 CE, DAR (TK), al-Kattāniyyūn.
70. Muḥammad al-Kattānī to ʿAbd al-Kabīr al-Kattānī, 27 Rabīʿ (I or II?) 1315 AH/August (or September) 27, 1897 CE, DAR (TK), al-Kattāniyyūn. This is similar to the formulation by al-Ḥasan al-Yūsī, the seventeenth-century saint and scholar, who was known in the Moroccan written tradition for speaking openly about the need for just rule and the role of the sultan in guaranteeing this. Al-Yūsī has become an important metaphor in the Moroccan imagination for supporting justice against an oppressive order. See Munson, *Religion and Power in Morocco,* 31. On the life and teachings of al-Yūsī, see Jacques Berque, *Al-Yousi: problèmes de la culture marocaine au XVIIième siècle,* 2nd ed. (Rabat: Centre Tarik bin Ziyad, 2001).
71. Although he did not mention the name of the order, a further disparaging reference to a certain Abū Bakr al-Taṭwānī—the *muqaddam* of the Kattāniyya *zāwiya* in Salé and someone who appears to have had contacts with the brotherhood as early as 1896—signals that it was indeed the Kattāniyya to which bin Khadrāʾ referred. Aḥmad bin Khadrāʾ to al-Ṭayyib al-Ṣabīḥī, [day not clear] Dhū al-ḥijja 1323 AH/ [January] 1906 CE, BS, series 1, no. 51, doc. 7252.

· THREE ·

Sufi Revivalism and Expansion of the Kattāniyya

In a letter written around 1903, Muḥammad al-Kattānī inquired after Abū Bakr al-Tiṭwānī, one of his close disciples and confidantes and the *muqaddam* (section leader)[1] of the Kattāniyya *zāwiya* in the Moroccan city of Salé located west of Fez. In a scolding tone, al-Kattānī began his letter: "Your correspondence has escaped me as well as news regarding your mystical state [*ḥāl*] and your interaction with God. And the results of your interactions with humanity—have they reduced your illumination or increased it?" In many respects, the contents of the letter to Abū Bakr al-Tiṭwānī reflected typical concerns of a Sufi master regarding one of his disciples. For example, al-Kattānī asked about al-Tiṭwānī's performance of spiritual exercises. Was he performing his daily prayers? So that al-Tiṭwānī would not forget the significance of regular mystical devotional practice, the shaykh warned his disciple that "concern in performing morning contemplation is the sign of the servant's concern for God. If you wish to know your place with God, look to God's place within yourself."[2]

Yet Muḥammad al-Kattānī's letter also expressed profane as well as spiritual concerns. "The *ṭarīqa* has spread in every place throughout Morocco—praise God!" exclaimed Shaykh al-

Kattānī. "I hope He brings forth the love of the world from your heart so that you may travel to the Hijaz [to] spread the order there," he added. Shifting the discussion away from the ambitious goal of expanding the Kattāniyya beyond Morocco, al-Kattānī questioned whether al-Tiṭwānī had completed the more immediate task of establishing a branch of the order in the northern Moroccan port city of Tangier.[3]

Muḥammad al-Kattānī's desire to see a Kattāniyya *zāwiya* established in Tangier partly reflected the brotherhood's relatively limited importance and influence beyond Fez. Muḥammad al-Kattānī's grandfather had founded the *zāwiya* in 1853 in the Ibn Ṣawwāl district of Fez, where the Kattanīs resided, and for the first thirty years of its existence, the Kattāniyya brotherhood remained primarily a local Fāsī institution. At the time of its inception, the Kattāniyya was but one of a number of Sufi *ṭarīqa*s that—beginning in the late eighteenth century with the foundation of the Tijāniyya and Darqāwiyya orders—had emerged in Morocco as part of a more sweeping mystical revivalism among the Moroccan ulama.[4] But unlike the Tijāniyya, for example, which had strong ties to wealthy patrons and to the patron-client networks associated with the *makhzan,* the Kattāniyya had remained with a limited reach and influence.[5] Other prestigious Sufi orders with longer histories than the Kattāniyya were dominating Fāsī and Moroccan mystical life.[6] Although the Kattāniyya shaykhs created affiliations with some tribal groups in the environs of Fez and drew disciples from Fez, the order was hardly distinguished among the numerous brotherhoods that existed at the time.

During the pre-Protectorate period, the *zāwiya*s served an important political role in Moroccan society. The *zāwiya*s of prominent mystics provided important venues for arbitration between different groups in society and the *makhzan.* In urban centers such as Fez or Ouezzane, *zāwiya*s were spaces of mediation between the urban populations and the central government, while in the countryside, shaykhs acted as interlocutors between the *makhzan* and the tribes. The Wazzāniyya represented the most successful relationships of this type. In exchange for their help in maintaining good relations and close ties between the *makhzan* and the tribes of the Ouezzane region, the Wazzānī *shurafā'* were entitled to oversee and draw income from large landed estates in the environs of Ouezzane.[7] The 'Alawī *makhzan* forged a similar relationship with the Sharqāwī *zāwiya* located in the southern Chaouia region of Morocco (between Marrakesh and the Atlantic coast) during the reign of Mawlāy Ḥasan (r. 1873–1894). Recognizing the influence of Sharqāwiyya leaders among the tribes of the region, the *makhzan* was forced to contend with their leaders to secure trade routes and the movement of goods between Marrakesh and the coastal region.[8] In the region of Fez, acts of arbitration with the tribes were useful for maintaining the often tenuous balance between the city and its rural environs. As a result of his influence among the Bahālīl tribe of the Middle Atlas region where Fez is located, for example, the *makhzan* summoned 'Abd al-Kabīr al-Kattānī (Muḥammad al-Kattānī's father) to mediate in a dispute between the people of Sefrou and members of the Bahālīl tribe in 1894 and later to intercede on their behalf for forgiveness from the sultan.[9]

But how did the Kattāniyya brotherhood expand under the leadership of Muḥammad al-Kattānī? And why were people drawn to the *ṭarīqa* from different sectors of Moroccan society? Present narratives about the Kattāniyya tend to address the question of its expansion by focusing on Muḥammad al-Kattānī's relations with the *makhzan* without adequately explaining his efforts to expand the influence of the Kattāniyya among a wider constituency. According to the existing framework for study of the Moroccan *ṭarīqa*s, the claims made by Muḥammad al-Kattānī in letters to disciples and others with whom he corresponded could easily be construed as empty and self-promoting rhetoric of a Sufi order bent on establishing its primacy among other brotherhoods with whom they were com-

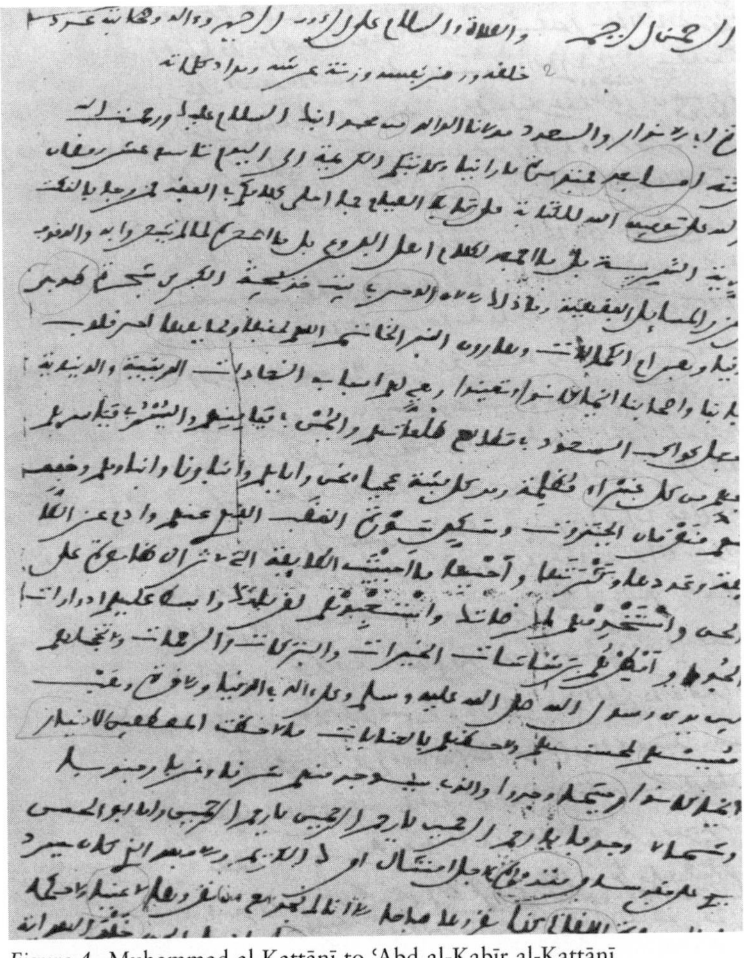

Figure 4. Muḥammad al-Kattānī to ʿAbd al-Kabīr al-Kattānī, 2 Ramaḍān 1314 AH/February 14, 1897 CE, DAR (TK), al-Kattāniyyūn.

peting for the favor of the state. That is, the Kattānīs were simply focused on their own narrow interests to accumulate wealth and prestige for the *zāwiya* and, by extension, for the Kattānī family. It certainly is the case that conflict sometimes existed between the Kattāniyya and other orders. And al-Kattānī spoke on several occasions of the supremacy of the Kattāniyya over other *ṭarīqa*s.[10] However, these interpretations do not explain why father and son were so determined to assert the orthodoxy of the rites of the Kattāniyya *ṭarīqa*. After all, if they were merely driven by the desire for family prestige and wealth, then why were they not satisfied with the alliance they had forged with the *makhzan* in 1896? The partnership with the *makhzan* would provide al-Kattānī with the support, resources, connections to the center of power, and prestige that he allegedly desired. Moreover, the makhzan's backing and support would also protect him against further accusations and reprisals by the ulama of Fez, who had accused al-Kattānī of harboring heretical beliefs. Clearly, Muḥammad al-Kattānī believed that something greater than the narrow interests of the *zāwiya* was at stake.

Indeed, Muḥammad al-Kattānī's desire to see the Kattāniyya grow beyond Fez was related to his deeply held conviction that the practice of mysticism in Morocco was in need of revival and that it was through the spread of Kattāniyya teachings that such a program of reform would emerge and be realized. In other words, al-Kattānī was motivated by his belief in the ideology of revivalism as an antidote to the problems plaguing Moroccan society. Shaykh Muḥammad al-Kattānī's activism focused on asserting the role of Sufi shaykhs as models of piety, as political exemplars, and as authorities in the interpretation of sharia. Between 1896, when he fled Fez for Marrakesh, and 1904, when he made the pilgrimage to Mecca and Medina, Muḥammad al-Kattānī worked assiduously to attract disciples to the Kattāniyya, to educate them regarding his revivalist notions, and to work toward a broader reform of Moroccan society.[11]

KATTĀNIYYA REVIVALISM AND THE REFORM OF MOROCCAN SOCIETY

Shaykh al-Kattānī's two-year sojourn in Marrakesh following resolution of the heresy affair sharpened his resolve about the need for a reinvigoration of the Sufi tradition in Morocco.[12] During his time in the southern capital, Shaykh al-Kattānī busied himself with teaching, writing, and practicing rituals of Sufism with other devotees of mysticism,[13] among them disciples of the Tijāniyya brotherhood,[14] which enjoyed great popularity and patronage in both Marrakesh and Fez in this period. At the time when al-Kattānī was in Marrakesh, the city hosted twelve different Tijāniyya *zāwiya*s.[15] Meanwhile, the shaykh continued frequent correspondence with his father regarding all matters of business relating to the order, both spiritual and profane.[16] Based on his observations, al-Kattānī concluded that the shaykhs of the large and prestigious Moroccan *ṭarīqa*s had failed to fulfill this broad range of expectations. There were shaykhs who "were propagandists for God and those who were propagandists for their ṭarīqa." God was "satisfied with those of the first group since they do not budge from their holy, lofty, sublime, and righteous position."[17] Al-Kattānī believed the shaykhs of the large brotherhoods had placed the narrow material interests of their orders above the higher goal of illuminating their disciples. Moreover, the failure of spiritual masters to fulfill their roles as guides and exemplars had resulted in a certain degree of decadence among their disciples. Instead of following a shaykh because of his knowledge *(maʿrifa)*, people preferred to follow those shaykhs who had garnered prestige through wealthy patronage and support. A shaykh's authority was no longer grounded in superior knowledge or spiritual perspicacity but rather in wealth: "If the hearts of the wealthy do not sympathize with [the *walī*]—even if his knowledge fills the sky and the earth—then he is nothing for them. It is the interest of the wealthy in the dead or the living [saint] that is necessary for such people to take interest in him."[18]

Al-Kattānī's critique was probably directed at leaders of the Tijāniyya order because in Marrakesh—where al-Kattānī spent one year observing the brotherhoods, practicing mystical rituals and praying with them—they were known to attract members from among the financial elite. Furthermore, the strength and prominence of the Tijāniyya in Marrakesh made it an obvious target for criticism by al-Kattānī.

Despite such feelings, al-Kattānī's earlier difficulties with the *makhzan* and juridical-minded ulama led him and his father to limit their discussions about esotericism, the role of the shaykhs, and the expansion of the Kattāniyya (that is, about subjects that could be viewed as controversial) to themselves and a select group of close disciples. After all, it was only two years since he had been forced to repent for his allegedly heretical statements regarding his authority as a saint and the Kattāniyya *zāwiya* of Fez had temporarily been closed. Furthermore, the reluctance of the Kattānīs to speak about esoteric matters reflects a more general practice. Sufis often spoke to only a select group of disciples about mystical experiences—such as illuminations, ecstatic utterances, and other subjects that were deemed to be complex or beyond the comprehension of the ordinary believer, therefore dangerous because of the potential for conflict between themselves and more juridical-oriented scholars.[19] In a similar manner, Muḥammad al-Kattānī believed that some things were better left unspoken to avoid having them be misunderstood or interpreted incorrectly. For instance, in response to an inquiry about the terminology associated with Kattāniyya prayers from one of al-Kattānī's disciples, Sīdī 'Alī al-Damnāṭī,[20] the shaykh cautioned, "Hidden things such as these are not written on paper because they fall into the hands of those who [should see them] and those [who should not]."[21] In this sense, Muḥammad al-Kattānī's concerns were similar to those of numerous Sufis before him who attempted to steer clear of the potentially devastating judgments of more legal-minded ulama.[22]

The Kattānīs' efforts to limit the circulation of contested ideas during this period may also reflect their belief that true theosophical illumination was exclusive and limited to a select few. "Divine offerings," declared Muḥammad al-Kattānī, "are given to those whom God desires."[23] Thus, although surely the shaykh wanted to express his opinions openly, in the immediate aftermath of the heresy affair the circumstances were not yet conducive to such open expressions. Through letter writing, far from the eyes and ears of suspicious authorities or sharia-oriented ulama, Muḥammad al-Kattānī, his father, and an inner circle of disciples freely expressed their attitudes to one another regarding the primacy of esoteric knowledge and Sufism, the power and authority of the shaykh, and the role of the Kattāniyya in the revival of Islam in Morocco.

FROM SUFI SHAYKH TO MUJTAHID

When he return to Fez in 1898 or 1899, Muḥammad al-Kattānī resumed teaching at the Kattāniyya *zāwiya* after a long hiatus, offering instruction in the canonical texts of Sufism and hadith (the corpus of traditions of the prophet Muḥammad). Even before Muḥammad al-Kattānī's tenure as shaykh of the Kattāniyya, his grandfather and father had provided instruction in the Quran and hadith to their disciples and affiliates. At the time of its foundation in 1853, the Kattāniyya *zāwiya* was unique among the *zāwiya*s of Fez for providing hadith instruction to disciples and others who came to participate in the activities of the Kattāniyya.[24] As shaykh of the Kattāniyya, Muḥammad al-Kattānī was celebrated for a series of gatherings he held in the Kattāniyya *zāwiya* for study of the *Ṣaḥīḥ of Bukhārī,* the most widely circulating hadith compendium among Moroccan ulama and students of law. His interest in the work compelled him to begin to compose his own *sharḥ* (exegesis), although it was never completed.[25]

Muḥammad al-Kattānī's interest in the study, transmission, and instruction of hadith reflected broader debates in pre-

Protectorate Moroccan intellectual life. From the late eighteenth century, prominent Moroccan ulama had developed a renewed interest in the study and instruction of the hadith. Responding to the doctrinal challenges of sharia revivalist movements, which developed throughout Islamic lands over the course of the eighteenth and early nineteenth centuries, the Moroccan ulama's willingness to reevaluate the importance of the traditions indicated a fundamental shift in the basis of legal interpretation through a rejection of the authority of the scholarly tradition as embodied in the principles established by the *madhhabs* (Islamic schools of law).[26] Hadith interpretation was central to this process, according to critics. They insisted that a return to the traditions was a necessary antidote to the decline in the interpretation and implementation of sharia. North African proponents of this perspective decried the declining state of religious instruction arguing for a more rigorous study of the traditions themselves instead of reliance on abridgments of the traditions (*mukhtaṣars*) that had become common practice in the study of *Mālikī fiqh* (law). Over-simplification, mistakes in transmission, and negligence among scholars due to deficiencies in their education had led to grave errors in understanding of the law and its implementation.[27] The Moroccan scholar, Muḥammad bin Ḥasan al-Bannānī (d. 1780), addressed the problem of the abridgments and their deficiencies in his *Fatḥ al-Rabbānī fī ma Dhahala ʿanhu al-Zurqānī,* as did the famed Moroccan jurist, Tawdī bin Sawdā (d. 1794).[28] Concern regarding the need for renewed focus on the traditions was even manifested at the institutional level through limiting the use of *mukhtaṣars* and more intensive focus on the corpus of the traditions in the curriculum of the Qarawīyīn University in 1788.[29]

Implicit in discussions about the revival of sharia was the issue of interpretive authority as expressed in the *ijtihād* (independent interpretation) versus *taqlīd* (the following of legal decisions laid out by the four schools of law) debate.[30] While critics of current interpretive practices believed a return to the original sources of sharia (the Quran and the hadith) was deemed necessary for its revival, the ulama held divergent opinions regarding who among them was qualified to carry out such interpretations. They debated over who had the right to practice *ijtihād* and to what degree, on one hand, and over what legal principles *ijtihād* should be based, on the other.

In al-Kattānī's view, the ideal Sufi not only embraced his role as a model of piety and leadership but also practiced *ijtihād*—the use of independent reason in matters of doctrinal interpretation. "Just as the *mujtahidūn* enjoined and [just as they] forbade . . . matters that were not sanctioned by the sharia in the realm of the exoteric," explained al-Kattānī, "the mystics [did the same] in the realm of the esoteric." In what appears to be a borrowing from the eleventh-century scholar, al-Ḥakīm al-Tirmidhī, al-Kattānī concluded that Sufism and *fiqh* were on equal footing as methods in the quest for understanding the meaning of divine revelation: "*Ijtihād* is factual in the two realms and neither realm is more valuable than the other, for *ḥaqīqa* without sharia is useless as is sharia without *ḥaqīqa*."[31]

To justify his perspective on the responsibility of Sufis (as well as their right) to engage in scriptural interpretation, al-Kattānī turned to the *Ṭarīqa Muḥammadiyya*—a complex of ideas formulated by the sixteenth-century scholar ʿAbd al-Wahhāb al-Shaʿrānī.[32] Shaykh al-Kattānī argued that some Sufis who experienced *kashf* (divine illumination) received it "written by the hand of the divine being on a stone or on a leaf" while others "hear the voice [say it]." Still other divinely inspired Sufis "learn it from the Prophet . . . during sleep or awake."[33]

In 1894, shortly after taking over leadership of the *zāwiya*, al-Kattānī revealed the results of his own encounter with the Prophet—that one recitation of the Kattāniyya *wird* had six thousand times the spiritual efficacy as one complete recitation of the Quran. Al-Kattānī's confidence in making such an overtly heterodox statement was based on his own spiritual illumination, which he claimed to have experienced as a result of waking visions he had had of the Prophet.[34] In the Islamic discursive tradition, allusions to the appearance of the Prophet in dreams and visions was a means of distinguishing and sanctifying the person who claimed to have experienced such an encounter. This dream trope was based on hadith-based arguments that the presence of the Prophet in dreams or in a waking state *(fī al-nawm aw yaqẓatan)* represented the conferral of God's distinction *(ni'ma)* on the seer.[35] The veracity of the Prophet's presence in a dream or vision was based on arguments grounded in hadith. Therefore, any instructions, utterances or legal interpretations that the Prophet pronounced during such an "encounter" with a saintly person were valid as long as they did not contradict Sunna.[36]

Muḥammad al-Kattānī argued that not only did he possess insight into the secrets of revelation through mystical experience, but also this knowledge qualified him as a *mujtahid*—someone who had the authority to interpret Islamic law.[37] He could rightfully act as a spiritual and social exemplar, provide leadership for his followers and thereby challenge the passivity of the *ṭarīqa* shaykhs and the inflexibility of sharia-oriented ulama in the process of reviving the sharia among the Moroccan Muslim community.[38] Quoting 'Abd al-Wahhāb al-Sha'rānī's *al-Yawāqīt,*[39] the shaykh defended his perspective: "Why do the Sufis not confine themselves to walking along the exoteric [side] of the Book and the Sunna only? Was that not enough for them as it was for others?" He responded, "If you reject the discovery of the Sufi [*al-'ārif*], then you must reject the discovery of the *mujtahid.* It is not possible for you to oppose the words of the *mujtahid* imams as they did not go beyond the rays of light of the sharia. Likewise, it is not permissible for you to oppose the Sufis who imitate the traces of God's Prophet in the exoteric and esoteric *adab.*"[40]

One of the reasons for Muḥammad al-Kattānī's decision to become more vocal regarding his views when he returned to Fez was the alliance he had forged with the *makhzan.* As is shown in the preceding chapter, this alliance provided protection and support for the Kattāniyya. But al-Kattānī must have been moved also by a sense of urgency regarding the task at hand. In 1900, shortly after his return to Fez, French troops occupied the Touat

Oasis region along the Moroccan-Algerian border, which indicated to many Moroccans that the country could soon face the fate of neighboring Algeria. The strategy of playing one European power off against another, which had succeeded in maintaining Moroccan independence, seemed to be faltering.[41] The inability of the Moroccan religious and political elite to adequately address the situation showed that a crisis of leadership existed, for nothing had proven effective in preventing European attacks against Moroccan sovereignty. As a Sufi, a sharīf, the shaykh of a mystical brotherhood, and a *mujtahid,* Muḥammad al-Kattānī was perfectly situated to challenge the Moroccan religious and political elite, calling on them to take action to reverse the decline of their society. Equipped with mystical doctrines of Sufism and sainthood and embracing the hadith revivalism of his peers, Muḥammad al-Kattānī was prepared to interpret and seek solutions that would address the power vacuum that was developing as the nineteenth century drew to a close and a new one began.

RESPONSES TO KATTĀNIYYA REVIVALISM

Expansion of the Kattāniyya involved intensive efforts on the part of Muḥammad al-Kattānī to maintain communication with affiliates and disciples regarding their activities, the pace of their spiritual instruction, and other news related to the functioning of the brotherhood. The shaykh and his closest affiliates used epistolary exchange to discuss doctrine and offer explanations of Kattāniyya practices to disciples in different cities and towns of Morocco.[42] One disciple even received the Kattāniyya *wird*—a standard practice indicating the initiation of a new disciple to the order—via correspondence.[43] Al-Kattānī also assigned instructors to teach new initiates the Quran after they had "taken the Kattāniyya *wird.*"[44]

Muḥammad al-Kattānī's efforts were aided by his efficient use of the new technology of printing. Print technology reached Morocco in 1864, when a Moroccan pilgrim, Muḥammad al-

Ṭayyib al-Rawdānī brought a printing press from Egypt after completing the Hajj. Shortly thereafter, Sultan Sīdī Muḥammad (r. 1859–1873) established the first Moroccan publishing house under the *makhzan*'s auspices. In the 1870s, printing became privatized, and several different printing establishments emerged in Fez, which then dominated the field until the establishment of the French Protectorate.[45]

Contrary to the view that members of the ulama rejected the use of printing on religious grounds, the Kattānis demonstrated their willingness to adopt the new technology for their needs.[46] Through contact with a printer named ʿAbd al-Salām Dhuayb, who was most likely a disciple of the Kattāniyya order, the Kattānīs—Muḥammad, his brother ʿAbd al-Ḥayy, and their father ʿAbd al-Kabīr—produced printed copies of materials such as epistles, prayers, and explanations of Kattāniyya practices.[47] Muḥammad alone published twenty-seven works, while his father, who was deeply involved in the activities of the Kattāniyya, published three of his own works on the lithographic press. These materials were intended for distribution among Kattāniyya disciples throughout the country. Letters between Muḥammad and his father contain numerous references to the use of printed materials for use among the disciples. In one letter, for example, Muḥammad al-Kattānī requested copies of texts that his father had written about mystical practice so that he could distribute them to Kattāniyya disciples in Marrakesh.[48]

Concern and interest in the education of the disciples on the part of Muḥammad al-Kattānī and his father is particularly relevant for understanding, in part, the gaining popularity of the Kattāniyya order in the early years of the twentieth century. Bypassing established institutions of instruction (most notably, the Qarawīyīn University), the Kattāniyya *zāwiya* provided an alternative channel for study and discussion relating to the subject of hadith scholarship.[49] Thus, the Kattāniyya provided an opportunity for traders, laborers, tanners, and students *(ṭalaba)* among the Fāsī population to participate in hadith circles without ever entering the world of institutionalized and elite scholarship. Indeed, al-Kattānī suggested that knowledge of prayer rituals and recitations were performed more accurately in the *zāwiya* than in the mosques as a result of poor knowledge on the part of the ulama. Thus, he encouraged his disciples to pray in the Kattāniyya *zāwiya* instead of the mosques, because, "most of the imams do not perform reading of the *Fātiḥa* correctly."[50]

Shaykh al-Kattānī's efforts to spread his view of reform and revival of Moroccan society did not fall on deaf ears during the early years of the twentieth century—a remarkable feat given his precarious position and even unpopularity only five years earlier. The shifting boundaries of reformist discourse in these years suggest the extent to which the situation in Morocco had become radicalized in this period. Indeed, following the Touat Oasis debacle in which French troops occupied Moroccan territory, a series of unprecedented attacks against the *shurafā'* took place. In 1901 the *makhzan* attempted to modernize its revenue collection by imposing a flat tax—the *tartīb*—which eliminated long-standing tax exemptions enjoyed by the shurafā' and thereby represented a direct challenge to their power as a loosely defined social group in Moroccan society.[51] Encouraged by Great Britain as part of sorely needed administrative and financial reforms, the *tartīb* represented one of the most radical expressions of Moroccan state centralization along modern European lines and away from the system of power sharing associated with Sharifism. Still another attack against the power and authority of the *shurafā'* occurred one year later in 1902. After the killing of an Englishman in Fez and the insistence of Great Britain's representative to the Moroccan court, the *makhzan*'s troops entered the most holy of Fez's sanctuaries, the tomb of Fez's founder and patron saint, Mawlāy Idrīs, to apprehend the Moroccan assailant who had sought sanctuary there. This act of defilement stood in grave violation of the concept of *ḥurm* (protection) which was yet another long-held privilege of the *shurafā'*.[52] These acts intended to assert the *makhzan*'s authority and at the behest of the foreign powers—appalled the city's inhabitants and caused great commotion and consternation among them.[53]

European-guided fiscal and disciplinary measures also occurred against the backdrop of a heightening sense of uncertainty in Fez as a result of the Bū Ḥmāra Rebellion, a rural uprising that began in 1902 in the territory to the east of Fez between the city and the Algerian border. Bū Ḥmāra (owner of a she-donkey) claimed to be the son of the strong-man sultan Mawlāy Ḥasan and the rightful heir to the ʿAlawī throne. Bū Ḥmāra and his supporters denied the legitimacy of Sultan ʿAbd al-ʿAzīz to rule and challenged the sultan's forces almost continuously from the rebellion's inception until it was finally put down in 1909. The rebellion greatly taxed the state's resources, forcing the already financially beleaguered *makhzan* to resort to borrowing from a European banking consortium in 1904 to forestall bankruptcy. People of the Middle Atlas region, the epicenter of the rebellion, experienced the effects of the Bū Ḥmāra Rebellion directly. The conflict disrupted trade between Fez and the eastern Moroccan border city of Taza, for example.[54] Bū Ḥmāra's millenarian-style rebellion forced the ulama of Fez to issue a collective statement denouncing the rebel while also reasserting ʿAbd al-ʿAzīz's legitimacy as the rightful heir to the sultanate.[55]

Muḥammad al-Kattānī began to capture the intellectual interest of members of the Moroccan religious and political elite. He was invited to read the *Ṣaḥīḥ of Bukhārī,* a major hadith collection, at Fez's illustrious Qarawīyīn.[56] Other instructional sessions, which were to be held in the Kattāniyya *zāwiya,* were continued in the Qarawīyīn as a result of overcrowding.[57] The assistant to the Qādī of Tangier and a disciple of the Nāṣiriyya *ṭarīqa,* Abū al-ʿAbbās Aḥmad b. ʿUmar al-Sūsī al-Ṭanjī, felt compelled to take the Kattāniyya *wird.* Likewise, the shaykh of the Mukhtāriyya *ṭarīqa* in the city of Meknes located west of Fez, Abū Muḥammad al-Saʿīd b. al-Mahdī al-Manūnī al-Ḥasanī, received the spiritual chain of transmission *(silsila)* from Muḥammad al-Kattānī.[58] The attention al-Kattānī received from his ulama and Sufi peers points to the fact that he was increasingly being viewed as a legitimate participant in the intellectual and political debates of the day. By this, I do not mean to suggest that skeptics were now convinced of al-Kattānī's positions. Rather, al-Kattānī was acting within an atmosphere of a heightened sense that crisis was imminent—an atmosphere in which the action-oriented efforts of Muḥammad al-Kattānī might be viewed with greater interest by Moroccans. An indication that al-Kattānī had moved from the margins of intellectual debate was the fact that, in 1903, he was one of numerous signers of a letter issued in the name of the ulama of Fez, which denounced the rebel leader and pretender, Bū Ḥmāra.[59]

In the opening years of the century, members of well-established and prominent brotherhoods also began to take interest in the activities of the comparatively neophyte Kattāniyya order. Like the Kattāniyya, the Darqāwiyya brotherhood had a penchant for Sufi activism. Al-ʿArabī al-Darqāwī, the Sufi master who developed the doctrines on which the Darqāwiyya was based, emphasized social engagement on the part of sufis as part of his own attempt to reinvigorate the mystical tradition some seventy years before the Kattāniyya was even founded.[60] The activism of the Darqāwiyya continued to the end of the nineteenth century when in 1892, for instance, Muḥammad al-ʿArabī al-ʿAlawī (d. 1309 AH/1892 CE), a shaykh of the Darqāwiyya in the Tafilalt region of Morocco, tried to rally support for a revolt against the *makhzan*.[61]

Amid the climate of impending political crisis and in response to weak leadership, Muḥammad al-Kattānī and his Darqāwiyya peers may have been brought together on the basis of a shared belief in the need for the Sufi orders to participate in social action in defense of Morocco.[62] Darqāwiyya shaykhs, disciples, and affiliates responded with seeming enthusiasm for al-Kattānī's call to Sufi activism. In Fez in this period, members of the Darqāwiyya were known to come to the Kattāniyya *zāwiya* to perform prayers and other Sufi rituals with Kattāniyya adepts.[63] And in Tangier, where the Kattāniyya was only newly established in the first decade of the century, Darqāwiyya affiliates showed great interest in the Kattāniyya. During his visit to the northern port city in 1903, the *muqaddam* of the Darqāwiyya *ṭarīqa* "came with all the disciples of his group with the intention of making a visitation [*ziyāra*] to Shaykh al-Kattānī and to form a bond of mutual friendship and respect [*ṣila*] with him."[64] As if to advertise his presence in the city, Muḥammad al-Kattānī and his disciples held a large gathering known as an *ʿamāra,* which was attended by Tangier's Muslim notables, among others. On that occasion, the Darqāwiyya *muqqadam* closed his *zāwiya* to attend.[65]

Much like the enthusiasm expressed by Darqāwiyya and others for the Kattāniyya and its leadership, disciples of the Tijāniyya order also were attracted to the shaykh and his *ṭarīqa.* For example, a certain Abū Muḥammad Zayyān b. Idrīs al-Marīnī al-Fāsī had been a Tijānī disciple for more than forty years, yet he desired to learn from Muḥammad al-Kattānī,[66] and al-Makkī Bū Adkir,[67] a *muqqadam* of the Tijāniyya, later became a close associate of Muḥammad al-Kattānī.[68]

Tijānī enthusiasm for the Kattāniyya was likely related to al-Kattānī's adoption and development of certain Tijāniyya practices and doctrines, among them his insistence that Kattāniyya disciples abandon the consumption of tea and sugar.[69] The abstention from the consumption of tea and sugar by Tijānī affiliates was a practice that had come to distinguish the Tijāniyya in Morocco. Aḥmad al-Tijānī, the eponymous founder of the brotherhood, was known for his refusal to take either product. He believed that human blood was used in the refining process of sugar, and this perception eventually led him to abandon the consumption of the highly popular mint tea, which was usually drunk heavily sweetened with sugar.[70] Although Tijānī never made a specific pronouncement regarding the prohibition of tea and sugar consumption, some Tijāniyya shaykhs required their disciples to abandon their use of these stimulants as a prerequisite for entry into the *ṭarīqa.*[71]

Various interpretations of the Kattāniyya injunction against tea and sugar exist, but none attribute the practice to the Tijāniyya. According to *the Tarjama,* Shaykh al-Kattānī was driven by nationalist sentiment to forbid the drinking of tea and sugar among his disciples. Tea and sugar—both items imported in large quantities from Europe—were economic weapons against Morocco, since Moroccans squandered precious resources on purchasing these commodities. Had the money used for purchasing tea and sugar been applied to military reforms, for instance, Morocco would not have been standing weak and helpless before European armies.[72] The nationalist sentiment, to which al-Kattānī's biographer attributes Kattāniyya injunctions against tea and sugar, is challenged in a small article about Muḥammad al-Kattānī, which appeared in the May 3rd, 1907, edition of the Tangier-based Arabic weekly newspaper, *Lisān al-Maghrib.* It was not nationalism that drove al-Kattānī to abandon tea and sugar but rather their allegedly insalubrious side-effects, explained the article's author.[73] Yet another interpretation, which al-Kattānī's brother, ʿAbd al-Ḥayy, put forward, frames abandoning tea and sugar in terms of Islamic orthodoxy. *Al-Maẓāhir* explains that milk and dates replaced tea and sugar at Kattāniyya *zāwiya*s, in accordance with the Sunna of the Prophet.[74]

Other important similarities between Muḥammad al-Kattānī and Aḥmad al-Tijānī and the Tijāniyya relate to potential overlaps in doctrine, most notably with regard to the source of saintly authority. The clearest expression of this relates to Muḥammad al-Kattānī's claims regarding the source of the Kattāniyya *wird.* Both Aḥmad al-Tijānī and Muḥammad al-Kattānī claimed to have received the *wird*s of their respective *ṭarīqa*s directly from the Prophet.[75] These claims were considered highly unorthodox by critics among the ulama, who interpreted them as near declarations of prophethood.[76] Like Aḥmad al-Tijānī, al-Kattānī told his disciples that recitation of the litany of special prayers associated with the Kattāniyya would bring them closer to spiritual illumination than sixty complete recitations of the Quran.[77] As mentioned earlier in this chapter, such a claim placed al-Kattānī above the authority of the ulama as interpreters of sharia on the basis of esoteric rather than exoteric knowledge, which was precisely the reason the ulama of Fez had charged him with heresy in 1895. Aḥmad al-Tijānī had made strikingly similar statements almost one hundred years before. According to Tijānī, one recitation of the Tijānī *wird* (called *Ṣalāt al-Fatḥ*) was more efficacious than six thousand complete recitations of the Quran—a claim that had also raised the ire of the ulama of Fez at the time.[78]

By drawing attention to the similarities between Muḥammad al-Kattānī and other important Sufis, I am not implying that al-Kattānī's doctrinal formulations were based on tactical considerations regarding the expansion of the Kattāniyya or that he adapted certain practices because he thought they would attract more disciples for the order. Rather, al-Kattānī's recognition serves to indicate that he operated within an intellectual environment that was defined by a simultaneous interest among his contemporaries in both hadith revivalism and in Sufism. It is certainly reasonable to suppose that he would look to the works of other Sufis he admired to supplement or influence his own thinking.[79] While al-Kattānī was certainly interested in putting his stamp on doctrines and practices that defined the intellectual and cultural environment, his adaptations alone do not explain why Tijāniyya and Darqāwiyya disciples would be drawn to the Kattāniyya, especially since their brotherhoods were well established and (at least in Fez) less controversial. Given the widespread participation in the various brotherhoods among Moroccans in this period, it is difficult to imagine that the practices of the Kattāniyya *ṭarīqa* did not reflect some continuity and overlap with existing practices.

NOTES

1. The *muqaddam* is a section leader of a *ṭariqa*. In the case of the Kattāniyya, we do not know how *zāwiya* shaykhs selected the *muqqadams* or what their specific duties entailed. It is most likely

that the shaykh made his choice on the basis of dedication to and involvement in the order.

2. *Rasā'il Abī al-Fayḍ al-Kattānī,* Ms. BGK 3297, pp. 3–4, BG.
3. Ibid.
4. Ḥarakāt, *Al-Tayyārāt,* 66. Muḥammad al-ʿAlawī confirms Ḥarakāt's assessment. See al-ʿAlawī, *Jāmiʿ al-qarawiyyīn wa al-fikr al-salafī, 1873–1912,* 47–48.
5. On the Tijāniyya, see Jamil Abun-Nasr, *The Tijaniyya: A Sufi Order in the Modern World* (London: Oxford University Press, 1965). See Mohamed El Mansour regarding the *makhzan*'s efforts to incorporate the *shurafā'* into their patron-client networks. Mohamed El Mansour, "Saints and Sultans: Religious Authority and Temporal Power in Pre-colonial Morocco," in Kisaichi Masatoshi ed., *Popular Movements and Democratization in the Islamic World* (London: Routledge, 2006), 24.
6. Le Tourneau, *Fès avant le Protectorat,* 606–612. See also Georges Dragues, *Esquisse d'histoire religieuse du Maroc: confréries et zaouïas* (Paris: J. Peyronnet, 1951).
7. Muḥammad Bū Salām, "Mūjaz Mashrūʿ Qirā'a fī Taṭawwur ʿIlāqāt baʿḍ al-Zawāya bi al-Sulṭa al-Markaziyya," *Majallat Tarikh al-Maghrib* 2 (April 1982): 86.
8. For more on relations between the *makhzan* and the Sharqāwī *zāwiya* under Mawlāy Ḥasan and ʿAbd al-ʿAzīz, see Dale Eickelman, *Moroccan Islam: Tradition and Society in a Pilgrimage Center* (Austin: University of Texas Press, 1976).
9. Muḥammad al-ʿAlamī bin Muḥammad al-Ḥasanī to Aḥmad bin Mūsā, 22 Rabīʿ al-awwāl 1312 AH/September 23, 1894 CE, DAR (TK), Fez 10, no. 6617.
10. Muḥammad al-Kattānī, *Kitāb fī al-Taṣawwuf,* Ms. BGK 3213, BG, 6. *"Ghālib man yushār ilayhi fī ṭarīqatihim laysa lahu fatḥ rawḥānī aṣlan."*
11. Several important caveats must be noted regarding the expansion of the Kattāniyya. First, in the absence of a thorough study of the writings, doctrines, and beliefs of the Kattāniyya shaykhs, our understanding of the Kattāniyya movement will be limited at best. Muḥammad al-Kattānī's esoteric doctrines and practices—an essential component of his spiritual authority, power, and his popularity—have yet to be studied in detail. To the best of my knowledge, no scholarly editions of these manuscripts have been

attempted. Dates of the manuscripts are missing, and the development of his thinking over time is difficult to trace. Second, tracing the emergence of the Kattāniyya from a local Fāsī phenomenon to a widespread and powerful brotherhood is difficult due to sparse and incomplete information about affiliates and disciples, their names, places of origin, intellectual lineages and biographies, and social positions. As I attempt to explain in the introduction of the book, it is also difficult to address the question of affiliation because official membership in an order did not exist, and affiliates and disciples of one shaykh often would study under different shaykhs or ulama simultaneously. Finally, in attempting to determine the social status of affiliates (i.e., ulama, *shurafā'*, and commoners), it is necessary to keep in mind that the two sources dealing with al-Kattānī's life mention only those affiliates from among the ulama. Given these caveats, however, it is possible to identify some general trends regarding the areas of Kattāniyya expansion.

12. The chronology of events is not clear at this point. According to Muḥammad al-Bāqir al-Kattānī's *Tarjama,* Muḥammad al-Kattānī remained in Marrakesh for fifteen months. He then went to the Chaouia region, where he stayed among the Chaouia tribe for three months. Al-Kattānī, *Tarjama,* 87–88. However, extant letters written between ʿAbd al-Kabīr and Muḥammad al-Kattānī indicate that Muḥammad returned to Fez in 1898. It is not clear whether he returned to Fez from somewhere other than Marrakesh or if he had returned there and then made other trips to Marrakesh between 1897 and 1898.
13. He was prolific in this period, having composed twenty works on Sufism and hadith. Ibid., 87.
14. Ibid., 79.
15. Abun-Nasr, 95.
16. For example, ʿAbd al-Kabīr al-Kattānī to Muḥammad al-Kattānī, 5 Rabīʿ al-thānī 1315 AH/4 September, 1897 CE, DAR (TK), al-Kattāniyyūn. We have fifteen extant letters for the period between September 1896 and January 1898.
17. ʿAbd al-Kabīr al-Kattānī from Muḥammad al-Kattānī, 27 Rabīʿ (I or II?) 1315 AH/July 27, 1897 CE or September 26, 1897 CE, DAR (TK), al-Kattāniyyūn.
18. Ibid.
19. Yohanan Friedmann has suggested that the contradictions that ap-

pear in the writings and teachings of the seventeenth-century mystic Aḥmad Sirhindī are attributable to his belief that esoteric doctrines should be revealed only to disciples who were spiritually capable of understanding them. Friedmann, *Shaykh Aḥmad Sirhindi,* 4. R. S. O'Fahey has suggested a similar explanation for apparent contradictions in the teachings of the early nineteenth-century mystic Aḥmad Ibn Idrīs. According to O'Fahey, Aḥmad Ibn Idrīs was selective about his students because he believed that there were few among them who could understand what he wanted to convey. O'Fahey, *Enigmatic Saint.*

20. Sīdī 'Alī's full name is 'Alī bin Muḥammad bin 'Abd al-Qādir al-'Adlūnī. However, his fellow disciples addressed him as Sīdī 'Alī al-Damnāṭī. Presumably, this was because he was from the town of Demnate, located to the northeast of Marrakesh. Sīdī 'Alī was al-Kattānī's *khalīfa* in Marrakesh. al-Kattānī, *al-Maẓāhir,* 204.
21. *Risāla ilā fuqarā' al-Kattāniyyīn,* BH10327, BH, 131.
22. Muḥammad al-Kattānī also appears to have hesitated regarding the spiritual capabilities of a certain Aḥmad bin Ṭayyib. In a letter most likely written to his father from Marrakesh, Muḥammad al-Kattānī requested that the aforementioned Aḥmad bin Ṭayyib not be informed about *al-haqā'iq* (divine truths), as such information might lead to his breaking with the *zāwiya.* Further along in the same letter, al-Kattānī warned that the *fuqarā'* should not mention these truths either. Perhaps uncertain about the students' depth of conviction, al-Kattānī warned that specific aspects of doctrine and belief should be withheld. The recipient of the letter is unknown because the top section is missing. However, the date falls within the period when Muḥammad al-Kattānī was in Marrakesh. Muḥammad al-Kattānī to an unknown recipient, 18 Ṣafar 1315 AH/July 20, 1897 CE, DAR (TK), al-Kattāniyyūn.
23. al-Kattānī, *Lisān al-Ḥujja,* 19.
24. In a description of the founder of the Kattāniyya order in 'Abd al-Ḥayy al-Kattānī's *al-Maẓāhir al-Sāmiyya,* the author highlighted his grandfather's hadith-centered orientation. *Al-Maẓāhir al-Sāmiyya* reports that, at the time of its foundation, the Kattāniyya *zāwiya* was the only one in Fez in which hadith was taught. Al-Kattānī, *al-Maẓāhir,* 380.
25. al-Kattānī, *Tarjama,* 153.
26. These included the Indian Shah Wali Allah (1703–1762), Muḥam-

mad Ibn ʿAbd al-Wahhāb (1703–1787), Muḥammad ʿAlī al-Sanūsī (1787–1859), and the West African scholar, ʿUthmān bin Fūdī (1754–1817). Dallal, "The Origins and Objectives of Islamic revivalist thought, 1750–1850."

27. Two particularly important abridgements of the canonical text, *The Mukhtaṣar of Khalīl*—highly influential among Mālikī students of the seventeenth and early eighteenth centuries—were written by the Mālikī scholars at al-Azhar University in Cairo. For an amusing description of a Maghrabī student's visit to Cairo to study under them, and his frustration with their interpretative mistakes, see Houari Touati, *Entre Dieu et les hommes: lettrés, saints et sorciers au Maghreb (17e siècle)* (Paris: Recherches d'Histoire et de Sciences Sociales, 1994), 58–59.
28. Ibid., 58–59.
29. This was implemented during the reign of the ʿAlawī sultan, Sīdī Muḥammad b. ʿAbd Allah (r.1757–1790). Sīdī Muḥammad b. ʿAbd Allah also initiated the practice of convening the most respected ulama at the palace for discussion of hadith. This practice was also taken up by Mawlāy Ḥasan (r. 1873–1894). O'Fahey, *Enigmatic Saint,* 34. With the introduction of printing in Morocco in the mid-nineteenth century hadith compendiums (particularly the *Ṣaḥīḥ of Bukhārī*) were among the most widely printed works. ʿAbd al-Razzāq, *Mamlakat al-Kitāb,* 56.
30. In the nineteenth century, religious reformers diverged from the opinions of the lawyers of the four schools of law and claimed the right to interpret the Quran and hadith independently. However, this argument was not new, for throughout Islamic history, scholars had attacked the notion of *taqlīd* (imitation) as obligatory. At the center of the *ijtihād/taqlīd* debate was the question of authenticity of prescription regarding the Quran and hadith, the bases of the Prophet's Sunna which, in turn, served as the only authentic knowledge of divine revelation. The argument against *taqlīd* is based on the belief that the opinions of the *madhhab*s introduced the element of human reasoning, which is not infallible. It therefore, forms an obstacle for believers who seek authentic prescriptions. However, *ijtihād* and *taqlīd* were rarely viewed in absolute terms and different degrees of *ijtihād* were recognized among the ulama. The founders of the schools of law were considered absolute *mujtahid*s. They were followed by *mujtahid*s within a particu-

lar *madhhab* and *fatwā mujtahids*, and finally, pure *muqallids*. See Rudolph Peters, "Idjtihad and Taqlid in Eighteenth and Nineteenth-Century Islam," *Die Welt des Islams* 20, no. 3–4 (1980): 131–145. For an excellent discussion of *taqlīd* as it relates to the sociology of law, see Mohammad Fadel, "The Social Logic of *Taqlid* and the Rise of the *Mukhtasar,*" *Islamic Law and Society* 3, no. 2 (1996): 194–233.

31. al-Kattānī, *Lisān al-Ḥujja,* 43.
32. ʿAbd al-Wahhāb al-Shaʿrānī (d. 1565) was known for his attempts to popularize the doctrines of the twelfth-century mystic Ibn al-ʿArabī. For a detailed examination of al-Shaʿrānī's influence among eighteenth- and nineteenth-century mystics and ulama, see Knut S. Vikør, "The Shaykh as Mujtahid: A Sufi Conception of Ijtihād?," in *El Sufismo y las Normas del Islam: trabajos del IV Congreso Internacional de Estudios Jurídicos Islámicos: Derecho y Sufismo, Murcia, 7–10 Mayo 2003/Edicion y traduccion, Alfonso Carmona* (Murcia: Editora Regional de Murcia, 2006), 351–375. I would like to thank Dr. Muhammad Shahab Ahmed for bringing this source to my attention. Bernd Ranke et al. have also examined the influence of al-Shaʿrānī on Aḥmad Ibn Idrīs and the nineteenth-century reformist Sufis. See Radtke et al., *The Exoteric Aḥmad Ibn Idris.* See also Michael Winter, *Society and Religion in Early Ottoman Egypt: Studies in the Writings of ʿAbd al-Wahhāb al-Shaʿrānī* (New Brunswick, NJ: Transaction Publishers, 2007).
33. al-Kattānī, *Lisān al-Ḥujja,* 37.
34. Yūsuf b. Ismāʿīl b. Ḥasan b. Muḥammad al-Nabahānī (1849–1932), *Jāmiʿ Karamāt al-Awliyāʾ,* on Muḥammad al-Kattānī's visions of the Prophet, quoted in al-Kattānī, *al-Maẓāhir,* 171.
35. Jonathan G. Katz, *Dreams, Sufism and Sainthood: The Visionary Career of Muḥammad al-Zawawi,* Studies in the History of Religions, ed. H. G. Kippenberg and E. T. Lawson, vol. 71 (Leiden: E. J. Brill, 1996), 222.
36. The hadith says this: "Whoever has seen me has seen me truly, and Satan cannot impersonate me." Quoted in Jonathan G. Katz, *Visionary Experience, Autobiography, and Sainthood in North African Islam,* Princeton Papers in Near Eastern Studies, ed. Charles Issawi and Bernard Lewis, no. 1 (Princeton: the Darwin Press, 1992), 86.
37. al-Kattānī, *Lisān al-Ḥujja,* 8. While the ulama were responsible for

establishing the limits of sharia based on *ʿilm,* the Sufis were responsible for establishing this limit on the basis of *maʿrifa.* Therefore, any argument about the heretical nature of his beliefs or about the practices of the Kattāniyya was moot because the two spheres of knowledge were not comparable. Al-Kattānī's opponents were not privy to the secrets of mystical knowledge *(al-'ilm al-bāṭinī)* and were incapable of understanding him.

38. See Muḥammad al-Kattānī's formulation of the Sufi-*mujtahid* in chapter 2 of this book.
39. On al-Shaʿrānī's *al-Yawāqīt wa al-Jawāhir fī Bayān ʿaqā'id al-Akābir,* see Chodkiewicz, "Quelques remarques sur la diffusion de l'enseignement d'Ibn Arabi."
40. Kattānī, *Lisān al-Ḥujja,* 42–43.
41. On the deteriorating situation see Burke, *Prelude to Protectorate,* and Katz, *Murder in Marrakesh.*
42. Muḥammad al-Kattānī to ʿAlī bin Muḥammad bin ʿAbd al-Qādir al-ʿAdlūnī, *Risāla ilā fuqarā' al-Kattāniyyīn* BH10327, BH, 130. The letter responds to an inquiry regarding the meaning of two terms associated with Kattāniyya doctrines.
43. al-Kattānī, *al-Maẓāhir,* 227. The disciple was the son of the Qāḍī of Tadla, Abū Muḥammad Sīdī al-ʿAlamī.
44. A letter to ʿAbd al-Kabīr al-Kattānī from an unknown correspondent (presumably a disciple) explained that when eighty-five new affiliates took the *wird* of the Kattāniyya, someone was assigned (also most likely by the correspondent) for their instruction. The letter specifies neither date nor place of writing. *Risāla ilā fuqarā' al-Kattāniyyīn* BH10327, BH, 155.
45. ʿAbd al-Razzāq, *Mamlakat al-Kitāb,* 138, 154–156.
46. Older scholarship on modernization in the Islamic world has incorrectly assumed that Muslim societies exhibited an aversion to printing. This has been viewed as evidence of Islam's role in holding back these societies in their trajectories of development. However, such perspectives have now been widely challenged by scholars in the field. For an excellent overview of these discussions, see Dana Sajdi, "Print and Its Discontents: A Case for Pre-Print Journalism and Other Sundry Print Matters," *Translator* 15 no. 1 (2009): 105–138.
47. ʿAbd al-Salām al-Dhuwayb had an affiliation with the Kattāniyya, although it is not clear what his relationship was to the order. A

reference to this affiliation is made in Muḥammad bin Muṣtafā Bū Jandar, *al-Ightibāṭ bi tarājim a'lām al-rabāṭ*, ed. 'Abd al-Karīm Karīm Kurayyim (Maṭābi' al-Aṭlas: Rabat, 1987), 413.

48. 'Abd al-Razzāq, *Al-maṭba'a al-ḥajariyya fī al-Maghrib* (Rabat: Maṭba'at al-Ma'ārif al-Jadīda, 1986), 170–172. As in chapter 2, during the height of the heresy controversy, 'Abd al-Kabīr al-Kattānī implored his son to send copies of a text explaining the Kattāniyya *wird* to convince skeptics among the disciples that there was nothing heretical about the prayer. Followers of the Mahdī in the Sudan used printing technology in the late nineteenth century to spread their ideas, as did members of the 'Jadidst' movement led by the Crimean Tater, Ismail Bey Gasprinskii, at the close of the nineteenth century. See Heather J. Sharkey, "A Century of print: Arabic Journalism and Nationalism in the Sudan, 1899–1999," *IJMES* 31, no. 4 (November 1999): 531–549 and Adeeb Khalid, "Printing, Publishing and Reform in Tsarist Central Asia," *IJMES* 26, no. 2 (May 1994): 187–200.

49. Some prominent Moroccan ulama, such as al-Tawdī bin Sawdā, discouraged hadith instruction among the masses *('āmm)* on the grounds that they did not possess the skills and training to interpret the traditions correctly. Ḥarakāt, *al-Tayyārāt,* 53.

50. Muḥammad Ḥamza ibn 'Alī al-Kattānī and Ghassān Abū Ṣūfa, eds., *Min rasā'il al-imām Muḥammad bin 'Abd al-Kabīr al-Kattānī fī al-ādāb wa al-sulūk* (Amman: Dār al-Rāzī, 1999), 272.

51. Cigar, "Socio-economic Structures and the Development of an Urban Bourgeoisie in Pre-Colonial Morocco." Cigar argues that the power of the *shurafā'* as political actors was slowly being undermined in the late eighteenth and early nineteenth centuries. The implementation of the *tartīb* signaled the end of sharīfan political power.

52. On the concept of *ḥurm* see el-Mansour, "The Sanctuary *(Ḥurm)* in Precolonial Morocco," 49–73.

53. Eugène Aubin, *Morocco of Today* (London: J. M. Dent and Co., 1906), 204–205. See also Burke, *Prelude to Protectorate in Morocco,* 49–53.

54. For a discussion about the economic consequences of Bū Ḥmāra's activities on trade in Fez, see Aubin, *Morocco of Today,* 102. Aubin also described battles between *makhzan* forces and tribes loyal to Bū Ḥmāra, see ibid., 103–108. See also Ross E. Dunn,

"The Bū Ḥmāra Rebellion in Northeastern Morocco: Phase 1," *Middle Eastern Studies* 17, no. 1 (1981): 30–48.

55. "Letter of the Ulama of Fez of 12 June 1903," in *Bulletin de la Société de Géographie d'Oran,* 223 (1903): 241–255.
56. al-Kattānī, *Tarjama,* 153.
57. Ibid., 150.
58. al-Kattānī, *al-Maẓāhir,* 223–224.
59. "Letter of the Ulama of Fez of 12 June 1903," in *Bulletin de la Société de Géographie d'Oran,* 223 (1903): 241–255.
60. On the rise of the Darqāwiyya and on Darqāwiyya doctrine, see ʿAbd al-Majīd al-Ṣaghīr, *Ishkāliyyāt iṣlāḥ al-fikr al-ṣūfī al-qarnayn 18 wa 19: Aḥmad Ibn ʿAjība wa Muḥammad al-Ḥarrāq* (Rabat: Dār al-Āfaq al-Jadīda, 1994); al-Ṣaghīr, *al-Taṣawwuf ka waʿī wa mumārasa.*
61. Al-ʿAlawī's call for jihad was a manifestation of shifting relations of power and authority between the *makhzan* and the *shurafāʾ* of the Tafilalt in favor of the *makhzan.* Susan G. Miller and Amal Rassam, "The View from the Court: Moroccan Reactions to European Penetration during the Late Nineteenth Century," *International Journal of African Historical Studies* 16, no. 1 (1983): 32–35.
62. Indeed, some scholars have viewed the Kattāniyya as an offshoot of the Darqāwiyya *ṭarīqa.* The French military intelligence officer, Georges Drague (a pseudonym for Georges Spillmann), viewed the emergence of all the major orders of this period (with the exception of the Tijānī) as branches of the Darqāwiyya. However, until detailed studies of Kattāniyya doctrines have been completed, the degree to which the Kattāniyya doctrines remained true to the original teachings of al-ʿArabī al-Darqāwī (or to what extent they were actually based on his teachings) cannot be determined. Drague, *Esquisse d'histoire religieuse du Maroc.*
63. When Muḥammad al-Kattānī was in Marrakesh, his father wrote informing him (among other things) that the Kattāniyya *zāwiya* had been empty and that the disciples preferred to practice prayers in the Darqāwiyya *zāwiya.* This may have been due to the controversy surrounding Muḥammad al-Kattānī at this time. ʿAbd al-Kabīr al-Kattānī to Muḥammad al-Kattānī, 3 [month not clear] 1315 AH/1898 CE, DAR (TK), al-Kattāniyyun.

64. ʿAbd al-Salām al-ʿUmrānī, *Al-luʾluʾa al-fāsiyya fī al-riḥla al-Ḥijāziyya,* Ms. BGK 3/1012, BG, 135. The term *ṣila* designates the practice of gift exchange and is "part of the semantic field of kinship and its obligations." Hammoudi, *Master and Disciple,* 51. Religious holidays provided the opportunity for families to reconfirm their *ṣila* and to renew a *ṣila* that had been broken due to family conflict or strife. For more on the inscribing of kinship in relations of power such as the *ṣila,* see Abdellah Hammoudi, "The Reinvention of Dar al-Mulk."
65. ʿAbd al-Salām al-ʿUmrānī, *Al-luʾluʾa al-fāsiyya fī al-riḥla al-Ḥijāziyya,* Ms. BGK 3/1012, BG, 135.
66. al-Kattānī, *al-Maẓāhir,* 226.
67. The name is written with the Arabic letter *dāl* but this probably reflects Moroccan dialect. It is very likely that the name is *Adhkir* and written with a *dhāl.*
68. al-Kattānī, *al-Maẓāhir,* 227.
69. Munson, *Religion and Power in Morocco,* 63.
70. Abun-Nasr, *The Tijaniyya,* 50.
71. Ibid.
72. al-Kattānī, *Tarjama,* 93.
73. "Domestic News." *Lisān al-Maghrib* 2 Rabīʿ al-awwal 1325 AH/ May 3, 1907 CE, Tangier, Morocco. According to the article, al-Kattānī considered tea and sugar addictive, although he did drink coffee. There is no mention in the article of either economic boycott or nationalist motives for al-Kattānī's position.
74. al-Kattānī, *al-Maẓāhir,* 381.
75. Aḥmad al-Tijānī claimed that the *Ṣalāt al-Fatḥ* (the name of the Tijāniyya *wird*) came directly from God. Abun-Nasr, *The Tijāniyya,* 172.
76. Criticism of the Tijāniyya was directed against the idea that the *Ṣalāt al-Fatḥ* was part of God's eternal speech. Abun-Nasr, *The Tijāniyya,* 176.
77. Muḥammad b. Rashīd al-ʿIrāqī to Aḥmad bin Mūsā, 12 Jumāda al-ūwlā 1314 AH/ October 20, 1896 CE, DAR (TK) Fez 11, no. 6338. This is the most controversial statement made by al-Kattānī known to this author. According to Jamil Abun-Nasr, Muḥammad al-Kattānī—like Aḥmad al-Tijānī—also claimed the title of *Khatm al-Walāya* (Seal of the Saints). However, I could not locate a copy

of the manuscript that contains this claim and which was cited by Abun-Nasr. See Abun-Nasr, *The Tijāniyya*, 95.

78. Ibid., 51.
79. Al-Kattānī was known to admire and praise al-Tijānī. al-ʿUmrānī, *Al-luʾluʾa*, 137.

· FOUR ·

New Contacts, New Horizons: the Kattāniyya beyond Fez

MUḤAMMAD AL-KATTĀNĪ PRIOR TO THE MOROCCAN CRISIS OF 1905

As the previous chapter illustrates, between 1900 and 1903, Muḥammad al-Kattānī made great efforts to establish his legitimacy as a *mujtahid* and to promote the role of the Kattāniyya brotherhood in a revival of the sharia. He did this through teaching and instruction, through discussion and debate with his disciples and other ulama, and through promotion of mystical knowledge and idioms of worship. On a broader level, however, Muḥammad al-Kattānī's efforts in these years set the stage for the Kattāniyya to play a leading role in challenging the *makhzan* and its supporters during the Ḥafīẓiyya uprising. He began to cast his net beyond the circle of Fāsī ulama and shaykhs (that is, the religiopolitical elite or *khāṣṣ*) and to ally himself with those who were willing to take action to prevent further catastrophes. Before 1904, al-Kattānī had been driven by his belief in the revival of Islam and in the activism of his Sufi peers in this process—that is, Shaykh al-Kattānī conceived of political action within the framework of Sharifism. This meant that he utilized his connections with the *makhzan* in order to shore up his *baraka* among other shaykhs and *shurafā'* (such as when he published his controversial defense of the Kattāniyya brotherhood—*Lisān al-Ḥujja*—in 1901). But it also implied that he articulated his program of change using language, metaphors, and symbolism associated with Sufism and sainthood. As al-Kattānī shifted focus in the years leading up to the 1907 Ḥafīẓiyya uprising, he also began to reconceptualize the meaning of Islamic revival and the qualifications of those who might see through its implementation. As a prelude to Kattāniyya participation in the events of 1907, let us turn to Muḥammad al-Kattānī's activities in the years immediately preceding the uprising.

Muḥammad al-Kattānī spent the better part of 1903 traveling in Morocco before embarking on the Hajj. These travels in Morocco were also instrumental in solidifying ties with followers in different regions of the country, thereby helping to extend the range of the Kattāniyya. Al-Kattānī departed from Fez in the early summer and traveled to Marrakesh. When he returned to the city after a five-year absence, he was greeted with great enthusiasm by his disciples and other well-wishers who came to welcome him back and later to bid him farewell as he continued on his itinerary.[1] Of the seventy-five people listed in *al-Maẓāhir al-sāmiyya fī al-nisba al-sharīfa al-Kattāniyya* (the biography of the Kattānī family written by ʿAbd al-Ḥayy al-Kattānī) as having some type of association with Muḥammad al-Kattānī (either as students or companions), fourteen were either from or resided in the Marrakesh region (including Demnate, located along a major trade route between the Tafilalt and Marrakesh, where a Kattāniyya *zāwiya* also existed).[2] Several of al-Kattānī's closest affiliates were also from Marrakesh and its environs, including ʿAbd al-Salām al-ʿUmrānī, who joined him in Marrakesh as his travel companion during the Hajj and documented the voyage in a book entitled *Al-luʾluʾa al-fāsiyya fī al-riḥla al-ḥijāziyya.* Correspondence between Muḥammad al-Kattānī and his father also indicates that they had dealings with groups and individuals from much of the Marrakesh region and its environs.[3]

From Marrakesh, al-Kattānī and his entourage headed northwest, stopping along the way to the Atlantic coast to meet with supporters and friends. The caravan of pilgrims passed through the regions of the Yāgūt and Azzamūr tribes to the region around Casablanca. Tribal delegations from the environs of Settat paid their respects to the shaykh, bringing with them donations and gifts.[4] Kattāniyya disciples from the cities of Salé, Rabat, and Marrakesh also came to participate in discussions with al-Kattānī.[5] The Moroccan portion of al-Kattānī's voyage came to an end in the northern port city of Tangier, the point of embarkation for pilgrimages headed for Port Said in Egypt, from where they would continue to the Hijaz. The voyage provided an important opportunity for the shaykh to reconnect with his disciples through the exchange and discussion of news, events, and religious and spiritual questions, thereby strengthening the bonds between them. Al-ʿUmrānī recorded numerous gatherings in which local tribal shaykhs, mystics, students, and ulama came to meet with al-Kattānī at each stop along the route to Tangier. Al-Kattānī's lectures on Sufism during a gathering held near Anfa inspired several attendees to take the *wird* of the Kattāniyya, marking their new affiliation with the brotherhood. According to al-ʿUmrānī, "where there had previously been but one Kattāniyya disciple [from the area], there were now twenty-one."[6]

TANGIER AND BEYOND

Muḥammad al-Kattānī's trip to the vibrant port city of Tangier—the point of embarkation for the pilgrimage—was his first experience in a place where a European presence was openly apparent. By the early twentieth century, Tangier accommodated an expanding community of European inhabitants and had assumed new significance for other regions of Morocco. Foreigners had yet to establish themselves in Fez in large numbers, but their growing presence in Tangier heightened the possibility that European control in Moroccan affairs could some day become a reality. Contact with Europe had already introduced new systems of regulation and control, which were unfamiliar to most Moroccans in the late nineteenth and early twentieth centuries. For instance, Muḥammad al-Kattānī, along with other pilgrims, was kept in quarantine for forty days in Tangier after returning from the Hajj as a result of regulations established by a sanitary commission under the auspices of the European representatives in Tangier.[7] Thus, while the rules of politics were being redefined at the state level through the implementation of reforms and the establishment of new administrative positions, on the ground, rules and regulations were also changing to reflect a new sense of order, control, and political organization.

As the seat of European political power in Morocco since the establishment of foreign consular legations in the eighteenth century, Tangier housed the office of the sultan's representative to European ambassadors stationed there. Correspondence between the *makhzan* and the European states was conducted principally through this office. As political involvement with Europe increased in the early twentieth century, so too did the city's importance as a site of politics. Apart from the heightened importance of Tangier for the politics of the *makhzan,* the city also assumed greater significance in matters relating to trade, transportation, and communication in conjunction with the rising importance of trade with Europe for the Moroccan economy.[8] Since the establishment of regular steamship service in the port of Tangier in the nineteenth century, large volumes of goods from Fāsī markets had begun moving through the city on the way to Europe and Suez. Moreover, increasing maritime transportation facilitated the movement of Hajj pilgrims through Tangier. What had once been a prosperous caravan route starting in Fez and extending eastward through the border cities of Oujda and Tlemcen and across the Algerian coastline had, by the late nineteenth century, been completely abandoned.[9] As a response to the rerouting of trade through Tangier, a sizeable community of Fāsī traders also established itself in the port to facilitate the movement of goods and information to and from Fez. Furthermore, Fāsī merchants and middling ulama also came to Tangier to fill positions in the newly expanding bureaucracy, most notably as customs officials and tax collectors *(umanāʾ)*.[10] It was among this group that al-Kattānī gained his first disciples in the city.[11]

MUḤAMMAD AL-KATTĀNĪ DURING THE MOROCCAN CRISIS OF 1905

Beyond his experiences in Tangier, Muḥammad al-Kattānī's visit to the eastern Mediterranean lands may have been of greater significance in influencing his understanding of politics and the possibilities of political, administrative, and financial reform for Moroccan society. After departing from Tangier, al-Kattānī and his entourage passed through Marseilles, Naples, Port Said, and Cairo before moving on to the Hijaz.[12] During his stay in Cairo, the shaykh, like thousands of Maghribī pilgrims before him, had the opportunity to meet with scholars from among the Azharites representing the different schools of law, leaders of Sufi orders, and leaders of the Moroccan trading community stationed in the city.[13] He also met with politically important figures such as representatives of the Ottoman Porte and even the Khedieve ʿAbbās.[14] From Cairo, the pilgrims moved on to the Hijaz, where they also met with other pilgrims from throughout the Muslim world.

Besides the contacts he surely made during the Hajj, al-Kattānī's travels also must have exposed him to new ideas about his spiritual and political relationship to the wider Islamic community. Historically, the pilgrimage had served as an important link between Muslims from disparate parts of the world. Scholars came together in Mecca and Medina to discuss doctrine, study with important thinkers residing in the area, and also share their views on all manner of affairs.[15] During his stay in Egypt, Muḥammad al-Kattānī experienced firsthand the results of almost one hundred years of social and economic reform. As one of the most important centers of pan-Islamic politics and Arab literary and cultural activity in the late nineteenth century, Cairo also attracted Muslims and Arabic speakers from all over who came to study, trade, and participate in the intellectual fervor of the day. Although we have no records of Muḥammad al-Kattānī's impressions about what he saw in Egypt and the Hijaz, his contacts surely must have provided new perspectives on questions of spiritual and political import.

Little is known about how and when Muḥammad al-Kattānī made contact with those people with whom he communicated during the crisis of 1905, also known as the First Moroccan Crisis. However, it would not be far-fetched to speculate that he had made many of them during the Hajj in 1903 and 1904. In 1904, the year when Muḥammad al-Kattānī returned from the Hajj, the Moroccan political and economic situation took a rapid turn for the worse. Since 1900, the *makhzan* had gone from having a sizeable treasury balance to owing almost 100 million francs to European banks.[16] Due to the state of near bankruptcy, the *makhzan* was forced to negotiate a loan agreement with a European banking consortium at high interest. The loan was necessary for the continuation of its costly campaign against the rebel Bū Ḥmāra and to alleviate financial pressures caused by overspending and poor financial planning.[17] Moreover, the terms of repayment jeopardized the *makhzan*'s autonomy and guaranteed France almost full economic leverage in Morocco in much the same way that the Caisse de la Dette had done in Egypt.[18] In 1904, Great Britain and France signed the Entente-Cordiale granting France supremacy in Moroccan affairs. With the new agreement in place, France could proceed with bringing Morocco into its political and economic orbit with less interference from the other European states.[19] Prior to the signing, the *makhzan* had maintained its autonomy (and that of Morocco) by playing the different European powers against one another in a game of shifting alliances.[20] Rumor of a secret agreement between France and Spain also began to raise suspicion among Moroccans. The agreement would result in the division of Morocco into a northern-run Spanish zone and a southern-controlled French region.[21] Continued French military activity on the Moroccan-Algerian border was an additional source of concern for Moroccan critics, who felt that in the absence of action on the part of the *makhzan,* foreign takeover would become imminent.[22] The final blow came several months after the signing of the Entente-Cordiale when a French mission to the court in Fez was planned. The mission was to be led by the ambassador of the minister of France, Georges Saint-René Taillander. Its purpose was to discuss with Sultan ʿAbd al-ʿAzīz French ideas for reform in all areas of Moroccan fiscal and administrative life. The combination of events led to the First Moroccan Crisis, during which Moroccan critics openly voiced their dissension against the *makhzan*'s collaboration with France on the question of reforming the state. It was during this period that Muḥammad al-Kattānī became involved with a group of Moroccan notables—ulama, *shurafāʾ,* and traders—who were alarmed by these political developments.

Even before the French mission actually took place, word of France's involvement had already begun to elicit negative responses from critics, who believed that without immediate action, French "treachery [would] continue to unfold."[23] In a letter to Muḥammad al-Kattānī, ʿAbdallah bin Saʿīd, a notable from the city of Salé, blamed the *makhzan* for its passive positions toward the Europeans: "[The French] aspire to [our land] because of what they have seen in some men who fear them."[24] In the conclusion of his letter, ʿAbdallah bin Saʿīd asked, "Should one fear the infidel?" And then he answered: "Only if they are lacking in religion or weak in their certainty [about Islam]."[25] Al-Kattānī also received warnings from a contact abroad regarding the immanent danger for Morocco posed by the French. A certain ʿAbd al-Ḥakīm al-Maz(z)ūghī[26] sent information to one of al-Kattānī's close disciples—Abū Bakr al-Tiṭwānī—about French government opinion concerning the 1904 loan as well as French attitudes regarding the best way to achieve its political goals in Morocco following the signing of the Entente-Cordiale.[27] The same correspondent conveyed similar ideas directly to Muḥammad al-Kattānī several years later during the negotiations in Algeciras (1906) between Morocco and the European powers.[28] Meanwhile, in Marrakesh, it appears that ʿAbd al-Ḥafīẓ, the sultan's brother and the *Khalīfa* of Marrakesh, was also forging ties with dissenters. These included the Glāwī *qā'id,* al-Madanī al-Glāwī, who would eventually play an important military role during the Ḥafīẓiyya uprising.[29]

The French delegation led by Saint-René-Taillander arrived in Fez in January 1905. Prior to the arrival of the Taillander mission, a group of notables led by Muḥammad al-Kattānī's cousin, the distinguished legal scholar, Muḥammad b. Jaʿfar al-Kattānī, met with Sultan ʿAbd al-ʿAzīz. In an effort to prevent the French from gaining total leverage in Moroccan affairs, the members of the delegation urged the sultan to seek Ottoman support and advisers for the reform process rather than become involved with France.[30] Moroccans were exposed to the idea of an Ottoman-style *Tanzimat* through travel to the Mashriq and through reading the Arabic-language press, which was becoming available in Morocco in the early twentieth century.[31] The Egyptian-based newspaper *al-Manār* (available in Tangier and Fez) had proposed Ottoman-style reform under the auspices of the Porte's advisers and had also criticized Sultan ʿAbd al-ʿAzīz for turning to the British and French instead of seeking Ottoman support for desperately needed reforms.[32]

Aware of the potential for political isolation that might result if the French mission was to leave Fez having secured itself a central role in reform of the Moroccan state, Sultan ʿAbd al-ʿAzīz decided to establish a consultative council of Moroccan notables. The council would be involved in evaluating French reform proposals and provide input into how the *makhzan* should proceed. Al-Kattānī was one of forty notables from the major cities and tribes of Morocco selected to participate in the council.[33] During negotiations, Muḥammad al-Kattānī pushed hard for Ottoman-guided reform as an alternative to proposals being forwarded by the French.[34] After several meetings and a series of negotiations, the council of notables finally rejected French reform proposals and called for the convening of an international conference to discuss the problem of reform and modernization. The Moroccans believed that an international forum would better serve their interests in keeping France in check. The *makhzan* undertook preparations for a conference to be held in the Spanish town of Algeciras the following year.[35] They had succeeded, if only temporarily, in keeping France at bay and in maintaining the *makhzan*'s autonomy.

Shaykh al-Kattānī's involvement in negotiations during the crisis revealed both his influence with Sultan ʿAbd al-ʿAzīz as well as among the Moroccan political elite.[36] As a result, al-Kattānī became the target of attack by the editors of the pro-French Arabic-language Tangier-based newspaper, *al-Saʿāda*. The newspaper's editor, Wadīʿ Karam, launched a scathing critique of al-Kattānī's involvement in political affairs. "It is said that every art is the provenance of those who are its masters," explained Karam. Yet "If this shaykh [al-Kattānī] was among those whose art was that of politics . . . and if he was among men of his [the sultan's] government . . . then he might have the right to delve into the waves of this ocean."[37] Muḥammad al-Kattānī responded to this attack by publishing a rebuttal in a short-lived news journal he established, which he called *al-Ṭāʿūn (The Pestilence)*.[38] As is shown in chapter 3, al-Kattānī and his family had already been using the technology of printing to impart information regarding the Kattāniyya to their disciples. For al-Kattānī, the revolutionary potential of the media of printing for expanded communication and for political mobilization was clear.[39] He urged the ulama to write about the need to defend Morocco and the sanctity of sharia and to "print thousands of copies and distribute them in the world."[40]

Since his visit to Tangier in 1903, the city had increasingly loomed large in al-Kattānī's mind. Although there were already Kattāniyya disciples in Tangier at the time of his visit, it appears that the order became more important and well-known after 1904.[41] By 1907, the year of the Ḥafīẓiyya uprising, it appears that the Kattāniyya had a well-entrenched cadre of contact points there. During the Ḥafīẓiyya uprising, activities in Tangier were carefully observed through communication between Muḥammad al-Kattānī, his brother ʿAbd al-Ḥayy, and Kattāniyya supporters and disciples in the city. Correspondents maintained regular contact and provided updates on the situation in both Tangier and Fez.[42]

Muḥammad al-Kattānī's involvement in the nascent anti-French coalition (which emerged in 1904) marked a departure from his earlier activities, which were centered primarily on the Kattāniyya and its affiliates. Until this time and in the aftermath of the heresy affair in 1896, al-Kattānī had focused his efforts on teaching, writing, printing, and communication with his disciples. He viewed these activities in terms of a larger process of sharia revivalism. Al-Kattānī's criticism in this period—from 1896 to 1904—was directed against the ulama and brotherhood shaykhs for their failure to be actively involved in this revival of the sharia. He believed that, as shaykh of the Kattāniyya, he had a vital role to play in this process. By extension, the Kattāniyya order also had a role to play as a religiopolitical institution associated with the *shurafāʾ* and with Sufism. But by the time of the Moroccan Crisis of 1905, Muḥammad al-Kattānī had begun to change focus somewhat by linking himself with critics of the *makhzan,* critics who condemned Sultan ʿAbd al-ʿAzīz for his weak position toward France. If the *makhzan* would not take action to resist French encroachment, then al-Kattānī was prepared to ally with those who were willing to challenge the sultan's authority. In turn, as a *sharīf* and shaykh, al-Kattānī's influence with the sultan and among his disciples could go a long way in forwarding the political goals of increasing numbers of anti-French contingents. No longer limiting his criticism to his peers among the ulama, Muḥammad al-Kattānī began to question the sultan's authority. In chapter 5, we shall see how al-Kattānī's new key of politics helped bring a new sultan to power, while simultaneously contributing to the undermining of the very system of power sharing from which he benefited—as a *sharīf* and a *ṭarīqa* shaykh.

NOTES

1. al-ʿUmrānī, *al-Luʾluʾa al-fāsiyya fī al-riḥla al-ḥijāziyya,* 111.
2. I have seen one letter written by the *muqqadam* of the Kattāniyya in Demnate to Muḥammad al-Kattānī; however, there is no date on the letter. *Risāla ilā fuqarāʾ al-kattāniyyīn,* BH10327, BH. According to Aḥmad Tawfīq, a Kattāniyya *zāwiya* existed in Demnate, but the date of its establishment is not mentioned. Aḥmad Tawfīq, *al-Mujtamaʿ al-maghribī fī al-qarn al-tāsiʿ ʿashar* (Casablanca: Maṭbaʿat al-Najāḥ al-Jadīda, 1983), 433.
3. References to names such as Shangīṭ, Bū Jaʿad, Ghujdāma, Ṣanhāja, Mdaghrī, Dukkāl, and Yāgūt are found in epistolary exchange.
4. Delegations from the Awlād Ḥarīz and Awlād Bū ʿAzīz tribes and from the town of Settat presented themselves to the shaykh. Al-ʿUmrānī, *al-Luʾluʾa,* 119.
5. Ibid., 117.
6. Ibid.
7. Muḥammad al-Ḥalū to Muḥammad b. al-ʿArabī al-Ṭurrīs, 21 Muḥarram 1322 AH/April 4, 1904 CE, DAR (TZ) 1322.
8. This was part of a larger trend toward the shifting of economic activities to the port cities and away from the interior.
9. Comité de l'Afrique Française, "Le commerce et l'industrie à Fez," *Renseignements Coloniaux, Supplément au Bulletin du Comité de l'Afrique Française,* 7 (July 1905): 229–253; 8 (August 1905): 295–321; 9 (September 1905): 337–350.
10. Burke, *Prelude to Protectorate in Morocco,* 34.
11. M. G. Salmon, "Confréries et Zaouyas de Tanger," *Archives Marocaines* 2 (1905): 111.
12. The only record of Muḥammad al-Kattānī's voyage that I have seen is al-ʿUmrānī's, *Rihla.* Information about where al-Kattānī went and whom he met is taken from this source, which reflects the attitudes and perceptions of its author, rather than those of al-Kattānī.
13. al-ʿUmrānī, *al-Luʾluʾa,* 160–167.
14. Ibid., 162, 168. We have no details about al-Kattānī's meetings with Ottoman officials or with Khedieve ʿAbbās. Yet these meetings could explain al-Kattānī's interest in promoting relations with the Ottomans after returning from the Hajj. One way that this

meeting might be verified would be through an examination of foreign records and spy reports. The author, al-ʿUmrānī, mentioned these political figures after having mentioned meetings with the ulama, the *shurafāʾ*, and the visits he and al-Kattānī made to the tombs of various holy figures.

15. Nehemia Levtzion and John Voll have argued that Mecca and Medina served as the launching point for the spread of revivalist ideas in different forms throughout the Islamic world in the eighteenth century. See Nehemia Levtzion and John Voll, *Eighteenth-Century Renewal and Reform in Islam* (Syracuse: Syracuse University Press, 1987).
16. Burke, *Prelude to Protectorate in Morocco,* 53.
17. By 1904, the *makhzan* had already made several unsuccessful attempts to capture the rebel and put an end to his activities. For more on the *makhzan*'s campaign against Bū Ḥmāra, see chapter 8 in Aubin, *Morocco of Today,* 89–108.
18. Burke, *Prelude to Protectorate in Morocco,* 75.
19. Ibid., 70. This was officially known as the Cambon-Lansdowne Agreement. It was signed on April 8, 1904.
20. Meanwhile, in an effort to counter the French after the signing of the Entente-Cordiale, Germany—whose commercial interests were focused on mining concessions in the south of Morocco—chose to support the anti-French faction within the *makhzan* regarding the loan. Conflict came to a head between France and Germany after the surprise visit of Kaiser Wilhelm to Tangier in March of 1905 after Taillander's departure for Fez. On German mining in Morocco and the visit of Kaiser Wilhelm, see Katz, *Murder in Marrakesh,* 13, 104. Regarding the German decision to get involved in inter-*makhzan* rivalries during loan negotiations see Burke, *Prelude to Protectorate in Morocco,* 80–81. For an overview of *makhzan* politics regarding the European powers in this period, see chapter 3 in Burke, *Prelude to Protectorate in Morocco,* 41–67.
21. Ibid., 76.
22. Ibid. French troops acting under General Lyautey's orders occupied the Moroccan oasis known as Rās al-ʿAyn.
23. ʿAbd Allah bin Saʿīd to Muḥammad al-Kattānī, in Muḥammad al-Manūnī, *Maẓāhir yaqẓat al-maghrib al-ḥadīth,* vol. 2. (Beirut: Dār al-Gharb al-Islāmī, 1985), 318–321.

24. Ibid.
25. Ibid.
26. We know virtually nothing about ʿAbd al-Ḥakīm al-Maz(z)ūghī. He does not appear to be Moroccan on the basis of his name, nor does he appear in the major bibliographic dictionaries of Moroccan ulama.
27. ʿAbd al-Ḥakīm al-Maz(z)ūghī to Abu Bakr al-Tiṭwānī, 20 Muḥarram 1322 AH/March 7, 1904 CE, DAR (TZ) 1322. It is very likely that al-Maz(z)ūghī was referring to a debate among French politicians at this time regarding whether a strategy of economic and political penetration or military action would be most successful in the realization of the French political agenda in Morocco. For more on this debate, see Burke, *Prelude to Protectorate in Morocco*, 75–76.
28. ʿAbd al-Ḥakīm al-Maz(z)ūghī to Muḥammad al-Kattānī, 3 Muḥarram 1324 AH/February 28, 1906 CE, quoted in al-Manūnī, *Maẓāhir yaqẓat al-maghrib al-ḥadīth,* 2: 322–326.
29. Burke, *Prelude to Protectorate in Morocco,* 102. Burke does not believe that there was any connection between the groups in Fez and Marrakesh at this time. Nevertheless, both groups were motivated to act as a result of the prevailing situation.
30. Ibid., 79–80.
31. Little information is available on the circulation of newspapers in Morocco in this period. Most observers and scholars agree, however, that circulation among Moroccans was quite limited at this time. See Le Tourneau, *Fès avant le protectorat,* 477; Jean-Louis Miège, "Journaux et journalistes à Tanger au 19ème siècle," *Hespéris-Tamuda* 1–2 trimestres 41 (1954): 191–228; Jacques Cagnes, "Presse et Salafisme au Maroc au début du Siècle," *Majallat Dar al-Niyāba,* 7 (Summer 1985): 1–5.
32. Two articles in *al-Manār*—one in 1902 and another in 1904—accused the *makhzan* of giving in to the European powers. *Al-Manār* was founded in 1897 by Rashīd Riḍā and was published in Cairo. Cagnes, "Presse et Salafisme au Maroc au début du siècle," 1.
33. Five meetings between the French delegates, the sultan's *wazīr*s, and fifteen members of the council of notables took place between February 22 and March 14, 1905. al-Manūnī, *Maẓāhir yaqẓat al-maghrib al-ḥadīth,* 2: 191–193.
34. Burke, *Prelude to Protectorate in Morocco,* 83–85.

35. Burke, *Prelude to Protectorate in Morocco,* 83–85. From the Moroccan perspective, an international conference would help check French ambitions.
36. Ibid., 83. Burke cites correspondence from the Archives of the Ministère de la Guerre d'Outre-Mer and *Documents Diplomatiques Français.*
37. al-Kattani, *Tarjama,* 186. It was in response to these attacks that al-Kattānī produced his own short-lived news journal entitled *al-Ṭāʿūn (The Pestilence)*—intended as a riposte to *al-Saʿāda (Happiness).* The paper did not survive long, but it is considered the first Moroccan news journal. It is not known whether copies of *al-Ṭāʿūn* exist. Some scholars believe there may be copies in French archives, but no contemporary historian has actually seen the publication. For more on *al-Ṭāʿūn,* see L. Mercier, "La presse musulmane au Maroc," *Revue du Monde Musulmane* 4 (1908): 619–630. See also Zayn al-ʿĀbidīn al-Kattānī, *al-Ṣaḥāfa al-maghribiyya: nashaʾtuhā waTaṭawwuruhā, 1820–1912* (Rabat: Nashr Wizārat al-Anbāʾ, 1969).
38. al-Kattani, *Tarjama,* 186.
39. Fawzi Abdulrazak has argued that it was competition among the different Sufi orders that led to the assimilation of print technology in Morocco. Fawzi Abdulrazak, *Mamlakat al-Kitāb: Tārīkh al-ṭibāʿa fī al-maghrib, 1865–1912,* 71.
40. al-Kattani, *Tarjama,* 36.
41. It is not clear when the Kattāniyya *zāwiya* was founded in Tangier. According to al-ʿUmrānī's *Riḥla,* however, there were already Kattāniyya disciples in the city when the group arrived in 1903 before leaving for Suez. Al-ʿUmrānī, *al-Luʾluʾa,* 129. The French Orientalist M. G. Salmon claimed that the Kattāniyya *zāwiya* was established after al-Kattānī returned from the pilgrimage. Salmon, "Confréries et zaouyas de Tanger," 106.
42. A series of extant letters written during the height of the Ḥafīẓiyya between Kattāniyya disciples in Tangier and Muḥammad and ʿAbd al-Ḥayy al-Kattānī provide detailed information about the situation in Tangier. DAR (TZ) 1326.

· FIVE ·

The Ḥafīẓiyya and Beyond

By 1907, political crisis, the *makhzan*'s financial insolvency, tribal discontent in the south, and famine due to drought formed the backdrop for rebellion across the country. Sultan ʿAbd al-ʿAzīz's legitimacy to rule increasingly came into question. In 1907, the sultan's brother, ʿAbd al-Ḥafīẓ, spearheaded a movement to dethrone the sultan. The Ḥafīẓiyya uprising brought together a shifting coalition of forces, united in its determination to dethrone ʿAbd al-ʿAzīz. Muḥammad al-Kattānī, whose reputation for action had spread since his return from Hajj in 1904, also joined the Ḥafīẓist coalition. The rebellion spread to Fez and throughout the north, and in January 1908, the ulama of Fez issued their oath of loyalty (*bayʿa*) to ʿAbd al-Ḥafīẓ, marking their acceptance of the new sultan—a signficant, albeit temporary, victory for Ḥafīẓist forces. However, while the interests of the Kattāniyya and ʿAbd al-Ḥafīẓ coincided briefly during the earlier months of the rebellion, conflict between them soon surfaced.

ʿAbd al-Ḥafīẓ's conflict with Muḥammad al-Kattānī was grounded in his efforts to crush the Kattāniyya as a political movement. Much like his conflict with the *makhzan* in the 1890s, al-Kattānī challenged the authority of the sultan during the Ḥafīẓiyya. In this chapter, I ask what was different about al-Kattānī's challenge in 1896 and his challenge in 1907. How had the role of the Sufi *mujtahid* changed? How did this reflect broader economic, political, and social transformations in Moroccan society?

Between the signing of the Algeciras Act in May 1906 and the outbreak of the Ḥafīẓiyya in 1907, hostilities occurred between Moroccans and Europeans residing or working in Moroccan cities.[1] Critics of ʿAbd al-ʿAzīz accused him of driving the *makhzan* into bankruptcy through his extravagant purchases and wasteful spending. Rumors circulated that he had converted to Christianity and that he surrounded himself with European advisers. In the south, tensions finally erupted in violence in March 1907 with the murder of Émile Mauchamp, a French medical doctor residing and working in Marrakesh. The killing was indicative of a much larger phenomenon of anti-European sentiment, dissatisfaction with the terms of the Algeciras Act of 1906, and a widespread sense among many Moroccans that the situation had reached a critical point beyond which negotiations were no longer possible. Mauchamp's death became a *cause celèbre* among both the French and the Moroccans. The killing set in motion a French campaign of reprisal, including demands for the payment of indemnities, the removal of the pasha of Marrakesh, and the arrest of those responsible for carrying out the attack. French reprisal culminated in the occupation of Oujda—a city located to the north-west of Fez not far from the Algerian border—on March 29.[2] For many Moroccans, Sultan ʿAbd al-ʿAzīz's response to the Mauchamps affair was not much better than that of the French. The sultan sent a letter to be read in the mosques of all the major cities of Morocco in which he condemned attacks on foreigners and blamed Moroccans for exacerbating the tense atmosphere through such incendiary actions.[3] The French occupation of Oujda and the sultan's ambivalent response further radicalized the population regarding how best to address the situation. The final blow came when, in July, the French bombarded Casablanca from ships anchored off coastal waters after attacks by tribes in the region had led to the killing of eight Europeans. The situation was ripe for rebellion, as popular anger and dissatisfaction with the terms imposed on Morocco by the European powers at Algeciras escalated. The Algeciras Act provided for the establishment of various institutions and control bodies headed by France or French business consortiums having broadly defined powers to intervene in Moroccan political and economic affairs. In August, Sultan ʿAbd al-ʿAzīz's brother and his *khalīfa* in Marrakesh, Mawlāy ʿAbd al-Ḥafīẓ, called for jihad against the European powers and for the dethronement of Sultan ʿAbd al-ʿAzīz. ʿAbd al-ʿAzīz's inability to thwart European plans, and his choice to surround himself with advisers who supported the terms of Algeciras, were seen as legitimate reasons for dethronement. On August 16, ʿAbd al-Ḥafīẓ was given the *bayʿa* by the ulama of Marrakesh. As word of the events in Marrakesh spread, forces drew ranks around the question of the legality of Mawlāy ʿAbd al-Ḥafīẓ's actions. In September 1907, Sultan ʿAbd al-ʿAzīz left Fez with his army and entourage in preparation for confronting ʿAbd al-Ḥafīẓ's forces, and by December, ʿAbd al-ʿAzīz's forces were involved in full-scale confrontation with ʿAbd al-Ḥafīẓ and his supporters.

ʿAbd al-Ḥafīẓ drew support for his claim to the throne from two important southern constituencies—from the tribes of the Chaouia region and from the Amazigh tribes of the Great Atlas.[4] During his tenure as *khalīfa* to his brother in Tiznit (1897–1901) and in Marrakesh (1901–1907), ʿAbd al-Ḥafīẓ had developed a strong understanding of tribal politics and customs and gained administrative experience, both of which helped in building his southern coalition.[5] Edmund Burke has highlighted the uniqueness of ʿAbd al-Ḥafīẓ's reliance on leaders like al-Madanī al-Glāwī for support in the insurgency. It was the first time a member of the ʿAlawī house had sought to create a political alliance with Berber tribes of the High Atlas, thus side-stepping traditional constituencies—namely, the ulama, the *makhzan* tribes, and notables of the major cities of the north.[6] Although, the Atlas tribal *qāʾids* helped to secure the sultanate for the Ḥafīẓist camp, ʿAbd al-Ḥafīẓ's reliance on them became the source of much resentment. After 1909, when it became clear that the new sultan had failed to alter the political situation in favor of Morocco, privileges granted to the southern tribes (such as tax collection among Middle Atlas tribes of the north) was the source of this great resentment against the new *makhzan*.

Aside from his support in the south, ʿAbd al-Ḥafīẓ still needed the support of Fez and the surrounding tribes to legitimate his claim to the imamate and to continue jihad against ʿAbd al-ʿAzīz and his European allies. The allegiance of Fez was significant for claimants to the imamate because the city was financially and intellectually important and because control of the city (the center of the cult of Idrīs) helped secure the support of northern Morocco, the traditional center of Idrīsī sharīfan power. The political leanings of the Fāsī population had often determined the outcome of political conflicts during the ʿAlawī period.[7] Therefore, shortly after the ulama of Marrakesh had given their *bayʿa* to Mawlāy ʿAbd al-Ḥafīẓ, the new sultan sent a letter to Muḥammad al-Kattānī. Choosing his words purposefully to highlight al-Kattānī's stature, ʿAbd al-Ḥafīẓ asked this "most sublime shaykh and Sufi, the complete saint [*al-walī al-kāmil*] and *sharīf*" for "support in strengthening this noble religion and for attending to the affairs of the Muslims."[8] Al-Kattānī's influence as the head of an important Sufi order would contribute to winning the sympathies of the population of Fez because, as a*sharīf*, Sufi and *ʿālim*, Muḥammad al-Kattānī was squarely situated as a member of the religiopolitical elite (albeit an elite that had effectively lost much of its power compared to the *makhzan*). Having expressed his vehement disapproval of the French reform agenda during the political crisis of 1905, al-Kattānī had also demonstrated his willingness to challenge Sultan ʿAbd al-ʿAzīz's judgment regarding his dealings with the European powers. Furthermore, benefits deriving from allegiance to the new sultan (assuming his ability to secure his position) would also provide an incentive for Muḥammad al-Kattānī and his family to give their support to ʿAbd al-Ḥafīẓ. This could include anything from ʿAbd al-Ḥafīẓ's patronage of the Kattāniyya *zāwiya*, the granting of favors to Kattāniyya disciples, and in general, the securing of the family's position within the fluid network of the *makhzan*'s patron-client relations.

Meanwhile, in Fez, the ulama and city notables were debating the legality of the dethronement of ʿAbd al-ʿAzīz. Was it permissible for Mawlāy ʿAbd al-Ḥafīẓ to seek the *bayʿa* and call on the people to desist in their support for the ruling sultan? In other words, did sharia mandate a perpetuation of the established order, or might it dictate revolt?[9] While debate ensued, large gatherings and demonstrations took place in the streets of Fez. It was reported that an estimated twenty thousand people gathered in the vicinity of the Qarawiyyīn mosque in December demanding the issuing of a *fatwā* declaring the dethronement of ʿAbd al-ʿAzīz.[10] In January, the ulama of Fez issued the oath of allegiance (the *bayʿa*) to ʿAbd al-Ḥafīẓ, marking an important victory for Ḥafīẓist forces.

THE "NEW KEY OF POLITICS" DURING THE ḤAFĪẒIYYA

With the support of the ulama and *shurafāʾ* of Fez, ʿAbd al-Ḥafīẓ obtained legal sanction to claim the sultanate. Keeping in mind the increasingly compliant behavior of the ulama toward the *makhzan* throughout the nineteenth century, the ulama's position regarding the *bayʿa* is rather remarkable. It marked an act of challenge on their part against Sultan ʿAbd al-ʿAzīz's authority. The spirit of ulama activism during the Fez *bayʿa* was manifested in their contribution to advancing a radical set of political demands through the inclusion of conditions to the *bayʿa* document; it also marked an attempt to implement the concept of the contractual *bayʿa* establishing consultation with the ulama as a prerequisite for political decision making.[11] The position of the ulama regarding the *bayʿa,* became a source of heated debate among the partisans of ʿAbd al-Ḥafīẓ and his dethroned brother. Accusations of intimidation and coercion spread. *Al-Saʿāda,* the French-sponsored newspaper known for its pro-ʿAzīzist position, claimed that the ulama of Fez had been forced to support

ʿAbd al-Ḥafīẓ because of fear from the crowds. However, ʿAbd al-Ḥayy al-Kattānī argued that, in fact, the ulama's initial decision to support ʿAbd al-ʿAzīz was taken under duress from the sultan himself and not from popular pressure. "They were forced, something that everyone confirms," wrote al-Kattānī. However, the ulama were quick to change their minds, continued ʿAbd al-Ḥayy. "Those who issued the *fatwā* regret [it], and the truth of the matter was not clear to them at the time as it is now. For, they did not know then that an occupation like that of Casablanca was coming."[12] Pro-ʿAzīzist supporters made counterclaims arguing (along with *al-Saʿāda*) that it was the decision to proclaim ʿAbd al-Ḥafīẓ as sultan that the ulama of Fez took under duress and out of fear of the angry mob.[13] ʿAbd al-ʿAzīz himself believed the events in Fez to be the riotous behavior of ruffians and members of the lowly artisan classes. Muḥammad Gharnīṭ, a close adviser of ʿAbd al-ʿAzīz, claimed "the most renowned of the scholars were under the control of insolent fools."[14]

The oath of allegiance issued by the ulama of Fez to the contender to the throne, ʿAbd al-Ḥafīẓ, stipulated fourteen conditions. These included ʿAbd al-Ḥafīẓ's rejection of the terms of the Algeciras Act, his rescinding of taxes that were not stipulated in the Quran (such as the *maks*), the return of territories seized by France, the termination of consultation with European advisers and experts, the ending of concessions to the European states and their protégés, and the requirement of consultation with Moroccan advisers regarding political matters, and finally, the protection of the rights of the *shurafāʾ* (such as exemptions from taxes).[15] We shall return to the Kattānīs' role in the *bayʿa,* but for now, it should be noted, that the conditions of the Fez *bayʿa* were allegedly known as *"al-shurūʿ al-Kattānīyya"* (the Kattānī conditions).[16]

The concept of the conditional *bayʿa* was not new; allegiance to the sultan was incumbent on his ability to ensure the well-being of the Muslim community by overseeing the proper implementation of sharia, by waging jihad when necessary, and by securing the cities and ports of Morocco against attack.[17] The Ḥafīẓ *bay'a* clearly reflected the grievances of the Ḥafīẓist coalition in Fez. Nevertheless, its form and language were familiar, emphasizing the divine obligation of the sultan to carry on the legacy of the Prophet in his capacity as Commander of the Faithful: "Through him, God Almighty desired to pull back the night of ignorance from [the eyes] of his servants, to renew religion . . . , to return the greatness of Islam to its youth . . . , to revive the legacy of the Rightly Guided caliphs and the great ancestors; he is Mawlānā, *amīr al-Muslimīn* . . . the cream of the 'Alawī elite, Mawlānā 'Abd al-Ḥafīẓ."[18] The *bay'a* affirmed that the ulama, *shurafā'*, notables, and *rumāt* of Fez had come together to give their allegiance to 'Abd al-Ḥafīẓ on the basis of his ability to carry out these duties, to wage jihad if necessary, and to defend the cities and ports of Morocco against further European incursions.

Although the Fez *bay'a* was a significant victory for 'Abd al-Ḥafīẓ because it legitimized his claim to the throne, it also marked a success for social groups previously politically marginalized, by articulating political demands that reflected their interests. This included merchants and a new class of urban notables and middling ulama—all of whom had benefited either directly or indirectly from Morocco's shifting economic and political relationship with Europe throughout the nineteenth century.[19] Therefore, the *bay'a* simultaneously opened the way for their participation in politics while also reaffirming the rights of the *shurafā'*, whose fortunes were tied to the existence of a strong *makhzan* and the maintenance of their traditional privileges.

The *bay'a* of Fez was an important expression of the new key of politics because it reflected the political demands of a wider constituency, which was united in its agreement that 'Abd al-'Azīz had failed to defend the autonomy of the Moroccan state. The success of the *bay'a* was due, in part, to the ulama's willingness to challenge the sultan and take their place as leaders in reform and revival, yet another component of the new key of politics. Although the form of the *bay'a* was not novel or unique, its contents reflected an attempt to redefine the relationship between the *makhzan* and the ulama (including the emergent class of middling ulama and scribes) by providing for consultation with the ulama as a condition for support; this was embodied in the notion of the contractual *bay'a*. The inclusion (in the *bay'a*) of conditions reflecting the interests of new classes also marked a definitive shift in relations between the *shurafā'* of Fez and new political elites—that is, between the merchant classes and protégés and the middling ulama who filled new administrative positions throughout the country. In other words, the conditional *bay'a* marked the culmination of a process that had begun almost one hundred years earlier of the diminution of sharīfan political power and authority, which was grounded in the legitimating principle of *sharaf*.[20] Given Muḥammad al-Kattānī's efforts to assert his political role and that of the Kattāniyya on the basis of his power and authority both as a *sharīf and* as a Sufi *mujtahid,* he must have considered the conditional *bay'a* of Fez a great success in terms of the wider interests of the Ḥafīẓiyya coalition, the ulama who stood for implementation of a contractual *bay'a,* and the more narrow interests of the Kattāniyya and the Kattānī *shurafā'*.

POLITICAL MOBILIZATION BEYOND FEZ

Securing the conditions in the *bay'a* of Fez was only one step in a series of efforts by Muḥammad al-Kattānī and other members of his family to assist in consolidating support for 'Abd al-Ḥafīẓ and for jihad. Other efforts included mobilizing popular support in the streets of Fez and among the tribes of the Middle Atlas, as well as rallying support in other cities, most notably in Tangier. 'Abd al-Ḥafīẓ, who departed from his base in Marrakesh to confront 'Abd al-'Azīz's forces, had yet to arrive in Fez by the early spring of 1908. In the sultan's absence and in the absence of any central authority in the city since the departure of 'Abd al-'Azīz in September of 1907, rumors of usurpation, extortion by *makhzan* officials, and unfair market prices began to circulate in Fez. An anonymous informant in the city warned of the vagaries of Fāsī opinion and urged 'Abd al-Ḥafīẓ to hurry to Fez, as the potential for an uprising against him grew with every passing day.[21] In 1873, the tanners of Fez had led a year-long uprising after the ascension of Mawlāy Ḥasan and in response to his implementation of certain taxes.[22] Their support was as essential to 'Abd al-Ḥafīẓ's bid for the sultanate as that of the ulama and *shurafā'* of the city.

Muḥammad al-Kattānī's influence among the tanners of Fez was key to supporting the Ḥafīẓist coalition in Fez. The shaykh led groups of armed men associated with the tanners' corporation in shooting practice outside the city walls. Jacob Niddam, an unsympathetic observer of these activities noted that "Une foule de 2000 Fassis doit infailliblement sortir, chaque soir, hors de la ville, à Bab El Fetouh, pour apprendre à viser. Le chef de ces imbéciles est Cheikh El Kittani." [23] Yet Niddam also recognized that al-Kattānī's influence among the combatants was great. He bemoaned the fact that "Avant que chacun ne déchargeânt son arme, il devait la présenter respectueusement a ce fameux marabout [al-Kattānī]. Ce dernier n'avait qu'a mettre la main sur la gachette pour que le propriétaire, du moins à ce qu'ils disent, pût atteindre le but."[24]

Muḥammad al-Kattānī's reputation as a saintly figure was not confined to Fez. Moroccans in other regions of the country also were inspired to participate in jihad against 'Abd al-'Azīz and his European allies. Captain Lechartier, leader of a French military mission to Morocco, reported that pro-Ḥafīẓist forces were encouraged to take up jihad against France. They drew inspiration from "agitateurs connus comme El-Kittani de Fez."[25] One of al-Kattānī's greatest efforts toward this end was the convening of a meeting in the city of Meknès of the region's most important tribal groups. His intention in bringing the tribes together was to strengthen support for 'Abd al-Ḥafīẓ. Preparations for the voyage to Meknès were made in Fez with the assistance of Kattāniyya affiliates from among the Bahālīl tribe, who provided fifty mules for transportation of the entourage and group of fighters.[26] The shaykh was received with great enthusiasm in Meknès, according to various observers.[27] The alliances formed at Meknes between the Kattāniyya and the Zammūr, Banī Mṭīr, and Aït Ndīr worked to the advantage of ʿAbd al-Ḥafīẓ, whose army's safe passage through these tribal regions on the way to Fez was dependent on the allegiances of the tribes inhabiting them.[28]

The Kattānīs also worked to muster political support for the new sultan. With the help of his brother, ʿAbd al-Ḥayy, Muḥammad al-Kattānī tried to influence the ulama of other cities, who had yet to give their allegiance to ʿAbd al-Ḥafīẓ. This included the major port city of Tangier, where Muḥammad al-Kattānī's name had become widely known for his political activities and for his spiritual and religious dedication since his visit there in 1904.[29] Muḥammad and his brother ʿAbd al-Ḥayy sent letters to their contacts in these cities, asking for support in "unit[ing] the word of Islam and the Muslims and to be one [united] hand against those who are at variance with them." Emphasizing the need for action, the brothers wrote to their contacts in Tétouan: "You are aware of what has happened in our Moroccan land in the way of the decline of our sharia and the rules of religion. This is due to Mawlāy ʿAbd al-ʿAzīz's concern with the Christians . . . such that France has occupied the cities of Oujda and Casablanca and has entered her borders from all sides." The Kattanis begged that the inhabitants of Tétouan follow the example of the people of Fez by casting their support in favor of ʿAbd al-Ḥafīẓ. The population of Tétouan should "rejoice" in the actions of their Fāsī compatriots and "deliver [their] *bayʿa* to [ʿAbd al-Ḥafīẓ] and inform the neighboring tribes" to follow suit.[30] The Kattānīs and their close associates in other cities also communicated among themselves about the political situation, observing and reporting with great detail the maneuvers of the European powers, the tide of popular opinion, and reports in both foreign and Arabic language newspapers regarding the Moroccan state of affairs.[31] Al-Kattānī even corresponded with representatives of foreign powers to obtain their support for the effort to secure ʿAbd al-Ḥafīẓ as sultan. In a letter to the American Consul in Tangier, for example, al-Kattānī asked that the Americans "not interfere in our internal political affairs." This, he argued, required that "none of the nations lean toward ʿAbd al-ʿAzīz, lend him money, or sell him arms."[32]

One of the most important Kattani efforts in support of the Ḥafīẓiyya was the publication and distribution of *Mufākahat Dhū al-Nubl,* a political pamphlet reflecting the spirit of ulama activism. The *Mufākaha* was written by ʿAbd al-Ḥayy al-Kattānī shortly after the *bayʿa* of Fez in response to an article published in the Tangier newspaper *al-Saʿāda* that criticized the people of Fez for their position supporting ʿAbd al-Ḥafīẓ in his bid for the throne. Much like the conditional *bayʿa* of Fez, the *Mufākaha* was also an important expression of the new of key of politics. Both through its rhetoric of unification of the *umma* around the struggle for better leadership and also through its mass printing and distribution, the Kattānī's wanted the *Mufākaha* to resonate among a wide audience.

In the *Mufākaha,* ʿAbd al-Ḥayy al-Kattānī argued for the role of the ulama as consultants to the sultan on the basis of their knowledge of sharia and as guarantors of its proper implementation. "Religion and kingship are brothers," began al-Kattānī. "One cannot subsist without the other—religion is the base, and kingship is its guardian." By conclusion, argued the author, "what has no bases will be destroyed, and what has no guardian will be lost."[33] Furthermore, al-Kattānī emphasized the sultan's need for knowledge and proper counsel "since it is from him that the general well-being springs." The responsibility of the sultan to protect his people implied that it was he who was "most in need of interacting with the ulama . . . and of gathering the *fuqahāʾ* around him." Critical of ʿAbd al-ʿAzīz's reliance on European advisers and in carrying out reforms, ʿAbd al-Ḥayy al-Kattānī complained that the dethroned sultan had "substituted convening with the learned class . . . by [convening] with those who are without knowledge."[34]

Responses to the *Mufākaha* were varied. Jacob Niddam noted great anticipation among Fāsīs of the completion of the writing of the *Mufākaha* by ʿAbd al-Ḥayy al-Kattānī.[35] Writing from Tangier in March 1908, a certain Abū Bakr al-Marīnī informed ʿAbd al-Ḥayy al-Kattānī that he had received ten copies of the *Mufākaha* and that other Kattāniyya disciples had also received copies. Al-Marīnī also explained that word of the *Mufākaha* had reached Tangier. They waited in great anticipation for its arrival. "How could we not?" explained al-Marīnī in admiration. "[The contents of the *Mufākaha*] have gratified the heart, satiated thirst, and made truth victorious through arguments and evidence. [The *Mufākaha*] is none other than a voice longed for by one who craves the truth."[36] The Tangier-based newspaper *Lisān al-Maghrib* also reported hearing about the *Mufākaha* before ever seeing it. Rumor had it that it was being printed in Fez and that it was lucid in "advanc[ing] the betterment of the country."[37]

Rumors that the *Mufākaha* challenged *al-Saʿāda*'s pro-ʿAzīzist sentiments were enough to illicit responses from the inhabitants of both Fez and Tangier. Niddam reported that when the mail delivery carrying copies of *al-Saʿāda* arrived in Fez from Tangier that day, a riot erupted in the street outside the office of the postal service. The rioters became so unwieldy that the *makhzan* issued a decree requiring that a government official inspect the contents of the mail before its distribution.[38] A potentially violent situation involving the commoners of Tangier also occurred in August 1908 when the editor of *al-Saʿāda,* Wadīʿ Karam, became the focus of their anger. An associate of the Kattānīs, Muṣṭafā al-Zūdī informed ʿAbd al-Kabīr al-Kattānī of the incident by letter. "Yesterday, Wadīʿ Karam was in the *sūq al-dākhilī* when the hashish smokers in the cafes and small children hissed . . . and cursed him," wrote al-Zūdī. He continued, explaining that the crowd told Karam "that if it were not for his running off and entering the houses of Christians, they would beat him wherever he published his lies."[39]

By the fall of 1908, with the help of Muḥammad al-Kattānī,

Sultan ʿAbd al-Ḥafīẓ had received *bayʿa*s from the most important cities, including Fez, Tangier, and Meknes. Guided by the new key of politics, the Kattāniyya leadership used their *zāwiya,* its resources, and affiliates, to bring ʿAbd al-Ḥafīẓ to power. During the Ḥafīẓiyya, the relationship between Muḥammad al-Kattānī and Mawlāy ʿAbd al-Ḥafīẓ was defined by the sultan's need to secure the allegiance of Fez and the north and by Muḥammad al-Kattānī's desire to ensure a role for himself in the political decisions of the new *makhzan.* This partnership was logical for many reasons. First, since the late seventeenth century (as is shown in chapter 1), a modus vivendi between the *shurafāʾ* and the ʿAlawī *makhzan* had formed the basis for a relatively stable political system characterized by highly diffuse power. Based on the political parameters defined by this system, both Muḥammad al-Kattānī (as an Idrīsī *sharīf* and Sufi shaykh) and Mawlāy ʿAbd al-Ḥafīẓ (as an ʿAlawī *sharīf* and sultan) had a shared interest in collaborating with one another. And second, both men believed that drastic measures were necessary to prevent further European involvement in Moroccan affairs. In an effort to put forward their political visions, al-Kattānī and Mawlāy ʿAbd al-Ḥafīẓ had reached beyond their traditional power bases for support and allegiance. Muḥammad al-Kattānī had reached out to merchants and the middling ulama of cities such as Tangier. Rather than rely on the elite ulama of Fez and the northern *makhzan* tribes, ʿAbd al-Ḥafīẓ created a coalition with the support of the tribal lords of the Great Atlas. Although this coalition was able to achieve a significant victory (the *bayʿa* of Fez) in the early phase of the Ḥafīẓiyya, it quickly lost its cohesion, thus straining the alliance between al-Kattānī and ʿAbd al-Ḥafīẓ.

Concern over the fate of the new *makhzan* reigned in Fez as it became increasingly apparent that ʿAbd al-Ḥafīẓ was both unwilling and incapable of fulfilling the demands stipulated in the *bayʿa* of Fez. The European powers refused to recognize the new government without ʿAbd al-Ḥafīẓ's acceptance of the conditions of Algeciras. Without European support, the transfer of desperately needed customs revenues would be denied to the *makhzan.* In an effort to avoid bankruptcy, ʿAbd al-Ḥafīẓ reimplemented the *maks* (gate tax).[40] His troops, drawn mostly from the south of Morocco, were also ordered to exact high taxes on the tribes in the region of Fez. As if this were not enough, ʿAbd al-Ḥafīẓ's choice of *wazīr*s also raised resentment and anger in Fez. His most important ministers were drawn from among his Berber tribal clients of the High Atlas, most notably the Glāwī.[41] Bankruptcy, declining morale, and military weakness contributed to a growing sense that ʿAbd al-Ḥafīẓ would not succeed in implementing the promises made in 1908 and enshrined in the *bayʿa* of Fez. ʿAbd al-Ḥafīẓ began to speak against the conditions put forward in the *bayʿa* of Fez. According to an eyewitness account, when a delegation of Fāsī ulama traveled to Meknès to greet the new sultan and congratulate him on his success, ʿAbd al-Ḥafīẓ refused to see them, on account of his anger over the conditional *bayʿa.* Later, when they finally met, the sultan scolded the ulama for their complicity in stipulating conditions. Their response was to blame Muḥammad al-Kattānī.[42]

Troubles between Muḥammad al-Kattānī and ʿAbd al-Ḥafīẓ also began to surface. Given the uncertainty of ʿAbd al-Ḥafīẓ's position, Muḥammad al-Kattānī must have seemed extremely threatening to him. After all, it was only a few months earlier that Muḥammad al-Kattānī had demonstrated the extent of his influence. He had mobilized fighters from among the Middle Atlas tribes and from among armed contingents in Fez, he had provided access to provisions and other resources necessary for supporting the Ḥafīẓiyya through the network of his disciples, and he had been instrumental in formulating the conditions of the Fez *bayʿa.* Muḥammad al-Kattānī, in other words, had tremendous power. He had military power and other resources at his disposal, as well as a plan of political action. Muḥammad al-Kattānī seemed to have captured the imagination of Moroccans from different parts of the country and from diverse social groups. Indeed, the shaykh's movements were closely observed by European intelligence, and his activities were noted in the Tangier-based Arabic and foreign-language press.[43]

How, then, could Sultan ʿAbd al-Ḥafīẓ undermine the power of the Kattāniyya? He began by criticizing Muḥammad al-Kattānī on the basis of his interest in Sufism. During a gathering of notables and ulama in which both men were present, ʿAbd al-Ḥafīẓ, who was known as a *faqīh* and for his legal rather than esoteric orientation, expressed his disapproval of ecstatic forms of Sufi practice and worship including dancing, singing, and the playing of musical instuments. ʿAbd al-Ḥafīẓ had studied with prominent shaykhs and was well-suited to spar intellectually with al-Kattānī. Although he participated in Sufi activities, he has been described by some scholars as a supporter of the Salafiyya. This assessment is based on the fact that he criticized Sufi orders such as the Wazzāniyya and Tjiāniyya. In addition, he supported scholars such as the Moroccan Abū Shuʿayb al-Dukkālī, known as one of the pioneers of Salafism in Morocco in the twentieth century.[44] Al-Kattānī responded by noting the sultan's vestiary that included silk and gold and pointed out that the Prophet did not display such items.[45] ʿAbd al-Ḥafīẓ began imprisoning Kattāniyya disciples and refusing to be swayed by al-Kattānī's attempts to achieve their release.[46] By the spring of 1909, the relationship between ʿAbd al-Ḥafīẓ and Muḥammad al-Kattānī had completely deteriorated. In March, the shaykh, along with a coterie of his closest disciples and family, departed from Fez and headed west toward the tribal lands of the Aït Ndīr, where they sought protection.[47]

Al-Kattānī's departure from Fez became a subject of immediate concern for the sultan. With the shaykh gone from Fez, ʿAbd al-Ḥafīẓ could not monitor his activities. Therefore, preparations were made to intercept the shaykh and his entourage. As word of al-Kattānī's departure spread throughout Fez and other parts of the country, rumors of tribal rebellion began to circulate. *Al-Moghreb al-Aksa,* an English biweekly published in Tangier, reported a sense of "excitement and fear owing to the departure of Shereef al-Kittani, who was said to have gone to raise the Berber tribes against the Sultan and preach holy war."[48] Meanwhile, the sultan ordered the closure of Kattāniyya *zāwiya*s throughout the country. Writing to the *qā'id* and notable of Salé, al-Ṭayyib al-Sabīḥī, the sultan's scribe described al-Kattānī's activites as "creat[ing] *fitna* among the Muslims and involv[ing] himself in [activities] that do not receive the blessing [of God]." The scribe warned al-Sabīḥī to be "aware of the truth of the situation . . . to close the *zāwiya* . . . to take notice of frivolous [Kattāniyya] disciples . . . until the time when we expose their harm."[49] In Tangier, *al-Moghreb al-Aksa* reported, "there is the greatest consternation among all those who belong to this most influential brotherhood or sect [regarding] the command to close three Kattāniyya *zāwiya*s [there]."[50] The *makhzan* made other efforts to curtail the activities of the Kattāniyya order by questioning adherents and forcing them to denounce the shaykh. In Tangier, the *muqaddam* of the Kattāniyya *zāwiya,* a certain al-ʿArabī Khamlīsh, was interrogated regarding his affiliation with the order.[51] The fact that Tangier-based newspapers reported the news of Muḥammad al-Kattānī's departure from Fez points to the shaykh's position as a prominent figure even outside the city.[52]

Al-Kattānī and his family were finally overtaken by tribesmen of the Banī Mṭīr tribe as they headed in the direction of Meknes. Acting on command from the sultan, the tribesmen abducted the group and marched them back to Fez. After their arrival, the travelers, including the family women and children and an entourage of disciples, were subjected to unprecedented public humiliations, which sent shock waves throughout the city and elicited reactions of utter dismay. The Kattānī men entered the city and were paraded through the streets on mules, their hands fettered, their beards shaved, and their head coverings removed. The family women and children rode solemnly behind. The group was eventually brought to the palace, where they were imprisoned, including the women. The incarceration of women, noted one source, had previously been unknown.[53] As an example to others who attempted to challenge the *makhzan*'s authority, ʿAbd al-Ḥafīẓ subjected the disicples who had accompanied the Kattānī clan to severe and gruesome punishment; first, they were beaten, and then their hands were cut off, the bleeding wounds then rubbed with salt.[54] Muḥammad al-Kattānī, his father, and his brother ʿAbd al-Ḥayy, were each subjected to lashings while their wives and servants looked on.[55] Muḥammad al-Kattānī died shortly after the beating. His body was then placed in an unmarked grave, its whereabouts unknown to the family or to disciples of the brotherhood.

The response in Fez to the death of Muḥammad al-Kattānī and to the humiliations suffered by the Kattānī *shurafāʾ* was one of shock and dismay. The Kattānīs were recognized as one of the oldest and most well-established families of the Idrīsī *shurafāʾ*. Muḥammad al-Kattānī was also celebrated as a great mystic and as an *ʿālim*. Furthermore, it was Muḥammad al-Kattānī's mobilization of the ulama of Fez that had helped to bring about the *bayʿa* for ʿAbd al-Ḥafīẓ. Despite all this, however, the shaykh's death was met with surprising silence and resignation by the ulama of the city, who had, by their words and actions, supported the efforts of the Kattāniyya only one year before during the uprising. Still lacking the cohesiveness of a corporate goup with clearly defined political interests, the ulama resumed their generally compliant position toward the *makhzan*, much like before the Ḥafīẓiyya. Even Muḥammad al-Kattānī's cousin, the famous *ʿālim*, Muḥammad b. Ja'far al-Kattānī, assumed this position of compliance toward the sultan. When summoned by ʿAbd al-Ḥafīẓ after Muḥammad al-Kattānī's murder to compose a compilation of hadith for use in study of the subject, he obliged.[56] The new key of politics envisioned by Muḥammad al-Kattānī, in which the ulama would become active participants in the politics of the state in the interest of the larger Moroccan Muslim community had clearly not been realized.

The execution of Muḥammad al-Kattānī was but one in a series of actions taken by ʿAbd al-Ḥafīẓ to preserve whatever control and authority remained to him. In 1910, after finally accepting the conditions of the Algeciras Act in 1909, the sultan signed another loan agreement with France, furthering the population's disillusionment in Fez.[57] Like his predecessor, ʿAbd al-ʿAzīz, ʿAbd al-Ḥafīẓ found himself at the head of a bankrupt state. ʿAbd al-Ḥafīẓ's dealings with the tribes of the Middle Atlas, also produced resentment and dissatisfaction among them. The *makhzan* sent a *maḥalla* (fighting force) against the Aït Ndīr tribe punishing them for protecting al-Kattānī as he fled from Fez; they were forced to provide fighters for ʿAbd al-Ḥafīẓ's army.[58] ʿAbd al-Ḥafīẓ's policy of strengthening alliances with the southern tribal leaders of the Great Atlas by placing them in high governmental positions and then using them as tax collectors among the tribes of the Fez region greatly contributed to general discontent.[59] Above this, Muḥammad al-Kattānī's execution undermined support for the *makhzan* among the tribes of northern Morocco, among Kattāniyya disciples in Fez and other cities, and also among the Idrīsī *shurafāʾ*. With support quickly fading and with French troops gaining ground throughout the country, the *makhzan*'s legitimacy had all but disappeared. ʿAbd al-Ḥafīẓ's only remaining ally was al-Madanī al-Glāwī, the most important and powerful of the High Atlas tribal lords. French troops finally gained the upper hand against the tribes of the Middle Atlas, who rebelled in 1911,[60] and in March 1912, the Treaty of Fez was signed establishing the French Protectorate in Morocco. In August of the same year, ʿAbd al-Ḥafīẓ agreed to abdicate the throne in exchange for protection and financial support from France. In many respects, the fate of ʿAbd al-Ḥafīẓ (and the ʿAlawī *makzhan*) was similar to that of Muḥammad al-Kattānī. However, whereas the Kattānīs failed to regain their lost religious and political authority as *shurafāʾ*, Sufis, and ulama, the ʿAlawīs emerged in the postindependence period as the ultimate religious and political power brokers, their authority drawing on the symbolism of prophetic descent (among other things).

NOTES

1. In Fez, a volatile situation already existed among the urban poor as a result of economic recession between 1905 and 1907, during which rioting was prevented only through the emergency importation of grain from Marseilles. Burke, *Prelude to Protectorate in Morocco,* 90.
2. The French announced that their actions were designed to "ensure the absolute respect on the part of the *makhzan* of the rights of France and to ensure its prompt response for the damages France suffered." Jacques Cagne, *Nation et nationalisme au Maroc* (Rabat: al-Maʿārif al-Jadīda, 1988), 263. For a detailed study of the Mauchamp Affair and the complicated political maneuvering among the European powers in Morocco surrounding it see Katz, *Murder in Marrakesh.*
3. Other attacks against foreigners included the murder of a Frenchman in Tangier in 1906, an attack against a French tourist in Fez in 1907, and other minor incidents in Marrakesh in the same year. Burke, *Prelude to Protectorate,* 91–93.
4. Mawlāy ʿAbd al-Ḥafīẓ's coalition was made up of a diverse group of supporters. First, he created alliances with the *qāʾid*s of the Great Atlas Berber tribes—of Glāwī, Mtūggī, and Gūndāfī. He also drew support from rural notables and tribal leaders in the Chaouia region, who had benefited from the expansion of Morocco's export-based economy and the emergence of Casablanca as a major port in the late nineteenth century. This group was empowered through their connections to various European states in their capacities as protégés. Burke, *Prelude to Protectorate,* 93–95, 102–104, 210.
5. His affiliations with al-Madanī al-Glāwī, leader of one of the strongest Great Atlas tribal confederations, seems to have been instrumental in gaining political support and financing for his efforts to overthrow Sultan ʿAbd al-ʿAzīz. ʿAbd al-Ḥafīẓ secured his alliance with Glāwī by marrying Glāwī's daughter. Burke, *Prelude to Protectorate,* 102.
6. Ibid., 107.
7. See chapter 1 for a discussion of politics in Fez during the ʿAlawī period.

8. Mawlāy ʿAbd al-Ḥafīẓ to Muḥammad al-Kattānī, 10 Rajab 1325 AH/August 20, 1907 CE, DAR (TK), Fez 13, no. 28213. On the significance of language in *makhzan* epistolary exchange, see Mohammed Ennaji and Paul Pascon, *Le Makhzen et le Sous al-Aqsa,* 9–12.
9. The first in a series of *fatwās* regarding the legality of Mawlāy ʿAbd al-Ḥafīẓ's actions was given by the ulama of Fez in response to a query submitted to them by ʿAbd al-ʿAzīz shortly after the *bayʿa* was declared in Marrakesh for ʿAbd al-Ḥafīẓ. The ulama's initial response was negative. However, the ulama later issued a statement declaring that the dethronement of ʿAbd al-ʿAzīz was legal. See E. Michaux-Bellaire, "Proclamation de la déchéance de Moulay Abd el Aziz," *Revue du Monde Musulman* 5 (1908): 425–435.
10. Munson, *Religion and Power in Morocco,* 70.
11. Ibid., 72.
12. ʿAbd al-Ḥayy al-Kattānī, *Mufākahat dhū al-nubl wa al-ijāda* (Fez: Lithographic Press, 1908), 15–16.
13. Muḥammad Gharnīṭ, quoted in Munson, *Religion and Power in Morocco,* 71.
14. Yet another interpretation posits that the ulama preferred to exercise caution in making a decision. With the sultan gone from Fez and the outcome of events still uncertain, the ulama waited to see how events would unfold before taking a final decision. Aḥmad Tawfīq, "Ta'amullāt fī al-bayʿa al-Ḥafīẓiyya," *Al-Maghrib min al-ʿahd al-ʿazīzī ilā sanat 1912, al-juz" al-awwal. (*Proceedings of the Summer Congress, Mohammadia, Morocco 21–31 July 1987) (n.p., n.d): 335–347.
15. Ibid., 343.
16. Ibid., 344.
17. Ibid., 343.
18. "The *Bayʿa* of Fez," in al-Manūnī, *Maẓāhir yaqẓat al-maghrib ḥadīth,* 2: 349–353.
19. Edmund Burke, "La Hafidiya (août 1907–janvier 1908): en jeux sociaux et luttes populaires," *Hespéris-Tamuda* 31 (1993): 101–115.
20. The process of the diminution of sharīfan political power and authority occurred simultaneously with an increasing influence in political affairs of the merchant class. Refer to chapter 1 for more on

political developments in the nineteenth-century and the position of the *shurafā'*.

21. Anonymous to Mawlāy 'Abd al-Ḥafīẓ, 21 Ṣafar 1326 AH/March 25, 1908 CE, DAR (TZ), 1326.
22. "Mulai Hassan moreover did not escape the usual obligation of laying siege to the town." La Martinière, *Morocco: Journeys in the Kingdom of Fez and to the Court of Mulai Hassan* (London: Whittaker and Co., 1889), 386.
23. "A crowd of two thousand Fāsīs must, without fail, leave the city from Bāb al Futūḥ in order to learn how to aim. The leader of these imbeciles is Shaykh al-Kattānī." Jacob Niddam, "Un correspondant de révolution: journal d'un Israélite de Fes, part 1," *Bulletin de la Société de Géographie d'Alger et de l'Afrique du Nord* 145 (1936): 36. Bāb al Futūḥ is one of the major gates of Fez. It served as the meeting point of the roads coming from Taza in the east and Sefrou in the south. See Le Tourneau, *Fès avant le protectorat*, 138.
24. "Before firing his weapon, each one must respectfully present it to Shaykh al-Kattānī. [Al-Kattānī] has merely to place his hand on the trigger, at least according to what they say, for the shooter to hit his target." Ibid., 38.
25. In a report describing the military situation in Morocco in 1908, Captain Lechartier wrote: "Aussi, ne cessèrent-ils d'envoyer partout des émissaiers pour fanatiser les populations dans des régions de plus en plus élongées. Ils étaient puissamment aidés dans cet appel à la guerre sainte par l'état de trouble dans lequel s'agite le Maroc depuis dix-huit mois; ils reçurent à plusieurs reprises des lettres d'encouragement; des agitateurs connus comme El-Kittani de Fez, leur annonçait leur prochaine arrivée" [Moreover, they do not stop sending sending emissaries everywhere in order to radicalize the populations in regions increasingly farther away. They were greatly assisted in this call to jihad by the troubled state gripping Morocco for the past eighteen months; on several occasions they received letters of encouragement; familiar agitators like al-Kattānī of Fez announced to them their next arrival]. Georges Lechartier, *La colone du Haut-Guir en septembre 1908* (Paris: Librairie Militaire R. Chapelot et Cie., 1908), 27.
26. Niddam, "Un correspondant de révolution," 51.
27. Ibid., 153. The Tangier-based Arabic newspaper *Lisān al-Maghrib*

also reported on the activities of the Kattānīs during the Ḥafīẓiyya. For example, the newspaper reports on Muḥammad al-Kattānī's departure for Meknès to attend a meeting of the Middle Atlas tribes. "Fez," *Lisān al-Maghrib,* no. 28, 9 Ṣafar 1326 AH/March 13, 1908 CE, 3.

28. Because of al-Kattānī's success at the Meknès meeting, Sultan ʿAbd al-Ḥafīẓ was forced to rely on al-Kattānī's assistance in facilitating his army's safe passage through tribal regions located between the Atlantic coast and Fez through the negotiation of agreements with the tribes controlling these regions. al-Kattānī, *Tarjama,* 207.
29. See chapter 4 for examples illustrating both al-Kattānī's fame and notoriety in Tangier.
30. An excerpt of this letter, which was written in January 1908 to the ulama of Tétouan, appears in the *Tarjama*. Kattānī, *Tarjama,* 202–203.
31. A series of letters written between April and September 1908 between the Kattānīs and their contacts in Tangier describe the political situation prior to the issuing of the bayʿa of Tangier in August 1908. DAR (TZ), 1326.
32. al-Kattānī, *Tarjama,* 204.
33. al-Kattānī, *Mufākaha,* 8.
34. Ibid., 5–6. The same discourse was put forward by Muḥammad al-Kattānī's cousin and prominent legal scholar, Muḥammad bin Jaʿfar al-Kattānī, in *Naṣīḥat ahl al-Islam*. Much like the *Mufākaha,* the *Naṣīḥa* emphasized that the sultan's consultation with the ulama was fundamental to his ability to rule justly and righteously. al-Kattānī, *Naṣīḥat ahl al-Islam.*
35. Niddam, "Un correspondant de la révolution," 44, 46, 57.
36. Abū Bakr al-Marīnī to ʿAbd al-Ḥayy al-Kattānī, 17 Ṣafar 1326 AH/March 22, 1908 CE, DAR (TK), Fez 13, no. 6617.
37. "Domestic News," *Lisān al-Maghrib,* 18 Muḥarram 1326 CE/ February 21, 1908 CE.
38. Niddam, "Un correspondant de la révolution," 45.
39. Muṣṭafā al-Zūdī to ʿAbd al-Kabīr al-Kattānī, 27 Rajab 1326 AH/ August 25, 1908 CE, DAR (TZ), 1326. A copy of this letter was received from the personal archive collection of Dr. Khaled bin Shrir, Rabat, Morocco.
40. Burke, *Prelude to Protectorate in Morocco,* 128–129.
41. Ibid., 150.

42. Munson, *Religion and Power in Morocco,* 72–73.
43. Numerous sources followed and reported the activities of the Kattānīs during the Ḥafīẓiyya including the reporter Jacob Niddam; the Arabic newspapers *al-Sa'āda* and *Lisān al-Maghrib,* and the English newspaper *al-Moghreb al-Aksa.*
44. As a result, Edmund Burke described the conflict between 'Abd al-Ḥafīẓ and Muḥammad al-Kattānī as a conflict between Sufi and *faqīh.* See Burke, *Prelude to Protectorate in Morocco,* 135. Henry Munson discredits this explanation on the grounds that Sultan 'Abd al-Ḥafīẓ was a Sufi himself. For Munson, their dispute was emblematic of the conflict between the righteous man of God (al-Kattānī) and the sultan, which, for Munson, constitutes a main theme in Moroccan history. See chapter 3 in Munson, *Religion and Power in Morocco.*
45. al-Kattānī, *al-Maẓāhir,* 112.
46. Ibid., 110. What is of interest is that once again, the debate revolves around the question of superior knowledge of sharia.
47. Burke, *Prelude to Protectorate in Morocco,* 134.
48. "The Situation in Fez," *al-Moghreb al-Aksa,* April 1, 1909, no. 1379.
49. Makhzan to al-Ṭayyib al-Sabīḥī, 2 Rabī' al-awwal 1327 AH/ March 25, 1909 CE, Wathā'iq, series 1, no. 915, BS.
50. "The Kittanin [sic] Zauias Closed," *al-Moghreb al-Aksa,* April 8, 1909, no. 1381.
51. Muḥammad al-Jabbāṣ to Mawlāy 'Abd al-Ḥafīẓ, 4 Rabī' (I or II?)1327 AH/March 27 (or April 26)/1909 CE, DAR (TK), al-Kattāniyyun.
52. Another Tangier-based newspaper, *Lisān al-Maghrib,* also reported on rumors of al-Kattānī's flight, capture and death. "Fez," *Lisān al-Maghrib,* 27 Rabī' al-awwal 1327 AH/April 18, 1909 CE; "Fez," *Lisān al-Maghrib,* 11 Rabī' al-thānī 1327 AH/May 2, 1909 CE.
53. "Captured Rebels' Torture," *al-Moghreb al-Aksa,* April 15, 1909, no. 1383: "Much excitement prevails in Fez owing to the whole of the Shereef Kitani's [sic] family, women and children alike, being imprisoned in irons. The imprisonment of women was hitherto an unknown thing in Morocco."
54. Ibid.

55. "Fez," *Lisān al-Maghrib,* 11 Rabīʿ al-thānī 1327 AH/May 2, 1909 CE, Tangier, Morocco.
56. Munson, *Religion and Power in Morocco,* 94.
57. Burke, *Prelude to Protectorate in Morocco,* 146.
58. Ibid., 134.
59. Ibid., 153.
60. On the events of 1911 in Fez and its environs, see Robert Ghastel, "Le coup de Fès ou Fès 1911," *Hespéris-Tamuda* 28 (1990): 71–90.

· SIX ·

Silence, Not Absence: The Kattāniyya and the Politics of History

Silence can be a plan rigorously executed, the blueprint to a life.
It is a presence. It has a history, a form.
Do not confuse it with any kind of absence.
—Adrienne Rich, "Cartographies of Silence"[1]

How should we interpret the conflict between Sultan ʿAbd al-Ḥafīẓ and Muḥammad al-Kattānī? According to the argument put forward in an article published in 1908 by Edouard Evariste Michaux-Bellaire—the French colonial administrator and editor and founder of *Archives Marocaines*[2]—the conflict reflected a struggle between the ʿAlawī and Idrīsī *shurafāʾ* over the control of the sultanate. Michaux-Bellaire argued that Muḥammad al-Kattānī's actions during the Ḥafīẓiyya were part of a larger plan on his part to overthrow the ruling ʿAlawī dynasty and restore the Idrīsī imamate with himself as caliph. Michaux-Bellaire likened al-Kattānī's involvement in the Ḥafīẓiyya to that of an earlier generation of Idrīsī *shurafāʾ*, who in 1465 established a short-lived Idrīsī imamate following the death of the ruling Merinid sultan. In Michaux-Bellaire's view, "certains passages de l'histoire de cette époque pourraient avoir écrits hiers."[3] At the heart of his argument is a vision of Moroccan history, society, and politics defined by incessant struggle between the center (the ruling dynasty) and the periphery (those ruled by the dynasty). The argument therefore assumes that relations between the ʿAlawī and Idrīsī *shurafāʾ* were characterized by inherent conflict.

ʿAbd al-Ḥayy al-Kattānī, Muḥammad al-Kattānī's younger brother, proposed a similar explanation in *al-Maẓāhir al-sāmiyya fī al-nisba al-sharīfa al-Kattānīyya*—a history of the Kattānī family that he wrote to shed light on "relations between the kings of Morocco and the House of Kattānī."[4] ʿAbd al-Ḥayy al-Kattānī also viewed the conflict between his brother and Sultan ʿAbd al-Ḥafīẓ in terms of ʿAlawī-Idrīsī rivalry. But unlike Michaux-Bellaire, ʿAbd al-Ḥayy al-Kattānī believed that the mutual respect that previously had defined relations between the ʿAlawī dynasty and the Kattānī *shurafāʾ* had been destroyed by the sultan's murder of Muḥammad al-Kattānī in 1909. The ʿAlawīs, who had transgressed against the rights of the Idrīsī *shurafāʾ*, were to blame for the rupture of relations. From ʿAbd al-Ḥayy al-Kattānī's perspective, the death of Muḥammad al-Kattānī was an act of martyrdom because he had stood firm against the arbitrary and unjust actions of the sultan. He explained that "when the *fuqahāʾ* of Fez went to congratulate the sultan, he reprimanded them and expressed enmity toward anyone who mentioned the conditions of the *bayʿa*." Referring to the sultan's disregard for the ulama, ʿAbd al-Ḥayy al-Kattānī added, "[T]he sultan became enemies with those who advised and counseled him."[5] The sultan's decision to close Kattāniyya *zāwiya*s and forbid the practice of rituals associated with the brotherhood constituted a violation against the sanctity of holy places. This breach of the principle of sanctuary *(ḥurm)* associated with the shrines and *zāwiya*s of holy men and women marked yet another transgression by the ʿAlawī *makhzan* against the rights of the Idrīsī *shurafāʾ*.[6] The 1962 *Biography* (*Tarjamat al-Shaykh Muḥammad al-Kattānī al-Shahīd* by Muḥammad al-Bāqir al-Kattānī, Muḥammad al-Kattānī's grandson) is the only extant work on the life of Muḥammad al-

Kattānī and the only source of information about him. It is based primarily on *al-Maẓāhir,* and it offers essentially the same arguments, reading like a vindication of the family's honor through the celebration of its vanquished ancestor.

The conflict between the 'Alawī and Idrīsī *shurafā'* played a role in Moroccan politics in the pre-Protectorate era. However, Michaux-Bellaire's argument fails to recognize significant historical developments that affected this relationship. Thus, his interpretation fails to take into account the fact that the 'Alawī dynasty came to power by creating a system of power sharing with other sharifan lineages. Despite the essentialist character of Michaux-Bellaire's explanation, his article forms the basis for later interpretations about Muḥammad al-Kattānī's role in the 1907 uprising.[7] Although no evidence has come to light indicating that Muḥammad al-Kattānī wanted to become sultan of Morocco, this argument has continued to define the scope of discourse about the events and their aftermath. According to popular wisdom, Muḥammad al-Kattānī's significance revolves around the question of his complicity in the effort to establish a restoration of Idrīsī power at the expense of the ruling dynasty.

Indeed, the conflict between Muḥammad al-Kattānī and Sultan 'Abd al-Ḥafīẓ marked the end of a system of power sharing that had existed for two centuries between the *makhzan* and the Fāsī *shurafā'*. The death of Muḥammad al-Kattānī and the demise of 'Abd al-Ḥafīẓ's *makhzan* later heralded the end of an era in Moroccan politics, in which the Idrīsī *shurafā'* (as Sufis and saints) and the 'Alawīs (as sultans) jointly wielded religiopolitical authority and legitimacy on the basis of their shared prophetic genealogies. Since the seventeenth century, Moroccan politics had been defined by this highly diffuse constellation of religious and political forces known as Sharifism. The subsequent development of a symbiotic relationship between the 'Alawī *makhzan* and other sharifan lineages was central to the maintenance of 'Alawī control, particularly in Fez and its environs.

During the nineteenth century, this highly fluid and diffuse constellation of religiopolitical power was shifting, reflecting larger external and internal socio-economic processes. These were, most notably, the rise of European economic, political, and military power over the Moroccan sultanate; the greatly increased importance of trade with Europe for the *makhzan;* and the rise of a new class of rural and urban notables, who had benefited from these developments but remained marginalized politically until the Ḥafīẓiyya. In an effort to face the economic and political challenges of the era, the *makhzan* began a process of state centralization and reform, thereby disrupting the tenuous system of power sharing that had existed for almost two hundred years. Furthermore, by increasingly relying on new elites to fill newly created positions in bureaucracy and expanding it (albeit slowly), the *makhzan* undermined this balance even further. Clearly the *shurafāʾ* were losing out. Although the concept of *sharaf* still carried symbolic weight at the end of the nineteenth-century and on the eve of French colonization, the new realities created by the demands of European economic and political agendas meant that the Kattānī *shurafāʾ* had to recast themselves and redefine their roles as political actors to participate in the politics of reform, which characterized the Moroccan transition to modernity.

Muḥammad al-Kattānī's activities as shaykh of the Kattāniyya were in conversation with and informed by these processes. During his life, he worked hard to garner religious and political support for himself according to principles of Sharifism, but he also relied on the active participation of Kattāniyya shaykhs and disciples in the process of revival and reform. Between 1895 and 1907, al-Kattānī struggled to put the Kattāniyya on the map as an institution, which could guide change in an era when the traditional Moroccan religiopolitical elite proved incapable of doing so. Having understood the need for a wide coalition of support to face the challenges of the day, al-Kattānī began to engage in a form of populist politics. This meant casting his net further afield—beyond the ulama, the *shurafā'*, and the heads of Sufi orders—by seeking alliances with a new class of urban elites.

During the Ḥafīẓiyya uprising, Muḥammad al-Kattānī tried to put this new activism into practice by encouraging the ulama to help in bringing together a wide coalition of forces for jihad. The Ḥafīẓiyya opened the way for the participation in politics of groups previously marginalized politically by bringing them into 'Abd al-Ḥafīẓ's coalition and by providing the occasion for them to articulate their political demands as conditions to the *bay'a* of Fez. However, the failure of the Ḥafīẓiyya movement to prevent a French takeover demonstrated that the "new key of politics" had ultimately failed to achieve the desired goal of reform that would ensure the independence of Morocco. Al-Kattānī's efforts to expand the Kattāniyya paradoxically furthered the demise of *sharaf* as the main legitimizing principle for political power by conceding to the participation of an emerging elite (as occurred during the Moroccan crisis of 1905) and by calling on all Moroccans to take up the struggle against European domination.

For the Kattānī family and for Kattāniyya disciples, Sultan 'Abd al-Ḥafīẓ's decision to bury Muḥammad al-Kattānī in an unmarked grave—its whereabouts unknown to anyone but the sultan and his closest advisors—was significant. The absence of a tomb marking al-Kattānī's burial would prevent the emergence of a saintly cult centered around the deceased, and his memory would eventually fade. Saintly veneration, pilgrimages to saints' shrines and tombs, and visits to living holy men and women were among the most important expressions of the power and authority of the Moroccan *shurafā'* in the pre-Protectorate period. Sultan 'Abd al-Ḥafīẓ's actions struck directly at the prestige of the Kattānī family and damaged Muḥammad al-Kattānī's legacy as a great Sufi shaykh for future generations. Yet 'Abd al-Ḥafīẓ's transgression against the Idrīsī *shurafā'* and the Kattāniyya was not without consequence. With his credibility greatly reduced as a result of the Kattānī affair and his sidelining of the *makhzan*'s *guish* tribes (by relying heavily on the

Great Atlas *qā'ids*), 'Abd al-Ḥafīẓ had, in essence, transgressed every rule of politics according to the logic of Sharifism.

After the establishment of the Protectorate, French authorities forced 'Abd al-Ḥafīẓ to abdicate the throne. Only one year earlier, the erstwhile sultan, 'Abd al-Azīz, had entered a similar agreement with the French. Again, through French pressure, the position of sultan was filled by a young prince of the 'Alawī house named Mawlāy Yūsuf (r. 1912–1927). During much of the Protectorate, the 'Alawī sultans functioned as mere figureheads with virtually no power, while France made and implemented policy decisions related to Morocco. For General Lyautey, resident general of Morocco and the architect of French indigenous policy during the Protectorate, the importance of the sultan for French policy could not be underestimated. Lyautey viewed the role of the Moroccan sultanate as a symbol of tradition and continuity in the lives of Moroccans, rather than their undergoing rupture and change. He explained, "C'est lui qui s'incarne toute la tradition [It is he (the sultan) who is the incarnation of all tradition]."[8]

The years 1909 through 1912 marked the end of one era, but they also inaugurated a formative period of Moroccan politics in which new concepts of political legitimacy and authority emerged in response to the reality of colonial domination. During the Protectorate, both the 'Alawī *makhzan* and the Kattāniyya—now under the leadership of Muḥammad al-Kattānī's brother, 'Abd al-Ḥayy—struggled separately to recover their damaged prestige and to reassert themselves as political actors. However, whereas the 'Alawī sultan, Muḥammad V (r. 1927–1953, 1957–1961), was successful in repoliticizing his role in the mid-1940s and 1950s through an alliance with the nascent Moroccan nationalist movement Istiqlāl, the Kattāniyya faded into oblivion, its leadership discredited and the family name tarnished.

Other political actors sought to position themselves within the changing landscape of Moroccan politics. During the early years of the Protectorate, for example, the ulama (some of whom had actively supported ʿAbd al-Ḥafīẓ and al-Kattānī during the Ḥafīẓiyya uprising) adopted ambiguous and often compromising positions toward France. Many—such as Abū Shuʿāyb al-Dukkālī, Muḥammad bin al-ʿArabī al-ʿAlawī, and Muḥammad al-Hajwī—began filling the positions within the newly formed French bureaucracy, thereby linking their interests to its fate. France successfully recruited some of the largest and most prominent Sufi brotherhoods in efforts to pacify regions of the country that remained beyond the control of the colonial government. In exchange, the French offered the brotherhoods religious autonomy against the increasingly *Salafī*-oriented ulama, who viewed Sufism as a degenerate and heterodox form of religious practice. This was yet another example in which French colonial authorities tried to use preexisting indigenous institutions to further the goals of the Protectorate. This policy pitted the religious elite against one another and reified a dichotomy between Sufism and sharia, which in the pre-Protectorate era had represented different modes of religious knowledge and forms of piety. This situation was a far cry from the goals of Muḥammad al-Kattānī to involve the religiopolitical elites in the process of reform and revival *(tajdīd)* of Morocco. The Glāwīs—the Great Atlas tribal *qā'id*s who supported ʿAbd al-Ḥafīẓ in 1907—achieved immense wealth and control over vast territories in the south as a result of their cooperation with French plans for the total pacification of Morocco. Marginal players in *makhzan* politics until the mid- to late nineteenth century, the Glāwīs had exchanged alliance with the *makhzan* for a more lucrative one with the French colonial government. Their elevation to such prominence was possible in a world in which prophetic lineage was no longer the basis of political legitimacy and in which a new legitimizing principle had yet to emerge.

The only member of the Kattānī family to remain involved in politics after the Ḥafīẓiyya and during the Protectorate was ʿAbd al-Ḥayy al-Kattānī, who eventually took over leadership of the Kattāniyya after his brother's death and after a succession struggle between himself and Muḥammad al-Kattānī's son.[9] As shaykh of the Kattāniyya, 'Abd al-Ḥayy oversaw the establishment of several new *zāwiyas* in the Dukkala region of southern Morocco, in the city of Azzemour, and in the Algerian cities of Tlemcen and Oran.[10] As with other Sufi shaykhs, the French brought 'Abd al-Ḥayy into their orbit of influence through the promise of religious and political autonomy for the Kattāniyya.[11] The French viewed the Sufi orders as a counterbalance to the sultanate, which, in any case, had all but lost its autonomy and become an extension of French colonial administration by the 1930s. On the request of General Lyautey, 'Abd al-Ḥayy al-Kattānī wrote letters to Middle Atlas tribal leaders from which he drew disciples—including the Banī Mṭīr, the Aït Yūsī, and the Banī Mglīd—to convince them to accept the authority of the puppet-sultanate.[12] According to Sī 'Abd al-Wahhāb bin Manṣūr, the royal historian and director of the Archives Royales in Rabat, al-Kattānī gained the support and trust of these tribes by performing "miracles" staged with the help of colonial authorities. Tribal leaders would then submit to the counsel of al-Kattānī, who would advise them to cooperate with French authorities.[13] Allegedly driven by anger and resentment against the 'Alawī dynasty, 'Abd al-Ḥayy al-Kattānī became one of several Moroccans who helped further the interests of the French government in Morocco. Although the extent of his collaboration and the motivations for such actions are not known, 'Abd al-Ḥayy al-Kattānī is known today in Morocco as one of the "symbol[s] of betrayal."[14] Just as the Glāwī came to power on the coat tails of the French Protectorate authorities, so too did 'Abd al-Ḥayy al-Kattānī.

Many of the Kattānī clan preferred to let their tragedy pass in silence and to abandon politics altogether. Like other Fāsī elites, they left Fez to pursue opportunities in Rabat and Casablanca, the new administrative and financial centers of Morocco.[15] Muḥammad bin Ja'far al-Kattānī, the renowned hadith scholar and cousin of the deceased Kattānī, responded to the new situation by leaving Morocco with his family permanently and taking up residence in Medina in the Hijaz and later in Syria. His decision to leave Morocco was based on the doctrine of *hijra,* which compelled Muslims to migrate from a place inhospitable for the practice of Islamic rites to one in which they could practice Islam unhindered or unsoiled while living by the laws of a non-Islamic government.[16] Muḥammad bin Ja'far al-Kattānī established contacts and close ties with ulama contemporaries during his first pilgrimage to Mecca in 1904 and had contacts with *Salafī* thinkers, such as Rashīd Riḍā and Shakīb Arslān. His affiliations and connection to the Ottoman Porte paved the way for his involvement in pan-Islamist politics.[17] The abandonment of his country and the city of his birth was both a spiritual and an ideological rejection of the new order of politics in which the *makhzan* experienced a great diminution of power and the sultan functioned as a figurehead rather than as an independent political actor.

One hundred years has passed since the events surrounding death of Muḥammad al-Kattānī at the hand of Sultan 'Abd al-Ḥafīẓ in 1909. It is still viewed as a dark moment in the history of both the Kattānī family and of the ruling 'Alawī dynasty. For some, al-Kattānī's endeavors constituted an act of national heroism, while for others, they represent the defilement of the sanctity of the sultanate. For the 'Alawīs, who continue to rule Morocco today, the closing years of the nineteenth century represent a dark moment in an otherwise glorious heritage, while the life of Muḥammad al-Kattānī is surrounded by the aura of betrayal and treason. As a result, even today few Moroccans are willing to discuss al-Kattānī's death or the movement he created. Clearly, the subversive nature of Muḥammad al-Kattānī's story has influenced the way the topic has been enshrined in memory.

The inability to discuss the Kattāniyya and Morocco at the end of the nineteenth century has important implications about the role of history and memory in the creation and sustenance of the Moroccan monarchy in the contemporary period. Today Moroccan nationalist history equates the monarchy with the movement for national independence from France and credits it as the driving force behind the reform and development of Moroccan society in its march toward modernity. To reconceptualize the pre-Protectorate period of Moroccan history as a period in which there were competing visions of power, authority, and reform opens up the horizon for new interpretations of the Moroccan past as well as new possibilities for the Moroccan present and future.

NOTES

1. Adrienne Rich, "Cartographies of Silence," *The Dream of a Common Language* (New York: W. W. Norton and Co., 1978): 16.
2. Michaux-Bellaire worked with Georges Salmon to start the publication of *Archives Marocaines* in 1904. From its initial publication until 1934, it made up part of the expanding colonial archive about North African society created by French scholars and colonial administrators. Burke, "The Creation of the Moroccan Colonial Archive, 1880–1930," 4.
3. E. Michaux-Bellaire, "Une tentative de restauration idrisite à Fès," *Revue du Monde Musulman* 51 (1908): 397.
4. al-Kattānī, *al-Maẓāhir,* 2.
5. Ibid., 110.
6. Ibid., 366.
7. See, for example, ʿAllāl al-Fāsī, *The Independence Movements in Arab North Africa,* trans. Hazem Zaki Nuseibeh (New York: Octagon Press, 1970).
8. Hubert Lyautey, cited in Robin Bidwell, *Morocco under Colonial Rule* (London: Frank Cass, 1973), 66. The remainder of the quote is interesting: "Or, comme c'est précisément la crainte que notre domination élague, morceau par morceau, tout ce qui est traditional, qui reste le principal obstacle á la conquête matérielle et la pacification morale . . . Le sultanat restauré une force d'attraction dont notre oeuvre pacificatrice a eu tout le profit [Well, it is precisely the fear that our domination prunes away, piece by piece, all that is traditional and that remains the main obstacle to material conquest and moral pacification . . . The sultanate restores the strength of appeal of which our pacification project has benefited]."

9. Mission Scientifique du Maroc, *Villes et tribus du Maroc,* vol. 10 (Paris: E. Leroux, 1915), 112.
10. For Dukkala and Azzemour, see ibid., 10: 111. For Tlemsen and Oran, see ʿAbd al-Kabīr b. Hāshim al-Kattānī, *Rawaḍ al-Anfās al-ʿĀliyya fī baʿad al-Zawāya al-Fāsiyya,* BG 12/1264 K, 294, BG.
11. John P. Halstead, *Rebirth of a Nation: The Origins and Rise of Moroccan Nationalism, 1912–1944* (Cambridge: Harvard University Press, 1967), 122.
12. Bidwell, *Morocco under Colonial Rule,* 34.
13. Sī ʿAbd al-Wahhāb bin Manṣūr related this story to me during a discussion about ʿAbd al-Ḥayy al-Kattānī. April 1998, Rabat, Morocco.
14. Aḥmad Qābīl, "20/8/1953: Dhikrā thawrat al-malik wa al-shaʿab wa dhikrā al-talaḥḥum bayna al-ʿarsh wa al-ḥaraka al-waṭaniyya," *al-Ittiḥād al-Ishtirākī,* August 20, 1998. The article includes a photograph of Thāmī al-Glāwī and ʿAbd al-Ḥayy al-Kattānī with the caption "rumūz al-khiyāna" (the symbols of treason).
15. Norman Cigar, "Socio-economic Structures and the Development of an Urban Bourgeoisie in Precolonial Morocco," *Maghreb Review* 6 (1981): 55–76.
16. On the concept of *hijra,* see Masud, "The Obligation to Migrate."
17. Idrīs al-Kattānī, Introduction, in al-Kattānī, *Naṣīḥat ahl al-Islām,* ed. Idrīs al-Kattānī.

Bibliography

UNPUBLISHED PRIMARY SOURCES

al-Kattānī, ʿAbd al-Ḥayy. *al-Maẓāhir al-sāmiyya fī al-nisba al-sharīfa al-Kattāniyya,* 1911. Photocopy of original manuscript, Private collection of Dr. Fawzi Abdulrazak, Cambridge, Massachusetts.

al-Kattānī, ʿAbd al-Kabīr b. Hāshim. *Rawaḍ al-Anfās al-ʿĀliyya fī baʿad al-Zawāya al-Fāsiyya* BG 12/1264 K, 294, Bibliothèque Générale, Rabat.

al-ʿUmrānī, ʿAbd al-Salām. *al-Luʾluʾa al-fāsiyya fī al-riḥla al-ḥijāziyya,* Ms., BGK 3/1012, 111–212, Bibliothèque Générale, Rabat.

Risāʾil Abī al-fayḍ al-Kattānī BGK 3297 Bibliothèque Générale, Rabat.

Risāla ilā fuqarāʾ al-kattāniyyīn BH10327 Bibliothèque Ḥasaniyya, Rabat.

Wathāʾiq, al-tartīb al-khāṣṣ Fez, Kattāniyyūn, Direction des Archives Royales, Rabat.

Wathāʾiq, al-tartīb al-zamanī, 1893–1909, Direction des Archives Royales, Rabat.

Wathāʾiq, series 1 (wāw) and (bāʾ) Bibliothèque Ṣabīḥī, Salé.

PUBLISHED PRIMARY SOURCES

Aubin, Eugène. *Morocco of Today.* London: J. M. Dent and Co., 1906.

"Captured Rebels' Torture." *Al-Moghreb al-Aksa,* April 15, 1909, no. 1383. Tangier, Morocco.

Comité de l'Afrique Française, "Le commerce et l'industrie à Fez." *Renseignements Coloniaux, Supplément au Bulletin du Comité de l'Afrique Française* 7 (July 1905): 229–253; 8 (August 1905): 295–321; 9 (September 1905): 337–350.

Delphin, G. *Fas, son université et l'enseignement supérieur musulman.* Oran: Paul Perrier, 1889.

"Domestic News." *Lisān al-Maghrib* 2 Rabīʿ al-awwal 1325 AH/May 3, 1907 CE, Tangier, Morocco.

"Domestic News." *Lisān al-Maghrib* 18 Muḥarram 1326 CE/February 21, 1908 CE, Tangier, Morocco.

Doutté, Edmond. *Merrâkech.* Paris: Comité du Maroc, 1905.

"Fez." *Lisān al-Maghrib,* 11 Rabīʿ al-thānī 1327 AH/May 2, 1909 CE. Tangier, Morocco.

"Fez." *Lisān al-Maghrib,* 27 Rabīʿ al-awwal 1327 AH/April 18, 1909 CE. Tangier, Morocco.

"Fez." *Lisān al-Maghrib,* 9 Ṣafar 1326 AH/March 13, 1908 CE. Tangier, Morocco.

Gleichen, Edward. *Journal of our Mission to Fez (1909).* London: Harrison and Sons, 1909.

Harris, Lawrence. *With Mulai Hafid at Fez: Behind the Scenes in Morocco.* Boston: Gorham Press, 1910.

al-Kattānī, ʿAbd al-Ḥayy. *Mufākahat dhū al-nubl wa al-ijāda.* Fez: Lithographic Press, 1908.

al-Kattānī, ʿAbd al-Ḥayy bin ʿAbd al-Kabīr. *Fihras al-fahāris,* 3 vols. Edited by Iḥsān ʿAbbās. Beirut: Dār al-Gharb al-Islāmī, 1982.

al-Kattānī, Muḥammad bin ʿAbd al-Kabīr. *Lisān al-Ḥujja al-burhāniyya fī al-dhabb ʿan al-Sharāʾiʿ al-kattāniyya.* n.p., 1908(?).

al-Kattānī, Muḥammad Ḥamza ibn ʿAlī and Ghassān Abū Ṣūfa, eds. *Min rasāʾil al-imām Muḥammad bin ʿAbd al-Kabīr al-Kattānī fī al-ādāb wa al-sulūk.* Amman: Dār al-Rāzī, 1999.

al-Kattānī, Muḥammad bin Jaʿfar. *Naṣīḥat ahl al-Islām*. Edited and Introduction by Idrīs al-Kattānī. Rabat: Maktabat al-Badr, 1989.

———. Muḥammad bin Jaʿfar. *Salwat al-anfās wa muḥādathat al-akyās bi man uqbira min al-ʿulamāʾ wa al-ṣulaḥāʾ bi fās*. Edited and with an introduction by ʿAbd Allah al-Kattānī et al. Casablanca: Dār al-Thaqāfa, 2004.

La Martinière, M. *Morocco: Journeys in the Kingdom of Fez and to the Court of Mulai Hassan*. London: Whittaker and Co., 1889.

"Letter of the Ulama of Fez of 12 June 1903." *Bulletin de la Société de Géographie d'Oran* 223 (1903): 241–255.

Mercier, L. "La presse musulmane au Maroc." *Revue du Monde Musulmane* 4 (1908): 619–630.

Michaux-Bellaire, E. "Proclamation de la Déchéance de Moulay Abd el Aziz." *Revue du Monde Musulman* 5 (1908): 425–435.

———. "Une Tentative de Restauration Idrisite à Fès." *Revue du Monde Musulman* 5 (1908): 393–423.

al-Nāṣirī, Aḥmad bin Khālid. *al-Istiqsā li akhbār duwal al-Maghrib al-Aqṣāʾ 3 vols*. Edited by Jaʿfar and Muḥammad al-Nāṣirī. Casablanca: Dār al-Kitāb, 1997.

Niddam, Jacob. "Un correspondant de révolution: journal d'un Israélite de Fès, parts 1 et 2." *Bulletin de la Société de Géographie d'Alger et de l'Afrique du Nord,* no. 145 (1936): 14–62 and no. 146 (1936): 133–192.

Salmon, M. G. "Confréries et Zaouyas de Tanger." *Archives Marocaines* 2 (1905): 100–114.

"The Kittanin [sic] Zauias Closed." *Al-Moghreb al-Aksa,* April 8, 1909, no. 1381. Tangier, Morocco.

"The Situation in Fez." *Al-Moghreb al-Aqsa,* April 1, 1909, no. 1379. Tangier, Morocco.

al-Wansharīsī, Aḥmad b. Yaḥyā. *al-Miʿyār al-Muʿrib wa al-Jamiʿ al-Mughrib ʿan Fatāwa ahl Ifriqiyya wa al-Andalus wa al-Maghrib*. Compiled by Muḥammad Ḥajjī. Rabat: Nashr Wizārat al-Awqāf wa al-Shu'ūn al-Islāmiyya, 1981.

SECONDARY SOURCES

Abdulrazak, Fawzi [ʿAbd al-Razzāq, Fawzī]. *Mamlakat al-Kitāb: Tārīkh al-ṭibāʿa fī al-maghrib, 1865–1912*. Translated by Khalid ibn al-Ṣaghīr. Casablanca: al-Najāḥ al-Jadīd, 1996.

Abun-Nasr, Jamil. *The Tijaniyya: A Sufi Order in the Modern World*. London: Oxford University Press, 1965.

al-ʿAlawī, Muḥammad al-Fallāḥ. *Jāmiʿ al-*qarawīyīn *wa al-fikr al-salafī, 1873–1914*. Casablanca: Maṭbaʿat al-Najāḥ al-Jadīda, 1994.

Alexander, Jeffrey C. *Fin de Siècle Social Theory: Relativism, Reduction and the Problem of Reason*. London: Verso, 1995.

Amar, Émile. "Introduction." In *La pierre de touche des fétwas de Ahmad al-Wanscharīsī: choix de consultations juridiques des faqîhs du Maghreb*, trans. and edited by Émile Amar, v–xiii. Paris: E. Leroux, 1908.

Anderson, Benedict. *Imagined Communities: Reflections on the Origins and Spread of Nationalism*. London: Verso, 1991.

Asad, Talal. *Genealogies of Religion: Discipline and Reasons of Power in Christianity and Islam*. Baltimore: Johns Hopkins University Press, 1993.

Bazzaz, Sahar. "Reading Reform beyond the State: Salwat al-Anfas, Islamic Revival and Moroccan National History." *Journal of North African Studies* 13 no. 1 (2008): 1–13.

Berkey, Jonathan P. "Tradition, Innovation and the Social Construction of Knowledge in the Medieval Islamic Near East." *Past and Present* 146 (February 1995): 38–65.

Berque, Jacques. *Al-Yousi: problèmes de la culture marocaine au XVIIème siècle*. 2nd ed. Rabat: Centre Tarik ibn Ziyad, 2001.

Bidwell, Robin. *Morocco under Colonial Rule*. London: Frank Cass, 1973.

Binebine, Ahmed-Chouqui [Bin bin, Aḥmad Shawqī]. *Histoire des bibliothèques au Maroc*. Rabat: Faculté des Lettres et des Sciences Humaines, 1992.

Bourqia, Rahma [Burqiyya, Raḥma]. "The Cultural Legacy of Power in Morocco." In *In the Shadow of the Sultan: Culture, Power and Politics in Morocco*, edited by Rahma Bourqia [Raḥma Burqiyya] and Susan Gilson Miller, 243–258. Cambridge: Harvard University Press, 1999.

———. "Don et théatralité: reflexion sur le rituel du don (hadiyya) offert au sultan au 19ème siècle." *Hespéris-Tamuda* 31 (1993): 61–75.

Brown, Daniel. *Rethinking Tradition in Modern Islamic Thought.* Cambridge: Cambridge University Press, 1996.

Brown, Kenneth. *People of Salé: Tradition and Change in a Moroccan City.* Cambridge: Harvard University Press, 1976.

Brown, Kenneth. "Profile of Nineteenth-Century Moroccan Scholar." In *Scholars, Saints, and Sufis: Muslim Religious Institutions in the Middle East since 1500,* edited by Nikki R. Keddie, 127–148. Berkeley: University of Califronia Press, 1972.

Bū Jandar, Muḥammad bin Muṣṭafā. *al-Ightibāṭ bi tarājim aʿlām al-rabaṭ.* Edited by ʿAbd al-Karīm Kurayyim. Rabat: Maṭābiʿ al-Aṭlas, 1987.

Burke, Edmund. "The Creation of the Moroccan Colonial Archive, 1880–1930." *History and Anthropology* 18, no. 1(March 2007): 1–9.

———. "The First Crisis of Orientalism." In *Connaissances du Maghreb: sciences sociales et colonisation,* edited by Jean-Claude Vatin et al., 213–226. Paris: Editions du Centre National de la Recherche Scientifique, 1984.

———. "La Hafidiya (août 1907–janvier 1908): enjeux sociaux et luttes populaires." *Hespéris-Tamuda* 31 (1993): 101–115.

———. "The Image of the Moroccan State in French Ethnological Literature: A New Look at Lyautay's Berber Policy." In *Arabs and Berbers: From Tribe to Nation in North Africa,* edited by Ernest Gellner and Charles Micaud, 175–199. London: Gerald Duckworth and Co., 1973.

———. "The Moroccan Ulama, 1860–1912: An Introduction." In *Scholars, Saints, and Sufis: Muslim Religious Institutions in the Middle East since 1500,* edited by Nikki R. Keddie, 93–125. Berkeley: University of California Press, 1972.

———. "Pan-Islam and Moroccan Resistance to French Colonial Penetration, 1900–1912." *Journal of African History* 8, no. 1 (1972): 97–118.

———. *Prelude to Protectorate in Morocco: Precolonial Protest and Resistance, 1860–1912*. Chicago: University of Chicago Press, 1976.

———. “Theorizing the Histories of Colonialism and Nationalism in the Arab Maghrib.” In *Beyond Colonialism and Nationalism in the Maghrib,* edited by Ali Abdullatif Ahmida, 17–34. Houndmills, Basingstoke, Hampshire: Palgrave, 2000.

Bū Salām, Muḥammad. “Mūjaz Mashrūʿ Qirāʾa fī Taṭawwur ʿIlāqāt baʿḍ al-Zawāya bi al-Sulṭa al-Markaziyya.” *Majallat Tārīkh al-Maghrib* 2 (April 1982): 83–94.

Cagne, Jacques. *Nation et nationalisme au Maroc.* Rabat: al-Maʿārif al-Jadīda, 1988.

———. “Presse et Salafisme au Maroc au début du siècle.” *Majallat Dār al-Niyāba* 7 (Summer 1985): 1–5.

Chakrabarty, Dipesh. *Habitations of Modernity: Essays in the Wake of Subaltern Studies.* Chicago: University of Chicago Press, 2002.

Chatterjee, Partha. *The Nation and Its Fragments: Colonial and Post-colonial Histories.* Princeton, NJ: Princeton University Press, 1993.

Chodkiewicz, Michel. “The Esoteric Foundations of Political Legitimacy in Ibn Arabi.” *Muhyiddin Ibn Arabi: A Commemorative Volume,* edited by Stephen Hirtenstein and Michael Tiernan, 190–198. Rockport MA: Element, Inc., 1993.

———. “Quelques remarques sur la diffusion de l’enseignement d’Ibn Arabi.” In *Modes de transmission de la culture religieuse en Islam,* edited by Hassan Elboudrari, 201–224. Institut Français d’Archéologie Orientale du Caire, 1993.

———. *Seal of the Saints: Prophethood and Sainthood in the Doctrine of Ibn Arabi.* Translated by Liadain Sherrard. Cambridge: Islamic Texts Society, 1993.

Cigar, Norman. “Conflict and Community in an Urban Milieu: Fez under the Alawis (ca. 1666–1830).” *Maghreb Review* 3, no. 10 (1978): 3–13.

———. “Socio-economic Structures and the Development of an Urban Bourgeoisie in Pre-colonial Morocco.” *Maghreb Review* 6 (1981): 55–76.

Clancy-Smith, Julia A. *Rebel and Saint: Muslim Notables, Populist Protest, Colonial Encounters (Algeria and Tunisia, 1800–1904).* Berkeley: University of California Press, 1994.

———. "In the Eye of the Beholder: Sufi and Saint in North Africa and the Colonial Production of Knowledge, 1830–1900." *Africana Journal* 15(1990): 220–257.

Combs-Schilling, Elaine M. "Performing Monarchy, Staging Nation." In *In the Shadow of the Sultan: Culture, Power and Politics in Morocco,* edited by Rahma Bourqia [Burqiyya] and Susan Gilson Miller, 176–214. Cambridge: Harvard University Press, 1999.

Cook, Michael A. *Commanding Right and Forbidding Wrong in Islamic Thought.* Cambridge: Cambridge University Press, 2000.

Cooper, Frederick. *Colonialism in Question: Theory, Knowledge, History.* Berkeley: University of California Press, 2005.

Cornell, Vincent. "Faqih versus Faqir in Marinid Morocco: Epistemological Dimensions of a Polemic." In *Islamic Mysticism Contested: Thirteen Centuries of Controversies and Polemics,* edited by Frederick De Jong and Bernd Radtke, 207–224. Leiden: Brill, 1999.

———. "Mystical Doctrine and Political Action in Moroccan Sufism: The Role of the Exemplar in the Tarqa al-Jazuliyya." *al-Qantara* 13 fasc. 1 (1992): 201–231.

———. *Realm of the Saint: Power and Authority in Moroccan Sufism.* Austin: University of Texas Press, 1998.

Cronin, Stephanie ed., *Subalterns and Social Protest: History from below in the Middle East and North Africa.* New York: Routledge, 2008.

Dakhila, Jocelyne. "Dans la mouvance du prince: la symbolique du pouvoir itinérant au Maghreb." *Annales ESC* 3 (May–June 1988): 735–760.

Dallal, Ahmad. "The Origins and Objectives of Islamic Revivalist Thought, 1750–1850." *Journal of the American Oriental Society* 113, no. 3 (July–September 1993): 341–359.

Dennerlein, Bettina. "Asserting Religious Authority in late Nineteenth-/Early Twentieth-Century Morocco: Muhammad b. Ja'far al-Kattânî and His Kitâb Salwat al-anfâs." In *Speaking for Islam: Religious Authorities in Middle Eastern Islam,* edited by G. Kramer and S. Schmidtke, 128–152. Leiden: Brill, 2006.

———. "Legitimate Bounds and Bound Legitimacy: The Act of Allegiance to the Ruler *(bai'a)* in Nineteenth-Century Morocco." *Die Welt des Islams* 41, no. 3 (2001): 287–310.

———. "Savoir religieux et débat politique au Maroc: une consultation des 'gens de Fès' en 1886." *Hespéris-Tamuda* 39, fasc. 2 (2001): 119–132.

Drague, Georges. *Esquisse d'histoire religieuse du Maroc: confréries et zaouïas.* Paris: J. Peyronnet, 1951.

Duara, Prasanjit. "Introduction: The Decolonization of Asia and Africa in the Twentieth Century." In *Decolonization: Perspectives from Now and Then,* edited by Prasanjit Duara, 1–20. London: Routledge, 2004.

———. *Rescuing History from the Nation: Questioning Narratives of Modern China.* Chicago: University of Chicago Press, 1995.

Dunn, Ross E. "The Bu Himara Rebellion in Northeast Morocco: Phase 1." *Middle Eastern Studies* 17, no. 1 (1981): 30–48.

Eickelman, Dale F. "Islam and the Languages of Modernity." In *Multiple Modernities,* edited by Shmuel N. Eisenstadt, 119–135. New Brunswick, NJ: Transaction Publishers, 2002.

———. *Knowledge and Power in Morocco: The Education of a Twentieth-Century Notable.* Princeton, NJ: Princeton University Press, 1985.

———. *Moroccan Islam: Tradition and Society in a Pilgrimage Center.* Austin: University of Texas Press, 1976.

Ennaji, Mohammed [al-Nājī, Muḥammad] and Paul Pascon. *Le Makhzen et le Sous al-Aqsa: la correspondance politique de la maison d'Iligh (1821–1894).* Paris: Éditions du CNRS, 1988.

Ernst, Carl W. *Words of Ecstacy in Sufism.* Albany: State University of New York Press, 1985.

Fadel, Mohammad [al-Fāḍil, Muḥammad]. "The Social Logic of Taqlid and the Rise of the Mukhtasar." *Islamic Law and Society* 3, no. 2 (1996): 194–233.

Fasi, Allal [al-Fāsī, 'Allāl]. *The Independence Movements in Arab North Africa.* Translated by Hazem Zaki Nuseibeh. New York: Octagon Books, 1970.

Friedmann, Yohanan. *Shaykh Ahmad Sirhindi: An Outline of His*

Thought and a Study of His Image in the Eyes of Posterity. Montreal: McGill-Queen's University Press, 1971.

García-Arenal, Mercedes and E. Manzano Moreno. "Idrissisme et villes idrissides." *Studia Islamica* 82 (October 1995): 5–33.

Ghastel, Robert. "Le coup de Fès ou Fès 1911." *Hespéris-Tamuda* 28 (1990): 71–90.

Ginzburg, Carlo. *The Cheese and the Worms: The Cosmos of a Sixteenth-Century Miller.* Translated by John and Anne Tedeschi. Harmondsworth, NY: Penguin Books, 1982.

Giorgi, Roberto. *Pour une histoire de la zandaqa*. Firenze: La Nuova Italia, 1989.

Gribetz, Arthur. "The *Sama'* Controversy: Sufi vs. Legalist." *Studia Islamica* 74 (1991): 43–62.

Halstead, John P. *Rebirth of a Nation: the Origins and Rise of Moroccan Nationalism, 1912–1944*. Cambridge: Harvard University Press, 1967.

Hammoudi, Abdellah [Ḥammūdī, 'Abd Allah]. *Master and Disciple: The Cultural Foundations of Moroccan Authoritarianism*. Chicago: University of Chicago Press, 1997.

———. "The Reinvention of Dar al-Mulk: The Moroccan Political System and its Legitimation." In *In the Shadow of the Sultan: Culture, Power and Politics in Morocco,* edited by Rahma Bourqia [Raḥma Burqiyya] and Susan Gilson Miller, 129–175. Cambridge: Harvard University Press, 1999.

Hannoum, Abdelmajid [Ḥannūm, 'Abd al-Majīd]. "Colonialism and Knowledge in Algeria: The Archives of the Arab Bureau." *History and Anthropology* 12 (2001): 343–379.

Ḥarakāt, Ibrāhīm. *Al-Tayyārāt al-siyāsiyya wa al-fikriyya bi al-Maghrib khilāla qarnayn wa niṣf qabla al-ḥimāya*. Morocco?: s.n., 1985.

Heller, Thomas C. and David E. Wellbery. Introduction. In *Reconstructing Individualism: Autonomy, Individuality and the Self in Western Thought,* edited by Thomas C. Heller, Morton Sosna, and David Wellbery, 1–15. Stanford: Stanford University Press, 1986.

Hobsbawm, Eric, and Terence Ranger, eds. *The Invention of Tradition.* Cambridge: Cambridge University Press, 1983.

Hoffman, Valerie J. "Annihilation in the Messenger of God: The Development of a Sufi Practice." *IJMES* 31 (1999): 351–369.

Holden, Stacy. "Modernizing a Moroccan Medina: Commercial and Technological Innovations at the Workplace of Millers and Butchers in Fez, 1878–1937." Ph.D. diss., Boston University, 2005.

Hoover, Ellen Titus. "Among Competing Worlds: The Rehamna of Morocco on the Eve of French Conquest." Ph.D. diss., Yale University, 1978.

Kafadar, Cemal. *Between Two Worlds: the Construction of the Ottoman State.* Berkeley: University of Califronia Press, 1995.

al-Kattānī, Muḥammad al-Bāqir. *Tarjamat al-Shaykh Muḥammad al-Kattānī al-Shahīd.* n.p., Maṭbaʿat al-Fajr: 1962.

al-Kattānī, Zayn al-ʿĀbidīn. *al-Ṣaḥāfa al-maghribiyya: nashaʾtuhā wa Taṭawwuruhā, 1820–1912.* Rabat: Nashr Wizārat al-Anbāʾ, 1969.

Katz, Jonathan G. *Dreams, Sufism and Sainthood: The Visionary Career of Muhammad al-Zawawi.* Studies in the History of Religion, ed. H. G. Kippenberg and E. T. Lawson. Vol. 71. Leiden: Brill, 1996.

———. *Murder in Marrakesh: Émile Mauchamp and the French colonial adventure.* Indianapolis: Indiana University Press, 2006.

———. *Visionary Experience, Autobiography, and Sainthood in North African Islam.* Princeton Papers in Near Eastern Studies. Edited by Charles Issawi and Bernard Lewis. No.1. Princeton: Darwin Press, 1992.

Katz, Stephen T. "Editor's Introduction." In *Mysticism and Philosophical Analysis,* edited by Stephen T. Katz, 1–9. New York: Oxford University Press, 1978.

Kenbib, Mohammed [Kenbīb, Muḥammad]. "Structures traditionnelles et protections étrangères au Maroc au XIXème siècle." *Hespéris-Tamuda* 22 (1984): 79–101.

Khalid, Adeeb. "Printing, Publishing and Reform in Tsarist Central Asia." *IJMES* 26, no. 2 (May 1994): 187–200.

Khuri-Makdisi, Ilham. *The Eastern Mediterranean and the Making of Global Radicalism, 1860–1914.* Berkeley: University of California Press, 2010 (forthcoming).

Knysh, Alexander. "Ibn Arabi in the Later Islamic Tradition," *Muhyiddin Ibn Arabi: A Commemorative Volume,* edited by. Stephen Hirtenstein and Michael Tiernan, 307–327. Rockport, MA: Element, Inc., 1993.

Kugle, Scott. *Rebel between Spirit and Law: Ahmad Zarruq, Sainthood, and Authority in Islam.* Bloomington: Indiana University Press, 2006.

Landau-Tasseron, Ella. "The 'Cyclical Reform': A Study of the Mujaddid Tradition." *Studia Islamica* 70 (1989): 79–117.

Laroui, Abdallah [al-ʿArawī, ʿAbd Allāh]. *Esquisses historiques.* Casablanca: Centre Culturel Arabe, 1992.

———. *Les origines sociales et culturelles du nationalisme marocain.* Casablanca: Centre Culturel Arabe, 1993.

Lechartier, Georges. *La colone du Haut-Guir en septembre 1908.* Paris: Librarie Militaire R. Chapelot et Cie., 1908.

Le Tourneau, Roger. *Fès avant le protectorat.* 2nd ed. Rabat: Éditions la Porte, 1987.

Le Tourneau, R., and L. Paye. "La corporation des tanneurs et l'industrie de la tannerie à Fès." *Hespéris* 20–21 (1935): 167–240.

Lévi-Provençal, Évariste. *Les historiens des chorfas: essai sur la litterature historique et biographique au Maroc du 16e au 22e siècle.* Paris: Larose, 1922.

Levtzion, Nehemia, and John Voll. *Eighteenth-Century Renewal and Reform in Islam.* Syracuse: Syracuse University Press, 1987.

Loubignac, V. "Un saint berbère, Moulay Bou Azza." *Hespéris* 31 (1944): 15–34.

Makdisi, Ussama. *The Culture of Sectarianism: Community, History and Violence in 19th Century Ottoman Lebanon.* Berkeley: University of California Press, 2000.

al-Manūnī, Muḥammad. *Maẓāhir yaqẓat al-maghrib al-ḥadīth.* Vol. 2. Beirut: Dār al-Gharb al-Islāmī, 1985.

el-Mansour, Mohamed [al-Manṣūr, Muḥammad]. *Morocco in the Reign of Mawlay Sulayman.* Cambridgeshire: Middle East and North African Studies Press, 1990.

———. "Saints and Sultans: Religious Authority and Temporal Power in Pre-colonial Morocco." In *Popular Movements and Democratization in the Islamic World,* edited by Kisaichi Masatoshi, 1–24. London: Routledge, 2006.

———. "The Sanctuary (Hurm) in Precolonial Morocco." In *In the Shadow of the Sultan: Culture, Power, and Politics in Morocco,* edited by Rahma Bourqia and Susan Gilson Miller, 49–73. Cambridge: Harvard University Press, 1999.

———. "Urban Society in Fez: The Rumat during the Modern Period (Seventeenth–Nineteenth Centuries)." *Maghreb Review* 22 (1997): 75–95.

Martin, B. G. *Muslim Brotherhoods in Nineteenth-Century Africa.* Cambridge: Cambridge University Press, 1976.

Masud, Muhammad Khalid. "The Obligation to Migrate: the Doctrine of Hijra in Islamic Law." In *Muslim Travellers: Pilgrimage, Migration and the Religious Imagination,* edited by Dale F. Eickelman and James Piscatori, 29–49. Berkeley: University of California Press, 1990.

McDougall, James. *History and the Culture of Nationalism in Algeria.* Cambridge: Cambridge University Press, 2006.

Miège, Jean-Louis. "Journaux et journalistes à Tanger au 19ème siècle." *Hespéris-Tamuda* 1–2 trimestres 41 (1954): 191–228.

———. *Le Maroc et l'Europe, 1830–1894.* 4 vols. Paris: Presses Universitaires de France, 1961–1963.

Miller, Susan Gilson. *Disorienting Encounters: Travels of a Moroccan Scholar in France in 1845–1846: The Voyage of Muhammad as-Saffār.* Berkeley: University of California Press, 1992.

Miller, Susan G. and Amal Rassam. "The View from the Court: Moroccan Reactions to European Penetration during the Late Nineteenth Century." *International Journal of African Historical Studies* 16, no. 1 (1983): 25–38.

Mission Scientifique du Maroc. *Villes et tribus du Maroc.* Paris: E. Leroux, 1915.

el-Moueddin, Abderrahmane [al-Mawdin, 'Abd al-Raḥmān]. "The Ambivalence of *Rihla:* Community Integration and Self-definition in Moroccan Travel Accounts, 1300–1800." In *Muslim Travellers: Pilgrimage, Migration and the Religious Imagination,* edited by Dale F. Eickelman and James Piscatori, 69–84. Berkeley: University of California Press, 1990.

———. "Sharifs and Padishahs: Moroccan-Ottoman Relations from the Sixteenth through the Eighteenth Centuries." Ph.D. diss., Princeton University, 1992.

Munson, Henry, Jr. *Religion and Power in Morocco.* New Haven: Yale University Press, 1993.

Oberoi, Harjot. *The Construction of Religious Boundaries: Culture, Identity and Diversity in the Sikh Tradition.* Oxford: Oxford University Press, 1994.

O'Fahey, R. S. *Enigmatic Saint: Ahmad Ibn Idris and the Idrisi Tradition.* Evanston: Northwestern University Press, 1990.

O'Fahey, R. S. and Bernd Radtke. "Neo-Sufism Reconsidered." *Der Islam* 70 (1993): 52–87.

Perité, M. "Les medrasas de Fès." *Archives Marocaines* 18 (1912): 257–372.

Peters, Rudolph. "Idjtihad and Taqlid in Eighteenth- and Nineteenth-Century Islam." *Die Welt des Islams* 20, no. 3–4 (1980): 131–145.

Powell, Eve M. Troutt. *A Different Shade of Colonialism: Egypt, Great Britain and the Mastery of the Sudan.* Berkeley: University of California Press, 2003.

Qābīl, Aḥmad. "20/8/1953: Dhikrā thawrat al-malik wa al-sha'ab wa dhikrā al-talaḥḥum bayna al-'arsh wa al-ḥaraka al-waṭaniyya." *al-Ittiḥād al-Ishtirākī,* August 20, 1998.

Radtke, Bernd, et al. *The Exoteric Ahmad Ibn Idris: A Sufi's Critique of the Madhhab and the Wahhabis.* Leiden: Brill, 2000.

Rudé, George. *The Crowd in History.* New York: Wiley, 1964.

al-Ṣaghīr, 'Abd al-Majīd. *Ishkāliyyāt iṣlāḥ al-fikr al-ṣūfī fī al-qarnayn 18 wa 19 M: Aḥmad ibn 'Ajība wa Muḥammad al-Ḥarrāq.* Rabat: Dār al-Āfāq al-Jadīda, 1994.

———. *al-Taṣṣawuf ka waʿī wa mumārasa: dirāsa fī al-falsafa al-ṣūfiyya ʿinda Aḥmad ibn 'Ajība.* Casablanca: Dār al-Thaqāfa, 1999.

Sajdi, Dana [Sajdī, Dānā]. "Print and Its Discontents: A Case for Pre-Print Journalism and Other Sundry Print Matters." *Translator* 15, no.1 (2009): 105–138.

Schimmel, Annemarie. *Mystical Dimensions of Islam,* 5th ed. Chapel Hill: University of North Carolina Press, 1983.

Schroeter, Daniel. "Royal Power and the Economy in Pre-Colonial Morocco: Jews and the Legitimation of Foreign Trade." In *In the*

Shadow of the Sultan: Culture, Power, and Politics in Morocco, edited by Rahma Bourqia and Susan Gilson Miller, 74–102. Cambridge: Harvard University Press, 1999.

Sebti, Abdelahad [al-Sibtī, ʻAbd al-Aḥad]. "Chroniques de la contestation citadine: Fès et la révolte des tanneurs (1873–1874)." *Hespéris-Tamuda* 29, fasc. 2 (1991): 283–312.

———. "Akhbār al-manāqib wa manāqib al-akhbār." In *al-Tārīkh wa adab al-manāqib: Proceedings of the Symposium in Rabat, Morocco, April 8–9, 1988*, 93–112. Rabat: al-Jamʻiyya al-Maghribiyya li al-baḥth al-tārīkhī, 1988.

———. "Au Maroc: sharifisme, citadin, charisme et historiographie." *Annales ESC* no. 2 (March–April 1986): 433–457.

Sharkey, Heather J. "A Century of Print: Arabic Journalism and Nationalism in the Sudan, 1899–1999." *IJMES* 31, no. 4 (November 1999): 531–549.

Sirriyeh, Elizabeth. *Sufis and Anti-Sufis: The Defence, Rethinking and Rejection of Sufism in the Modern World*. Richmond, Surrey: Curzon Press, 1999.

Slyomovics, Susan. *The Performance of Human Rights in Morocco*. Philadelphia: University of Pennsylvania Press, 2005.

Tawfīq, Aḥmad. *al-Mujtamaʻ al-maghribī fī al-qarn al-tāsiʻ ʻashar*. Casablanca: Maṭbaʻat al-Najāḥ al-Jadīda, 1983.

———. "Ta'amullāt fī al-bayʻa al-Ḥafīẓiyya." *al-Maghrib min al-ʻahd al-ʻazīzī ilā sanat 1912, al-juz' al-awwal: Proceedings of the Summer Congress, Mohammadia, Morocco 21–31 July 1987*, n.p., n.d. 335–347.

Terzioğlu, Derin. "Sufi and Dissident in the Ottoman Empire: Niyazi-i Misri (1618–1694)." Ph.D. diss., Harvard University, Cambridge, 1999.

Thompson, E. P. *The Making of the English Working Class*. New York: Vintage Books, 1963.

Thomson, Joseph. *Travels in the Atlas and Southern Morocco: A Narrative of Exploration*. London: George Philip and Son, 1889.

Touati, Houari. *Entre Dieu et les hommes: lettrés, saints et sorciers au Maghreb (17e siècle)*. Paris: Recherches d'Histoire et de Sciences Sociales, 1994.

Trimingham, Spencer J. *The Sufi Orders in Islam.* Foreword by John O. Voll. New York: Oxford University Press, 1998.

Turner, Bryan S. *Orientalism, Postmodernism and Globalism.* London: Routledge, 1994.

Vikør, Knut S. "The Shaykh as Mujtahid: a Sufi Conception of Ijtihād?" In *El Sufismo y las Normas del Islam: trabajos del IV Congreso Internacional de Estudios Jurídicos Islámicos: Derecho y Sufismo, Murcia, 7–10 Mayo 2003/Edicion y traduccion, Alfonso Carmona,* 351–375. Murcia: Editora Regional de Murcia, 2006.

Winter, Michael. *Society and Religion in Early Ottoman Egypt: Studies in the Writings of ʿAbd al-Wahhāb al-Shaʿrānī.* New Brunswick, NJ: Transaction Publishers, 2007.

Zaman, Muhammad Qasim. *The Ulama in Contemporary Islam: Custodians of Change.* Princeton: Princeton University Press, 2002.

Zilfi, Madeline. *The Politics of Piety: The Ottoman Ulema in the Postclassical Age (1600–1800).* Minneapolis: Bibliotheca Islamica, 1988.

Index

ʿAbd al-ʿAzīz: 1, 9, 96, 119; criticism against, 118, 120, 125, 126; dethronement of, 127–129

ʿAbd al-Ḥafīẓ: 3, 118; abdication of, 142, 154; attempt to control the Kattāniyya, 139–142; *bayʿa*s in support of, 127, 128, 136–137; conflict with al-Kattānī, 1, 13, 125, 138–139, 140–142, 147n44, 150, 151; decline of support for, 142, 153–154; descendants of, 4; and dethronement of ʿAbd al-ʿAzīz, 125, 127; European attitude toward, 137–138; failure to fulfill the *bayʿa* of Fez, 137–138; political alliances of, 127–128, 137, 143nn4,5, 153–154; reliance on al-Kattānī, 128, 133–135, 137, 146n28

ʿAbd al-Raḥmān, 29–30, 39

adhān (call to prayer), 53

al-ʿAlawī, Muḥammad bin al-ʿArabī, 97, 108n61, 155

ʿAlawī dynasty, 27, 59–60, 63, 72n8, 142; competition with Idrīsī *shurafa'*, 149–150, 151

Algeciras, 118, 119; Algeciras Act of 1906, 126, 127, 137, 142

Amīr al-Mu'minīn (Commander of the Faithful), 5

ancien regime in Morocco, 3

anti-French coalition, 120

Archives Marocaines, 149, 158n2

ascetic practices, 54

baraka, 11, 27–28

bayʿa (oath of allegiance), 127–131. *See also* Fez: *bayʿa* of

bidʿa, 53, 56, 71, 73n12; vs. sharia, 72

bin Mūsā, Aḥmad, 50, 58, 61, 63, 64, 66

bin Saʿīd, ʿAbdallah, 117

Bū Ḥmāra/Bū Ḥmāra Rebellion, 96, 97, 116, 122n17

Bū Yaʿzā, Mawlāy, 36

Burke, Edmund, 21n23, 22, 127, 147n44

Cairo, 115, 116

Casablanca, 58, 126, 130, 134, 143n4

Cornell, Vincent, 28, 34, 75n22

cult of saints, 26

Dār al-Islām, 3

al-Darqāwī, Al-ʿArabī, 97

HARVARD MIDDLE EASTERN MONOGRAPHS

1. *Syria: Development and Monetary Policy,* by Edmund Y. Asfour. 1959.
2. *The History of Modern Iran: An Interpretation,* by Joseph M. Upton. 1960.
3. *Contributions to Arabic Linguistics,* Charles A. Ferguson, Editor. 1960.
4. *Pan-Arabism and Labor,* by Willard A. Beling. 1960.
5. *The Industrialization of Iraq,* by Kathleen M. Langley. 1961.
6. *Buarij: Portrait of a Lebanese Muslim Village,* by Anne H. Fuller. 1961.
7. *Ottoman Egypt in the Eighteenth Century,* Stanford J. Shaw, Editor and Translator. 1962.
8. *Child Rearing in Lebanon,* by Edwin Terry Prothro. 1961.
9. *North Africa's French Legacy: 1954-1962,* by David C. Gordon. 1962.
10. *Communal Dialects in Baghdad,* by Haim Blanc. 1964.
11. *Ottoman Egypt in the Age of the French Revolution,* Translated with Introduction and Notes by Stanford J. Shaw. 1964.
12. *The Economy of Morocco: 1912-1962,* by Charles F. Stewart. 1964.
13. *The Economy of the Israeli Kibbutz,* by Eliyahu Kanovsky. 1966.
14. *The Syrian Social Nationalist Party: An Ideological Analysis,* by Labib Zuwiyya Yamak. 1966.
15. *The Practical Visions of Ya'qub Sanu',* by Irene L. Gendizier. 1966.
16. *The Surest Path: The Political Treatise of a Nineteenth-Century Muslim Statesman,* by Leon Carl Brown. 1967.
17. *High-Level Manpower in Economic Development: The Turkish Case,* by Richard D. Robinson. 1967.
18. *Rebirth of a Nation: The Origins and Rise of Moroccan Nationalism, 1912-1944,* by John P. Halsted. 1967.
19. *Women of Algeria: An Essay on Change,* by David C. Gordon. 1968.
20. *The Youth of Haouch El Harimi, A Lebanese Village,* by Judith R. Williams. 1968.
21. *The Problem of Diglossia in Arabic: A Comparative Study of Classical and Iraqi Arabic,* by Salih J. Al-Toma. 1969.

22. *The Seljuk Vezirate: A Study of Civil Administration,* by Carla L. Klausner. 1973.

23. and 24. *City in the Desert,* by Oleg Grabar, Renata Holod, James Knustad, and William Trousdale. 1978.

25. *Women's Autobiographies in Contemporary Iran,* Afsaneh Najmabadi, Editor. 1990.

26. *The Science of Mystic Lights,* by John Walbridge. 1992.

27. *Political Aspects of Islamic Philosophy: Essays in Honor of Muhsin S. Mahdi,* by Charles E. Butterworth. 1992.

28. *The Muslims of Bosnia-Herzegovina: Their Historic Development from the Middle Ages to the Dissolution of Yugoslavia,* Mark Pinson, Editor. 1994.

29. *Book of Gifts and Rarities: Kitāb al-Hadāyā wa al-Tuḥaf.* Ghāda al Hijjāwī al-Qaddūmī, Translator and Annotator. 1997.

30. *The Armenians of Iran: The Paradoxical Role of a Minority in a Dominant Culture: Articles and Documents,* Cosroe Chaqueri, Editor. 1998.

31. *In the Shadow of the Sultan: Culture, Power, and Politics in Morocco,* Rahma Bourqia and Susan Gilson Miller, editors. 1999.

32. *Hermeneutics and Honor: Negotiating Female "Public" Space in Islamic/ate Societies,* Asma Afsaruddin, editor. 1999.

33. *The Second Umayyad Caliphate: The Articulation of Caliphal Legitimacy in al-Andalus,* by Janina M. Safran. 2000.

34. *New Perspectives on Property and Land in the Middle East,* Roger Owen, editor. 2001.

35. *Mystics, Monarchs, and Messiahs: Cultural Landscapes of Early Modern Iran,* by Kathryn Babayan. 2003.

36. *Byzantium Viewed by the Arabs*, by Nadia Maria El Cheikh. 2004.

37. *The Palestinian Peasant Economy under the Mandate: A Story of Colonial Bungling*, by Amos Nadan. 2006.

38. *The Moral Resonance of Arab Media: Audiocassette Poetry and Culture in Yemen*, by W. Flagg Miller. 2007.

39. *Islamicate Sexualities: Translations across Temporal Geographies of Desire*, Kathryn Babayan and Afsaneh Najmabadi, editors. 2008.

40. *Spiritual Wayfarers, Leaders in Piety: Sufis and the Dissemination of Islam in Medieval Palestine,* by Daphna Ephrat. 2008.

41. *Forgotten Saints: History, Power, and Politics in the Making of Modern Morocco,* by Sahar Bazzaz. 2010.

42. *Violent Modernity: France in Algeria,* by Abdelmajid Hannoum. 2010.